Strategic Implications of
the All-Volunteer Force

Studies on Armed Forces and Society

Published in Association with the
Inter-University Seminar on Armed
Forces and Society

Series Editors:
Sam C. Sarkesian, Professor of Political Science,
Loyola University
Ellen Stern, Syracuse University

Strategic Implications of the All-Volunteer Force

The Conventional Defense of Central Europe

By Kenneth J. Coffey

The University of North Carolina Press

Chapel Hill

ISBN 0-8078-1403-2
ISBN 0-8078-4057-2 pbk.
Library of Congress Catalog Card Number 79-19110

Library of Congress Cataloging in Publication Data
Coffey, Kenneth J
  Strategic implications of the all volunteer force.
  Bibliography: p.
  Includes index.
    1. United States—Armed Forces. 2. United States—Military
policy. 3. Military service, Voluntary—United States. 4. Europe—
Defenses. 5. North Atlantic Treaty Organization—United States.
I. Title.
UA23.C578   355.03'3073   79-19110
ISBN 0-8078-1403-2
ISBN 0-8078-4057-2 pbk.

The present work draws upon research undertaken for the
American Enterprise Institute (AEI) and published in
Manpower for Military Mobilization (American Enterprise,
1978). Portions of that study are reprinted herein by
permission of AEI.

The present work also has been approved by the University of London for the award of the degree of Ph.D.

To my wife Osa
without whose interest,
encouragement, and support
this book would not
have been possible.

Contents

Preface

Following the Vietnam War, most Americans became disinterested in U.S. military policies and capabilities. As the decade of the 1980's begins, however, Americans are getting concerned again. Increasingly, questions are being raised about the All-Volunteer Force and its capability to provide the realistic and cost-effective defense needed to respond to the strategic eventualities of the near future. Furthermore, mounting revelations of serious deficits in the resources thought necessary have put in serious doubt the ability of U.S. forces—particularly the army—to respond to the most likely non-nuclear contingency.

A crucial and intense national debate on the issue of the appropriateness of our strategic commitments and capabilities will no doubt occur in the very near future.

The following text should be considered a contribution to as well as a catalyst for such a major national discussion.

Strategic Implications of
the All-Volunteer Force

Introduction

The adoption of the All-Volunteer Force (AVF) in 1973 marked a clear departure from previous U.S. military policy and strategic capabilities.

The draft years produced large active forces, even larger reserve components, and a guaranteed supply of new trainees for all forseeable contingencies. Since the end of conscription in 1972, however, fundamental changes have taken place in the composition, strength, structure, mobilization/reinforcement, and war-sustaining capabilities of the armed forces. These changes have been particularly evident in the army's ability to defend Central Europe as part of an overall NATO effort to contain a conventional attack by forces of the Warsaw Pact.

This study aims to analyze the impact on U.S. strategic capabilities of the changes which have occurred in the AVF years; to evaluate in more specific terms the impact of these changes on the army's ability to fulfill its role in the NATO defense; and to assess the range of possible policy changes which might reconcile, or rationalize, the gap that has developed between U.S. capabilities and strategic commitments.

The personnel policies of the U.S. armed forces should support the attainment of major strategic objectives. Thus AVF policies should provide active and reserve forces with the numbers and quality of personnel needed for the nation's non-nuclear military contingencies. Yet since the draft was abruptly abandoned in the wave of opposition to the Vietnam War, the services, particularly the army, have experienced significant manpower problems. These problems developed despite major planned reductions in the strength of the armed forces caused primarily by President Richard M. Nixon's decision to adopt the strategy of the Realistic Deterrence. In calling for the maintenance of a 1½ war capability rather than the previous planning goal of a 2½ war capability, the new strategy de-emphasized the U.S. commitment to fight a major land war in Asia while reaffirming the commitment to join with NATO members in the conventional defense of Central Europe. In addition, the new strategy prompted the total force policy, a fun-

damental change in U.S. military concepts that placed an unprec-
edentedly high level of responsibility on the reserve forces.

According to this new strategy, a strong ground force capability, able to meet the commitments of NATO's extended conflict
scenario, has become a priority for American military and civilian
leaders. In the event of a Warsaw Pact attack on NATO in Central
Europe, the well-trained U.S. forces already in Europe, and those
units stationed in the U.S. which could be rapidly moved overseas
would play a crucial role. Yet reinforcements and a sustained war
capability could also be needed, and this eventuality has revealed
the greatest problems of the AVF.

No doubt a partial resolution of these problems will be achieved
through relatively easy policy changes within the Department of
Defense, Congress, and the Administration. But if the armed forces
are to have the resources to meet the requirements of an extended
conventional conflict, more serious decisions must be made. These
could include a return to some form of compulsory service, the
expenditure of additional billions for new manpower programs,
or other such departures from current policy. Whether such actions are desirable or necessary is still open to question and analysis.

This study therefore attempts to analyze the social and political
processes by which the nation's conscription policies were first
amended and then abandoned, and to assess the impact of these
decisions on the structure of U.S. forces and the capabilities for
the conventional defense of Central Europe.

The study begins by appraising the anti-draft opposition during
the Vietnam War and its impact on the decision to adopt an AVF.
The first three chapters consider the impact of conscientious objection, draft-dodging, draft-law violation, and anti-draft/anti-war
activities; the efforts of Congress and the Administration to pacify
the growing opposition by various draft reforms; and, finally, the
circumstances surrounding the decision to stop the draft.

In the following chapter, the changes in force composition
which resulted from the decision to end the draft are documented
and analyzed, with a focus on the actual and perceived impact
of these changes on the ability of the services to carry out their
assigned missions. Changes in the numbers and utilization of

women and blacks are discussed, as are changes in recruit quality and representation.

Considering, then, the requirements for full mobilization, Chapter V analyzes changes in the strength of the various active and reserve forces. Particular attention is paid to the army, including the structure of the active army, the mobilization capabilities of the army national guard and army reserves, and the ability of the army's individual reserve pools to provide the fillers and combat replacements needed to support a conventional conflict in Central Europe.

Chapter VI then discusses the special problems which have arisen during the AVF years concerning the adequacy of the volunteer recruiting processes and the draft to supply new trainees under conditions of full mobilization. The focus is on the role of the Selective Service System in providing manpower resources required for a prolonged conflict.

Chapter VII examines the ability of the army to fulfill its primary mission: to meet the requirements for the "worst case" scenario of a conventional war between NATO and the Warsaw Pact forces. Special emphasis is placed on assessing the war-sustaining capabilities of the Seventh Army in Germany and of problems in transporting, equipping, and supplying reinforcements for U.S. on-site forces.

In light of the problems that have developed in the AVF years regarding the war sustaining capabilities of the army, Chapter VIII then questions the validity of the total force policy and the U.S. commitment to fight a prolonged conventional ground conflict.

Chapter IX discusses the possibilities of correcting AVF-related problems through major policy alterations, including increased funding or the adoption of Selective Service, Universal Military Training, or Universal Service schemes.

Finally, Chapter X advances other policy changes that could resolve—or reconcile—strategic capability/commitment differences, assesses major policy alternatives open to Americans, and sets forth the conclusions of the study.

Chapter I

Growing Opposition to the Draft and the Vietnam War

The strong strategic capability of the armed forces of the United States during the postwar decades of the 1950's and 1960's was due largely to the draft. Because of legislated conscription, the armed forces were able inexpensively to obtain enough qualified personnel to support large mass armies with even larger reserve components.[1] While B. H. Liddell Hart could write in 1950 that "conscription has been the cancer of civilization," in most communities, service on draft boards was a singular honor, and young men unquestioningly accepted their board's decisions.[2]

Political leaders believed, therefore, that the armed forces had the tools to respond to any contingency in the indefinite future, including extended conventional conflicts in Southeast Asia and Central Europe. As events of the late 1960's and early 1970's were to prove, however, this assumption was in error.

The root cause of the change in the nation's military manpower procurement policies was the Vietnam War and the use of the draft to supply the bulk of combat manpower.[3] While the initial involvement in Vietnam was hailed by many as another commendable effort on the part of the United States to stop communist aggression, the inability of the political and military leadership to bring the war to a quick and successful conclusion caused progressively deepening divisions within the country over the wisdom of intervention and the need to persevere. As draftees, more than any other identifiable group, were paying the price for what was becoming a tragic military venture, it was not surprising that the Selective Service System became the symbol and target of antiwar elements.

For very young man inducted into the army, three to four times as many could avoid service, so the equity of calling only a few also became a major issue. The call-up of only a limited proportion of eligible youth created an attitude, as Eli Ginzberg explained, "that the young man who gets caught and who serves for two or more years on active duty is likely to consider himself a sucker."[4]

Protests by concerned youths were prompted by a variety of motives, ranging from the selfish and frivolous to the self-sacrificing and morally committed. Many youths conscientiously opposed their participation in the war, others believed the war was wrong and therefore opposed the draft. Still others tried to avoid service for reasons of self-interest. While many were earnest in their desire to avoid the draft, others were largely responding to peer pressure. Even among those who deliberately violated the draft law, most expected to avoid prosecution, although some resisters were willing to pay any price—including jail—for their beliefs.

Conscientious Objectors

Those men who applied for Conscientious Objector (CO) status, more than any other group, had strong emotional objections to the war. Many of them deeply and sincerely opposed participation in all wars (a legal requirement for CO status) while others applied for the designation as a protest action—often prompted by anti-draft groups and aimed at overloading the draft machinery, disrupting the delivery of inductees, or provoking media coverage of anti-draft and anti-war activities. Others applied for purely selfish reasons: they saw an opportunity to void their military service obligation, and they took it.

Just who were these young men? In general, they were middle-class youth with considerably greater education than the men being inducted into the army. On the average, they had almost fifteen years of formal education (three years more than high school); more than four of ten were college graduates; more than seven of ten had some college education, and only one of twenty-five had not graduated from high school. Very few blacks or other minority representatives appeared among their ranks.[5]

The legal basis for granting CO status to these men was contained in the Selective Service Act of 1948 (Public Law 759, 80th Congress, and subsequent legislation that modified or amended this law). Under these congressional mandates, local draft boards could grant exemptions from combatant service on grounds of conscience to two categories of young men: (1) those who opposed combatant training and service but were willing to perform noncombatant duties; and (2) those opposed to both combatant and noncombatant service.[6] This latter group was required to perform such alternative civilian service as would contribute to the maintenance of the national health, safety, or interest.

Before the Vietnam War, most men requesting CO status were members of the historic Peace Churches (Mennonite, Brethren, Friends, and certain other denominations), whose claims were easily decided by local draft boards. Furthermore, the number of men applying was small (estimated to be no more than two thousand or so applications per year). Their processing caused no administrative problems nor in any way troubled local boards in meeting their monthly calls for inductees.[7]

The beginning of ground combat action in Vietnam in 1965–66, together with large increases in draft calls, marked the point at which the volume of CO requests began to escalate far beyond what might have been expected because of higher induction levels. By 1970–71 the numbers had become nearly overwhelming. In World War II, when more than ten million men were inducted, an estimated 72,000 CO claims were received.[8] In 1970–71, only 153,000 men were inducted, yet more than 121,000 men applied for CO status—a rate more than one hundred times greater than the rate of application during World War II.[9]

This enormous number of claims caused increasing backlogs in processing workloads. For example, although more than 88,000 CO applications were considered during 1970–71, 33,000 requests were still pending, and the number of such cases was growing. Further administrative headaches for the Selective Service System were caused by the unusually high proportion of young men (33 per cent) who appealed the initial rejection of their claims.

The system also had a responsibility to assist and then place in civilian employment those approved CO's who were unwilling to serve in the armed forces under any circumstances. This too be-

came an administrative problem. As no government funds or facilities were provided, the CO's had to compete for employment in
the labor market. Before the Vietnam War years, the finding of
alternative service jobs was relatively easy. Most of the CO's were
willing seekers of employment. There was a need for such workers
in low-skill public service jobs, such as in mental hospitals, and
the number of men seeking such employment was relatively small.
During the war years, however, the vast increase in the number of
approved applications, an unwillingness on the part of some CO's
to find or keep suitable employment, and a scarcity of jobs in the
public sector due to the worsening economy created an ever-growing backlog of men waiting to be assigned. By 1971 more than
34,000 were awaiting placement, and many of them had been
waiting for several years.[10] In fact, many were able to extend their
waiting period until their twenty-sixth birthday, when their liabil-
ity for alternative service ended.

Two Supreme Court decisions in 1965 and 1970 helped to open
the door for the vast increase in the number of CO claims submitted during 1966–73. Before these decisions, membership in one
of the Peace Churches or a clearly established objection based on
lengthy religious training were the commonly accepted criteria
for granting CO status, and it was easy for local draft boards to
decide claims. The Court decisions, however, so complicated the
criteria for granting CO claims that the submission of lengthy
dissertations based on college philosophy courses or readings became common practice. As a result, most local draft board members had great difficulty comprehending the requests, let alone
deciding on them, and were exposed to criticism. Their position
was well summarized by Walter Goodman: "The reaction of the
nation's local boards when confronted with a CO these days
ranges from something like sympathy to something like antag-
onism, with a good measure of bafflement included."[11]

The first case that so dramatically altered the ground rules on
CO claims concerned Daniel A. Seeger, who had placed quotation
marks around the word "religious" on his application form. After
denial of his claim by the local draft board and appeal bodies,
Seeger appealed his case through the judicial system to the Supreme Court. On 8 March 1965, it unanimously ruled that he was
entitled to CO status.[12] In its opinion, the Court essentially broad-

ened the definition of "religious" to include beliefs which occupied "in the life of its possessor a place parallel to that filled by the God of those admittedly qualified for the exemption."[13]

The Court's second decision concerned the case of Elliott Welsh II.[14] This 1970 ruling was thought by many further to expand the acceptable definition of conscientious objection. Yet, like the Seeger decision, the lengthy Welsh decision lacked specific, easily applicable criteria for determining acceptable claims.

One of the continuing worries of officials during this period was that the "just war" theory of opposition to the Vietnam War alone would also be approved by the Supreme Court. As the statutes authorizing conscientious objection required that opposition be "to all wars," the adoption of the "just war" criteria would have opened the way to still more CO claims. Finally, however, in 1971, the Supreme Court ruled that opposition to a *particular* war was not sufficient grounds for CO status.[15]

Whereas the Selective Service System avoided the difficulties that could have been caused by adoption of the "just war" criteria, the Seeger and Welsh decisions presented it with serious problems. Indeed, an unfortunate result of these decisions was that some truly conscientious objectors were refused CO status. While the confusion over CO criteria in the minds of draft board members may be faulted in such cases, a basic communications gap between youthful applicants and older members of local boards was also responsible. Most local board members assumed that CO's should have arrived at their beliefs rationally, that their objections should have been based on a system of beliefs, and that the young men should have been able to articulate these beliefs. But many of the youths could not accept the need for a rational approach, and believed that their views were too complex to be fit into structured patterns, neat concepts, or well-formed phrases. As a result of these differences, many young men who probably met the legal requirements for CO status were unable to convince their local or appeal boards of their qualifications.[16]

In retrospect, the Supreme Court decisions came close to invalidating the ability of the local boards to decide the truthfulness of CO claims. It can be argued that Congress and the Selective Service System should have removed the decision-making authority on CO claims from the local boards, perhaps by establishing special regional panels of theologians and other experts. But Selective

Service had been founded and operated successfully on the concept of local draft board autonomy—local citizens making decisions about local young men. To change this concept would have resulted in a basic surrender of Selective Service principles, an action which the system could not have seriously considered. As a consequence, local boards muddled through and the seeking of CO status became one of the major methods of opposing the draft and the Vietnam War.

Draft Dodgers

Young men who applied for CO status showed a willingness to cooperate with the system within the boundaries established by law. Other young men, however, challenged the right of the government to conscript—often successfully—by "gaming" the draft procedures.[17]

Draft-dodging efforts were concentrated in certain areas of the country, most often at the locations of large colleges or universities. The activities in New York City were typical. In that large metropolitan area, at the height of draft resistance, seventy-seven of every hundred men who willingly submitted to examination were disqualified (the highest national disqualification rate during this period was approximately fifty-five of one hundred).[18]

The physical examination given to all candidates for induction offered the greatest opportunities for draft dodging. In addition to disqualifications based on false or exaggerated documentation concerning back injuries, football knees, and asthma (these were almost impossible to detect upon examination and generally prompted immediate rejection), the candidates learned a whole variety of tricks and passed them on to others by word of mouth and counseling.[19]

While one group of youth was trying to "game" the system in order to avoid military service altogether, another group was trying indefinitely to delay induction through yet other forms of dodging. One of the most common techniques was to take advantage of every procedural right. These actions included requests for various deferment/exemption or conscientious-objector classifications; as long as there were reasonable grounds for consideration, men could apply for each of the available draft categories.

They also could request personal appearances before local boards in order to explain each request. Further, as each request was denied, they could file formal appeals. Each of these actions placed an administrative burden on the Selective Service System. When the volume of such procedural actions reached its Vietnam War high, resulting delays in processing at most local boards were many months and in some cases years.

The number of men whose processing was delayed because of pending personal appearances is but one indicator of these draft-delaying actions. While 14,468 men were awaiting personal appearances in June 1966, the number had climbed to more than 27,000 by June 1967, to 36,000 by June 1968, to almost 52,000 by June 1969, and to a Vietnam era high of almost 55,000 by June 1970.[20]

The rise in the number of appeals submitted during the Vietnam War years is another indication of the extent of protest action against draft policies. Whereas the number of appeals in fiscal year 1966 equaled some 15 per cent of the more than 343,000 men who were inducted, this percentage rose dramatically in the next five years. For example, in fiscal year 1967 the number of appeals reached 64 per cent. The Vietnam War high was reached in the following year when 136,256 appeals represented 67 per cent of the 203,707 men inducted.[21]

Of course, all registrants who took advantage of procedural rights, personal appearance or appeal were not draft dodgers. Indeed, many legitimate requests were filed, particularly in CO cases. Yet the vast increases in personal appearances and appeals add weight to the argument that many registrants used these processes to "game" the system and contribute to the administrative breakdown of their local boards or the entire Selective Service. In fact, many draft counseling groups and publications openly urged men to take advantage of their rights in order to achieve these purposes. While the great increases in personal appearances and appeals did not prevent local boards from delivering men for induction on schedule, the near overwhelming workload and long delays in processing requests increased the inequities in the handling of draft cases between local boards, geographical areas, and socio-economic groups. They also contributed to a growing dissatisfaction among the press, public, and Congress with Selective Service policies.

Draft Law Violators

Youth's revolt against the management of their lives by the Selective Service System during the Vietnam War years also was evident in draft law enforcement activities. The federal courts were the final arbitrators of violations, yet local boards were responsible for initiating the rather long and complex process between violation and eventual trial. The first of these local board actions—at least during the 1965–69 period—was to declare the violators delinquent. Local boards took this step when young men failed to obey orders for physical examinations or inductions, or to register within required time periods. As there were no firm deadlines for local boards to declare men delinquent, most boards waited several months, giving second and third chances to registrants.

When a local board actually declared a violator delinquent, one of two actions followed: either his case was referred to the Department of Justice (after review for legal sufficiency by Selective Service attorneys) for investigation and possible prosecution; or the delinquent was subject to accelerated induction into the armed forces (at least until this practice was halted by the Supreme Court in 1970).[22]

If a case was referred to the Department of Justice, the FBI attempted to locate the delinquent and determine whether he was willfully violating the law. At this point, if a young man contacted his local board and agreed to obey the Selective Service order, the investigation was dropped. The visits of FBI agents and the prospects of possible indictment also convinced other would-be violators to agree to induction.

If the FBI determined that the violation was willful, or if the delinquent could not be found because he had gone "underground," to Canada, or the like, the case was referred to the U.S. Attorney for the judicial district where the violation took place. Thereafter, many of the cases were presented to grand juries for indictment, others were rejected, and yet others were dropped; even at this late stage, men who agreed to enter the army were allowed to do so unless there were aggravating circumstances.

Putting this entire process into the perspective of draft resistance during the Vietnam War years, one must consider the full range of these actions. For example, during 1963, before major U.S. involvement in Vietnam, the FBI investigated 18,190 cases and had almost 5,000 additional cases pending. By 1965 the numbers had grown only slightly. By 1967, however, the number of cases investigated had increased to 29,128 with an additional 10,000 cases pending. By 1971 the cases awaiting FBI investigation or Department of Justice review had climbed to 27,000, with more than 30,000 cases having been investigated during the year.

The number of men being tried for violations of the draft law was considerably lower. Only 339 men were brought to trial in 1963, though the number began to climb thereafter. In 1966, 516 men were tried. By 1968 the total had more than doubled, and by 1970, 2,833 men were tried. The sharpest increase occurred in 1972, when 4,906 men were brought to trial, due in large part to the special efforts of the Department of Justice and Selective Service lawyers to cut down on their backlog of some 27,000 cases.[23]

The Anti-Draft Movement

Public pressures on lawmakers for corrective actions on the draft issue also were caused by the activities of the anti-draft movement. Through widespread publicity and direct-confrontation tactics, these groups were able to bring their views on the inequities of the Selective Service System, its role in the war, and the moral question of the war itself to those in the country who were not directly facing military service. As a result, more and more Americans took part in their demonstrations, counseling activities, disruptions, and other protest actions. While one may argue that the movement was initially prompted by idealistic young men who faced the possibility of induction, there can be no doubt that the movement grew to include many who did not face military service.

Young college students were the early leaders, spokesmen, and activists of the movement; in the later years of the war, however, the vanguard was composed of respected educators, clergy, businessmen, veterans of Vietnam, and older college students who had been or probably would be excused from military service.

Organized resistance began to burgeon on college campuses across the country in 1965–66. There had been vocal opposition to

U.S. policy in Vietnam before that. But dissent did not move sharply toward defiance of the draft until the war became large enough to have personal impact on the lives of many young people. Thereafter, the minuscule anti-draft movement became a major phenomenon of social protest.[24]

During the late 1960's, as resistance to the war and the draft hardened, a different pattern of opposition—described by Francine Gray as the "ultra resistance"—was also evolving.[25] This form consisted of direct assaults on the Selective Service System itself. Such actions generally were conducted by those who were excluded by sex or age from direct resistance to the draft but wanted an active role in the resistance movement. Demonstrations and the signing of statements seemed adequate to these protesters in the early years of the movement, but as their frustrations increased over their inability to stop the escalation of the Vietnam War, many took more direct action.

By the fall of 1970, such disruptive actions had become commonplace. The Selective Service System admitted 271 "anti-draft occurrences" in the first eight months of that year. The episodes ranged from minor harassments, such as sit-ins and bricks thrown through windows, to destruction of draft board files and facilities, and occasionally attacks on personnel.[26]

The induction capabilities of damaged facilities were impaired for varying periods of time, but in all cases the files were eventually reconstructed from duplicate records, and inductions were resumed. Furthermore, during the months in which these attacks occurred, the overall capability of the system to deliver men to the army was never in jeopardy. In practice, when certain local boards were "inoperative," their share of the induction load was spread to other local boards within the state.

In analyzing the effect of disruptive actions on the Selective Service System, the relative significance of these actions must be considered. For example, during the period of the Vietnam War, the Selective Service System operated approximately four thousand local draft boards, many of them co-located with one or more other boards at central administrative sites. Even during the peak year of disruptions, the several hundred reported incidents involved only a small percentage of potential local board targets. And the disruptive actions were concentrated in areas of the country that coincided with areas of high individual draft resistance.

The disruption of the draft was the immediate objective of the protesters. Yet disruption was only a means to an end. The ultimate goal was an end to the Vietnam War. Draft resistance simply presented itself to opponents of the war as the most effective, and possibly the only, means available to influence that policy. Whereas most of the movement's members attempted to effect change through normal channels of social and political pressure, the "ultra resistance" minority determined to make it as uncomfortable as possible for the government to continue the draft and the war.

Conclusion

The degree of youth's opposition to the war and the draft was without precedence in recent American history. In the 1950's and early 1960's there had been a modicum of draft resistance as well as several attempts to modify or repeal the draft law. The scope of these resistance activities, however, never reached the proportions of those during the Vietnam War years. Nevertheless, in relation to the number of men who willingly accepted induction, even the number of Vietnam-era draft resisters was relatively low.

In light of this, one may ask how so relatively few resisters had so much political influence. There is no simple answer, but two factors deserve mention. First, unlike resisters in earlier wars, the Vietnam resisters were almost exclusively from the ranks of the better educated and the upper economic classes. Through their parents, friends, teachers, employers, and others, they had contact with the leadership of the country, who quickly recognized the depth of the opposition. The sons of unemployed, unskilled workers from inner cities could evade the draft without much public notice. Similar actions by the sons of prominent businessmen, politicians, teachers, and others prompted both heavy media coverage and concern. Second, and equally significant, the degree of draft resistance was higher at the nation's more influential universities—Harvard, Yale, Stanford, the University of Wisconsin, and the University of California, among others—than it was at lesser schools.

While the Selective Service System was able to deliver inductees on schedule during the entire Vietnam War period, there is serious question whether it could have done so without (1) the draft reform measures of 1969–71 which were designed to achieve greater equity of service among young men and to reduce the degree of opposition to the draft, and (2) the defusing of the draft issue by decisions to abandon the draft and adopt AVF recruitment policies. Had these actions not been taken, draft opposition probably would have reached a level at which the system would no longer have functioned. Changes in opinion polls support this view. Throughout the post-World War II years, public support for the draft remained at a consistently high level. At its peak in 1956, some 77 per cent of those surveyed believed that the draft should be continued.[27] Even by the late 1960's, more than 60 per cent still believed that the draft was needed.[28] By January 1970, however, a noticeable drop in the level of public support was evident.[29] Thereafter, support for the draft evaporated in quick order and by 1972 one survey reported that only 13 per cent favored a continuation of conscription.[30]

No doubt the inequitable ways in which the draft provided manpower for the Vietnam War was a major cause of the anti-draft movement, though some draft opposition had existed in earlier years. Yet the draft was but one issue in a range of citizen complaints against U.S. military policy. Despite the fact that a large minority of Americans supported a strong military and defended U.S. actions in Vietnam, it soon became clear that most citizens opposed not only U.S. involvement but also the continuation of a strong military capability. Through their opposition to the draft and to the war, these citizens served notice on military and political leaders alike that they would no longer unquestioningly support a military capability for intervention in foreign wars or the maintenance of a draft mechanism which could manage the youth of the nation and provide unlimited manpower for military build-ups.

As anti-draft and anti-war activities reached their peaks of bitterness and intensity, President Nixon implemented his new foreign and military policy which reduced the strategic capability of the armed forces from a planned 2½ war capability to a 1½ war capability, with an emphasis on participation in the defense of Western Europe. Many factors contributed to this retrenchment, among them a devastating slide in the U.S. balance of payments and growing concern over reductions in U.S. equipment and manpower in Europe which, by 1970, found many units at 40 per cent strength, led by young and inexperienced officers and NCO's and equipped with deteriorating stocks. In addition, the U.S. faced growing international opposition to its involvement in Vietnam and rapidly decreasing support from the NATO allies. Nevertheless, there can be no doubt that the new U.S. policy was caused in large measure by the reaction of the American people to the involvement of American forces in a land war in Asia. The implications of this shift toward a more conservative public attitude were clear: citizens were no longer willing to support a system of conscription for involuntary service in an unpopular war, particularly in Asia. Military leaders could no longer count on the Selective Service System to provide manpower quickly and in sufficient numbers to meet all reasonable contingencies. This restriction on the strategic capabilities of the armed forces did not appear to be significant at the time, but it was the first step toward a major reduction in the ability of U.S. forces to respond to the demands of a major conventional war in Europe.

Notes

1. For an accurate and concise summary of Selective Service legislative and procedural history from 1939 through 1965, see Selective Service System, *Outline of Historical Background of Selective Service* (Washington, D.C., GPO, 1965).
2. B. H. Liddell Hart, *Defence of the West* (London, Cassell, 1950), p. 338.
3. The draft was the major tool for increasing the size of the army and the force level in Vietnam; there were major increases in yearly draft calls (which had averaged 119,000 during 1955–64). During the Vietnam War, more than 1.72 million men were inducted (382,010 in 1966). An additional 3.7 million men (many of whom were draft motivated) and women enlisted, and almost twelve million men were rejected, exempted, indefinitely deferred, or excused through the lottery.
4. Eli Ginzberg with James K. Anderson and John L. German, *The Optimistic Tradition and American Youth* (New York, Columbia University Press, 1962), pp. 79–81.

5. "Survey Shows CO's Talented," *Selective Service News,* January, 1973, p. 4.
6. While most CO's were opposed to all military service, significant numbers (25,000 during World War II) entered the armed forces. Many performed with distinction, including several who won the nation's highest awards for valor while serving as medical corpsmen in combat.
7. J. Harold Sherk, "The Position of the Conscientious Objector," *Current History,* June 1968, p. 21.
8. Selective Service System, *Conscientious Objection,* Special Monograph No. 11 (Washington, D.C., GPO, 1950), pp. 315–332.
9. Selective Service System, *Semi-Annual Report of the Director of Selective Service, July 1, 1970–December 31, 1970* (Washington, D.C., GPO, 1971), p. 8; *Semi-Annual Report of the Director of Selective Service, January 1, 1971–June 30, 1971* (Washington, D.C., GPO, 1971), p. 58.
10. Selective Service System, *Semi-Annual Report of the Director of Selective Service, January 1, 1975–June 30, 1975* (Washington, D.C., GPO, 1975), p. 82.
11. Walter Goodman, "They March to Different Drummers," *New York Times Magazine,* 26 June 1966, p. 42.
12. *United States* v. *Seeger,* 380 U.S. 163 (1965).
13. 85 *Supreme Court Reporter,* pp. 850–851.
14. *Welsh* v. *U.S.,* 398 U.S. 333 (1970).
15. In this case, the defendant, Guy Gillette, had been convicted for failing to report for induction after his claim had been denied. Gillette had based his claim on his belief that he was morally opposed to serving in Vietnam, though he would have been willing to fight in defense of the United States or in a UN peacekeeping mission. In ruling on the case, the Supreme Court held, by an 8-1 margin, that opposition to a particular war was not sufficient basis for exemption and that denial of the "just war" argument did not violate Gillette's 1st Amendment rights. See *Gillette* v. *U.S.,* 401 U.S. 437 (1971).
16. As Richard Killmer, Robert Lecky, and Debrah Wiley explained: "Most groups and individuals in our society accept the Selective Service definition of conscience, and believe that a system of belief, a rational approach and articulateness are necessary 'proofs' of sincerity." See *They Can't Go Home Again* (Philadelphia, Pilgrim Press, 1971), pp. 98–99.
17. All violations of the *Military Selective Service Act,* ranging from burning of draft cards to refusing induction, were subject to

the same penalties, a maximum of five years in prison, a
$10,000 fine, or both.

18. For a detailed discussion of the draft avoidance activities in New
York City, see Mel Zeigler, "Selective Service Meets Massive Resistance," *New York Magazine,* 29 June 1970.

19. Among the ways of "beating the system" were faking homosex-
uality, acting out the symptoms of mental breakdown, taking
heroin or marijuana, or creating the illusion of drug addiction
by puncturing one's arms with a hypodermic needle. Other
ways included getting drunk, as well as faking suicidal ten-
dencies. Men also could be disqualified for getting arrested on a
variety of minor charges, or by reporting to the examination
without having washed or shaved for several weeks. Some men
were even rejected on the basis of substitute blood, urine, or
feces samples which had been obtained from men with disqual-
ifying diseases and then smuggled into examination sites.

20. Statistics on pending personal appearances were compiled from
Annual Reports of the Director of Selective Service for 1966,
1967, and 1968, and from Semi-Annual Reports of the Director
of Selective Service for 1969, 1970, 1971, and 1972.

21. Data from Annual and Semi-Annual Reports of the Director of
Selective Service for the years cited. These reports were published by the Government Printing Office (GPO) in Washington, D.C.

22. *Breen* v. *Local Board No. 16,* 396 U.S. 295 (1970); *Gutknecht* v.
U.S., 396 U.S. 295 (1970).

23. A summary of the extent of draft law violations was provided by
Walter H. Morse, General Counsel, Selective Service System,
before the Judiciary Subcommittee, House of Representatives,
on 8 March 1974. According to Morse, 191,840 registrants
failed to respond for induction into the armed forces during the
Vietnam conflict (when 1.8 million men were inducted). Most
of these men eventually agreed to enter the army, though
19,153 were indicted or put under a criminal complaint. Of
these, 10,035 had their indictments dismissed. Of the remaining
9,118, 1,186 were acquitted while 7,932 were convicted.

24. According to Irving L. Horowitz, there were more than one thousand anti-war demonstrations, including more than fifty major
demonstrations, during the four years 1965–68. Although the
draft was not the specific target of all these protest actions,
many of them included anti-draft speeches, draft card burnings,
draft card turn-ins, and sit-ins and walk-ins at Selective Service
offices. See Irving L. Horowitz, *The Struggle Is the Message:*

The Organization and Ideology of the Anti-War Movement (Berkeley, Glendessary Press, 1970), pp. 148–167.

25. See Francine du Plessix Gray, *Divine Disobedience: Profiles in Catholic Radicalism* (New York, Knopf, 1970).
26. Selective Service System, Office of Public Information, Press Release, "Disruption of Selective Service Local Board Operations," 7 September 1970.
27. *Gallup Poll: Public Opinion* (New York, Random House, 1972), p. 1452.
28. *Christian Science Monitor*, 26 February 1969.
29. According to the *Washington Post*, 26 January 1970, only some 52 per cent of those surveyed favored a continuation of the draft.
30. See *Attitudes of Youth Toward Military Service* (Alexandria, Virginia, Human Resources Research Organization, 1972).

Chapter II

Government Response:

Equity and Draft Reform

On 5 March 1963, the Committee on Armed Services of the House of Representatives voted 37 to 0 to extend the policies of the Selective Service System for another four years. The vote followed less than five hours of hearings. Six days later, the full House approved the extension, 388 to 3. Four days later, the Senate passed the bill by a voice vote after only ten minutes of debate. President Kennedy signed the bill into law on 28 March 1963. From start to finish, the whole process had taken less than a month. As Hanson Baldwin noted, "The opposition is apathetic and politically unimportant."[1]

Yet within the next decade, the question of fundamental change in the policies and procedures of the Selective Service System became a major political issue of bitter divisiveness which required the extended involvement of the Administration and Congress.

The stakes in this battle were clear. To supporters of the status quo, the issue centered on the ability of the United States to maintain a strong military force able to defend national interests in all possible contingencies, including a conventional conflict in Europe between the forces of NATO and the Warsaw Pact. To this end, they saw the draft, with its widespread channeling activities, as managing the youth of the nation in support of these strategic objectives. They also saw the uncomplicated induction procedures of the draft as a viable deterrent during periods of peace and a source of manpower augmentation during periods of international crisis and military emergency. In short, to this constituency the draft was a vital component of the national defense effort.

Advocates of draft reform focused on the right of Selective Service to such absolute control over the lives of young people. In this judgment, the system's authority was too great, and corrective action could be taken without seriously affecting the nation's national defense capabilities. To this end, reformers hoped to obtain greater legal protection for draft-age youths and to remove many of the discretionary decisions from local draft boards. (Local boards had great freedom in deciding which young men from their communities would be deferred or exempted from service and which young men would be inducted.) Thus, in seeking policy changes, the reformers directly challenged the need for Selective Service to retain all of its traditional authority. In a sense, therefore, they also challenged the strategic policies which depended on the draft—among other resources—to provide required military capabilities.

This issue was of course directly related to the war in Vietnam and to the large role of the draft in supplying manpower for that conflict. And there is no doubt that the deep concerns and emotions which developed as a result of the war focused attention on those many young men who had been involuntarily inducted and on the seeming unfairness of draft board decisions which had sent them off to war without extensive safeguards for their individual rights.

Early Reform Attempts

The first attempts to challenge Selective Service policies occurred during the 1964 session of Congress. On some two dozen occasions, one or another member critiqued current induction practices—an effort equal to the sum of such criticisms during the preceding ten years. In addition, bills were introduced to create a study commission for review of draft policies and to require a plan for ending the draft by mid-1967. Thus the embryo of a serious congressional challenge to Selective Service policies developed at the same time the nation's military leaders were beginning to involve American forces in Vietnam. Although more of an irritant than an actual threat to existing draft policies, the 1964 question-

ing of the draft prompted President Lyndon B. Johnson to an-
nounce his approval of plans for a comprehensive study of Selective Service to be conducted by the Department of Defense.

The results of the Johnson-ordered study of the draft were presented to the House Committee on Armed Services in mid-1966.[2]
While the Department of Defense report did little more than
"rubber stamp" the existing draft system, the congressional hearings marked the first extensive public review of Selective Service
since the Korean War, the first ever conducted without a specific
legislative proposal at hand. No doubt they opened the door for
more extensive challenges to the system in later years.

After mid-1965, however, opportunities for reform were ob-
scured by increased demands for military manpower and the
corresponding buildup of U.S. ground combat forces in Vietnam.
At the same time, as James W. Gerhardt points out, large numbers
of unmobilized reservists, deferred students, fathers, and marginally qualified youths, together with rising and disproportionate
casualties among draftees in Vietnam, sharpened public perception of the anomalies and inequities in the nation's military manpower policies, and growing protests against both the war and the
role of the draft in supporting the war heightened the reformers'
sense of urgency.[3]

Year of Hope and Despair

The year 1967 offered draft reformers high hopes for action within Congress. Not only had President Johnson appointed
a twenty-member National Advisory Commission on Selective
Service, chaired by Burke Marshall; but, responding to the President's move and apparently interested in a different set of views,
the House Armed Services Committee had appointed its own Civilian Advisory Panel on Military Manpower Procurement, chaired
by retired General Mark Clark. Both reports were due in 1967.
Although the Clark Report was expected to be another rubber
stamp of Selective Service policies, reformers believed that the
Marshall Commission would be highly critical of the draft and
would provide the stimulus for legislative change. Prompted by
growing opposition to the draft (and perhaps eager to stifle further criticism), the President had in the Marshall Commission

appointed a truly independent and experienced membership. The Clark panel, by contrast, was heavily weighted toward traditional military views of manpower policy.

The Marshall Commission submitted its report to President Johnson in early 1967, and its recommendations delighted the draft-reform bloc. The Commission found that Selective Service operations produced two kinds of inequities in the distribution of military service among young men. First, there were different opportunities for avoiding service among different socio-economic groups. Physical and mental requirements weighted the incidence of service toward relatively healthier and brighter youths and prevented many of the disadvantaged from serving. In addition, the Commission noted that deferments for study and occupation, often convertible to exemptions, weighted the chances of service avoidance in favor of more highly educated and economically better off youths. Second, decentralized and local board autonomy produced myriad variations in deferments for study, occupation, and hardship among youths in similiar circumstances living in different parts of the country or simply registered with different local boards.[4]

The Report of the Clark panel gave draft reformers much less to cheer about, for, as expected, it endorsed a continuation of existing policies.[5]

Following publication of the Marshall Commission and the Clark reports, President Johnson formally requested another four-year extension of the Selective Service induction authority (the induction authority was the only section of the long Selective Service legislation that had a limited life). He also asked Congress to enact certain reform measures in Selective Service policies. While rejecting many of the more revolutionary changes recommended by the Marshall Commission, the President proposed to end a number of inequities, including the calling of "oldest-first" and deferments for graduate students.

The congressional debates which followed were, if measured by the variety of specific proposals, long and complicated; but the fundamental alternatives at stake were simple. One was to preserve existing policies and programs more or less intact. Defenders of this alternative continued to emphasize the principle of a universal service obligation either in the armed forces or in a "shortage" civilian profession. In their view, this was vital to the preservation of a military force able to respond to all forseeable contingencies. The other alternative offered important changes in the principles and process of selection. Those seeking reform urged greater concern for equity and a reduced role for the system in providing for nonmilitary needs. Totally absent from the debate was serious consideration of abandoning conscription in favor of all-volunteer procurement policies. Yet the meaning of the challenge was clear: a growing number of Americans were unhappy with existing practices.

The debate was extensive and, at least in the House, heated. But the Military Selective Service Act of 1967 (Public Law 40, 90th Congress), signed into law by President Johnson on 30 June 1967, contained few changes. Among other new provisions, the 1967 law made college undergraduate deferments mandatory unless the President formally declared that the needs of the armed forces required the drafting of college students. It also required the President to obtain the specific approval of Congress if he wished to introduce any sort of lottery plan for choosing inductees, and it denied draft-exempt status to doctors who served the Peace Corps overseas or who worked for the Food and Drug Administration. Perhaps the major reform provision of the new law was the change in policy concerning deferments for graduate students. Their fate now would be in the hands of the National Security Council, which recommended on 15 February 1968, that no further graduate student deferments be given to persons in fields other than medicine, dentistry, veterinary medicine, osteopathy, and optometry.

A number of conclusions may be drawn from the legislative process of approving the 1967 draft law. First, Congress was not willing to accept the Administration's quest for equity in Selective Service processing, though several small steps in this direction were approved. Second, the failure of Congress to make significant changes in the draft law was a personal victory for Chairman L. Mendel Rivers of the House Armed Services Committee, and others who believed that the national defense capabilities of the armed forces depended heavily on the existing conscription system. Third, Draft Director General Lewis B. Hershey emerged once more as an immovable object in his resistance to any change in the administration or operation of the draft. In sum, while the majority agreed with Congressman Rivers, many others echoed the sentiments of the *New York Times*, which commented, "The draft bill is a small but regrettable victory for the know-nothing sentiment prevailing in the House Armed Services Committee."[6]

Mounting Support and Limited Success

By 1968 calls for draft reform were mounting, and the lack of equitable treatment of youth by local draft boards was a subject of continuing and increasing criticism in the nation's media.[7]

Influential members of Congress also were beginning to call for draft reforms. Among them was Senator Edward M. Kennedy of Massachusetts, who championed the lottery system of selecting young men for induction (even though such a system had been prohibited by the 1967 law).[8] Other members of Congress joining the call for draft reform included Representatives John E. Moss of California and Robert Stafford of Vermont. In fact, Stafford and four other members of Congress wrote a book entitled *How to End the Draft*, which argued for sustaining the armed forces with volunteers by making service pay rates competitive with private industry.

Despite growing opposition to the draft within Congress, the power of General Hershey and his supporters on the House and Senate Armed Services Committees remained formidable. Whereas Stafford's group, which introduced a bill calling for several procedural reforms in the draft, could issue a stinging criticism of both Hershey and the Administration for rejecting the recommendations of the Marshall Commission, Stafford acknowledged that without a widespread national clamor for change, "there's no chance of getting anything through this session of Congress."[9]

Stafford's prediction was correct: 1968 proved an uneventful year. But emotions were mounting, draft resistance and demonstrations were reaching a peak, and the newly elected President Nixon was under pressure to pacify these elements by championing various procedural reforms in the draft. Committed to such changes by promises made during the presidential campaign of 1968, Nixon submitted the first of his draft reform proposals to Congress on 13 May 1969. Reaffirming his commitment to seek an AVF (when the Vietnam War ended), he requested authority to

institute a lottery system to select men for induction, and authority to induct men on a youngest-first rather than an oldest-first
basis.[10]

The President submitted the proposals despite earlier indications of opposition. For as the *Wall Street Journal* commented in
1966, "The public is 3 to 1 against it. The American Legion is
against it, too. And the man who has to put it into effect (General
Hershey) hates the thought of it."[11]

General Hershey's objection to the lottery proposal was deep-
rooted. In his view, unchanged by 1969, a lottery would limit the
prerogatives of local draft boards and thus have a negative impact on strategic capabilities. Nevertheless, the idea of using a
lottery to select young men for the draft had gained support in
Washington, with many Administration leaders and Congressmen
going on record in favor of a lottery to help eliminate the "uncertainties and inequities" of the draft. The new interest largely reflected rising public dissatisfaction with the operations of the
draft, and the chorus of complaints grew louder as draft calls
mounted. As a result, there was little serious opposition in Congress to the Nixon proposals. Although the Old Guard of Hershey
supporters tried once again to block the reform measure, their
efforts were unsuccessful, and the bill was signed into law by
President Nixon on 26 November 1969 (Public Law 124, 91st
Congress).[12]

While the lottery authorization reduced some of the uncertainties for young men facing possible induction, it did not eliminate
major inequities in Selective Service policies. Further, while many
who had objected to the lottery proposal did so on the grounds
that there would be "winners" and "losers," the fact that there
would be winners and losers under any selection system was often
forgotten. The problem lay not in the method of selection; it lay
in the fact that only a small minority of those eligible for induction would actually be called.

Despite its failure to remedy these continuing problems, the
1969 authorization for a lottery and a youngest-first order of selection was a major draft reform. Some supporters of the draft hoped
it would reduce pressures for further policy changes. Instead, agi-
tation mounted, and the new target for reform became one of the
bastions of local board operations: occupational deferments.

At the time such deferments were the cornerstone of the system's program for managing the youth of the nation. Through selective deferments, Selective Service could channel young men into "critical" civilian occupations and "essential" activities.

Hershey was especially proud that the draft, as he saw it, had used its deferments to promote and protect society's larger interest. Testifying before the House, he said:

> Deferment is the carrot we have used to get individuals
> into occupations and professions that are said by those
> in charge of Government to be the necessary ones. I am
> convinced that this Nation has paced the world techno-
> logical advance of recent years in large part because
> scores of thousands of people have become scientists,
> engineers, teachers and acquired and applied other tech-
> nical skills because they were deferred to do so.[13]

The Director of Selective Service was typical of many military men and government officials who saw the draft as a way of forcing young men into vocations chosen for them by the government. They advocated not a smaller draft in peacetime, but a draft that was used in both peace and war to direct the energies of young men into military service or needed civilian professions. To many others, however, such policies reflected what Kenneth Boulding called "a wide control over civilian life that is characteristic of totalitarian regimes."[14]

Many others objected to the channeling practices on different grounds. One of these was Congressman John V. Lindsay, who explained:

> Deferments, then, are extended to nuclear scientists,
> but not to classicists, sociologists or political scientists,
> who, says the Government, are less essential to national
> security. Thus, in the name of national security and
> Government interest, the future course of emphasis in
> our society may be changed by the State, indeed by
> the military apparatus.[15]

Collectively, opposition to the channeling policies was widespread and mounting. Whereas many supporters of the draft maintained that such deferments were needed for reasons of national defense, the growing opposition, together with increasing public awareness of gross inequities in the management of the program, as well as some inappropriate public statements and actions by General Hershey, convinced the President that action was essential. In late 1969 he relieved General Hershey as draft director; on 23 April 1970, he issued an Executive Order which canceled the authority of the system to issue occupational deferments.[16]

The channeling policy had provided many skilled workers and educated professionals in times of national need. Since the end of the Korean War, however, more deferments had been granted to persons employed in community service, such as policemen, firemen, teachers, and social workers, than to those working in defense-related industries. By 1970 there was no great need for deferred men in war-essential industries. The use of the deferment authority to steer men toward community-related service employment, however, was thought by many to be a policy in the national interest. At the time, many such professions were understaffed, owing largely to low salary schedules. Community leaders welcomed the channeling of young men into these professions, and they strongly opposed the ending of the occupational deferment authority. As events proved, however, during the post-Vietnam War years of high unemployment, community service positions that had often been hard to fill were no longer open. Indeed, there were long lines of candidates. By the mid-1970's, therefore, even the community service justification for the occupational deferment program had evaporated.

Many officials mourned the passing of the occupational deferment program. Yet, with the exception of some civic leaders, this regret was based primarily on fear of being unable to meet future requirements in times of national emergency. Even in this context, however, the program would have been of great value only in a major mobilization, when a quick and massive conversion of civilian industries to manufacturers of war materials would be needed. And while such a major mobilization was not completely discounted by military planners, the growing realization among the military services that a future conflict would likely become nuclear before it reached the conventional level of past major wars dampened the enthusiasm of those who supported a continuation of channeling efforts. As a result, there was little opposition to the President's decision within the Pentagon or Congress.

The Final Draft Reform Measures

The ending of occupational deferments pacified some draft reformers. But others found a new target in the inequity of granting undergraduate deferments while drafting non-college men, and the inequitable methods used by local draft boards in selecting men for induction.[17]

By 1970 anti-draft and anti-war activities had reached such a high level that few observers expected serious objections to still further draft reform measures. Indeed, when the President asked Congress in April 1970 for authority to phase out undergraduate deferments and induct men across the nation on the basis of a Uniform National Call (so that men with the same lottery numbers would be inducted at the same time, regardless of their local boards), he drew near overwhelming support. Many Congressmen called for even more changes in draft policies in order to provide registrants with greater procedural safeguards.

Despite the growing commitment of most Congressmen for further draft reform, Nixon's proposal met with initial resistance from key congressional committees. It was not until 1971 (after the President had resubmitted his request) that Congress undertook the final Vietnam-era consideration of draft reform. While the debate was the longest of the year, the outcome was never in doubt. In addition to authorizing an end to undergraduate deferments and the utilization of a Uniform National Call, the legislation also directed extensive changes in Selective Service operations, including the granting of many more procedural rights to registrants. The new law was signed by President Nixon on 28 September 1971 (Public Law 129, 92nd Congress). This last draft reform measure of the Vietnam War period took effect as American forces were accelerating their withdrawal from Vietnam and draft calls were ending.

Conclusion

In 1967 and 1968 (and perhaps in 1969), challenges to Selective Service policies did not pose a severe threat to existing practices. Over the next two years, however, the defenses of the status quo crumbled. Strong sentiment opposing the draft and the war caused a fundamental readjustment of power in Congress, where the rank-and-file successfully challenged the older leadership. This does not happen often in American politics, nor does it happen quickly. But the bandwagon of anti-draft feelings, buttressed by ever-growing public dissatisfaction with the war and draft policies, and ever-increasing resistance to the draft by American youth, provided an unstoppable assault on Selective Service programs.

Certainly General Hershey and other supporters of a strong national defense capability should have seen the potential dangers in the challenge to Selective Service policies. They might have agreed early on to reasonable policy adjustments. With the wisdom of hindsight, it is easy to see that their stiff resistance to change fanned emotions over the draft issue and strengthened the resolve of draft reformers. Indeed, the confrontation over draft reform kept the issue of the war and the draft in the public mind, with more and more citizens recognizing, as Theodore H. White explained, that "the draft could not work in a war for which there was no consent, either of Congress or of the public, and which required so little manpower that choice for service became a matter of fate, bad luck or trickery."[18]

Still, any set of draft policies—including those championed by reformers during 1967–71—would likely have been attacked. By whatever system, large numbers of men would still have been excused from service, at a time when the sacrifice of those being called up was great by contrast. The critics would not have been pacified.

For all the proposals, debates, discussions, protests, and decisions concerning the draft, the immediate impact of the reforms was negligible. True, certain registrants, their parents, and antidraft proponents were pacified; yet, after the final draft reform measure was instituted, the system was still granting some deferments and exemptions and generally deciding who would be inducted into the armed forces. Furthermore, the changes were not effected until the end of the Vietnam War. In 1970, for example, the first year in which the lottery was used, only 162,746 men were inducted (the Vietnam War high was reached in 1966 when 382,010 men were inducted); and in 1972, the first year in which men were called by the Uniform National Call, only 49,524 men were inducted. During each of these years, approximately two million young men had become eligible for induction.

Regardless of the limited impact on draft policies during the Vietnam War, however, the changes did create two potential weaknesses in U.S. strategic capabilities. First, and of lesser significance, by removing the authority of the Selective Service System to channel youth into educational programs and professions judged to be in the national interest, the government also removed the ability of the armed forces to manage young people in support of a major mobilization effort. In short, restricting the use of deferment authorities removed the ability of the system to develop and support a critical industrial base. One may argue, of course, that such channeling activities were appropriate for World War II, but that the development of nuclear weapons and the rising costs of military equipment made such a total national mobilization an obsolete concept. Indeed, even if a conflict of World War II dimensions developed, the complexities of modern weapons systems would disallow quick expansions of the industrial base. Consequently, even in such an extreme scenario, a sudden need for deferred workers would be highly unlikely. And if such a need evolved, the deferment policies could be restored. For this reason, then, there would appear to be little military value in retaining the occupational deferment policy. While some would argue that the policy was cheap insurance, it appears that the possibilities for utilizing the authority are so remote that even a modest insurance premium would be too high.

The second and greatest weakness in strategic capabilities caused by the draft reform measures concerns the ability of the system quickly and effectively to process inductees in the event of a national crisis. Because of the various procedural rights instituted as part of the last draft reform package, large numbers of youth could delay their induction process and administratively overload the draft machinery. If this were to occur, Selective Service could be prevented from meeting its national emergency commitments.

The chances of such a widespread opposition to induction policies taking place in an atmosphere of national crisis are remote, however. In the aftermath of the Vietnam War, it is inconceivable that the military services would call for massive numbers of conscripts unless the military emergency was a clear and present danger and unless the force expansion had the support of a majority of national leaders and citizens. The enactment of the War Powers Resolution (Public Law 93–148) supports this contention. The resolution, which was passed in 1973 over President Nixon's veto, requires that the President consult with Congress "in every possible instance" before American troops are introduced "into hostilities or into situations where imminent involvement in hostilities is clearly indicated by the circumstances."

With the passage of time, the frenzied emotions of the waning days of the Vietnam War have faded. As the decade was ending, the American people were moving back toward a greater level of support for the armed forces than they demonstrated in the years immediately after the Vietnam War.[19] Consequently, the draft probably would be resumed in an emergency which had less than full public support. And in such a situation, the ability of Selective Service to provide conscripts could be curtailed by an abnormally high rate of procedural rights requests.

In a sense, the legislation of these new procedural rights reflected the changing view of American lawmakers on the issue of the draft and the responsibility of citizens to serve. Before, the manpower needs of the armed forces were thought to be paramount; in view of the new procedural rights, however, it can be argued that the legislators came to view the welfare of individual registrants as more important than military needs.

In summary, then, it is not likely that national defense capabilities would have been so abruptly changed if the opposition to the draft and the war had been pacified by draft reform measures and the withdrawal of forces from Vietnam. Rather, the growing undercurrent of opposition to the draft in the years before the Vietnam War would eventually have forced legislators to grapple with draft law changes. Indeed, Morris Janowitz has suggested that the process of abandoning the draft in favor of an AVF was due to changes in both technological and socio-political factors, associated with World War II, which had been underway for more than twenty years prior to the draft reform efforts of the late 1960's.[20]

Nevertheless, because of the impetus provided by draft law abuses during the Vietnam War years, the momentum for change quickly led to an effort to repeal conscription altogether. Thus the movement for draft reform should be viewed in context of overall changes in U.S. military manpower policies since 1969 and their resulting impacts on strategic capabilities. In this light, the draft reform movement, which resulted in large measure from the revolt of youth against the war and the draft, was another step on the road toward a new military strategy based on a reduced national defense capability.

Notes

1. Hanson W. Baldwin, "New Attitudes on Peacetime Draft," *New York Times*, 8 March 1963, p. 10.
2. Thomas D. Morris, Assistant Secretary for Defense (Manpower), Statement before the House Committee on Armed Services, *Report on Department of Defense Study of Draft*, 30 June 1966.
3. James M. Gerhardt, *The Draft and Public Policy: Issues in Military Manpower Procurement 1945–1970* (Columbus, Ohio State University Press, 1971), p. 358.
4. The National Advisory Commission on Selective Service, *Report* (Washington, D.C., GPO, 1967), pp. 4–8.
5. Civilian Advisory Panel on Military Manpower Procurement, *Report to the Committee on Armed Services, House of Representatives*, 90th Congress, 1st Session (Washington, D.C., GPO, 1967), pp. 3, 21–25.
6. *New York Times*, 21 June 1967, p. 40.
7. The following comment from the *International Herald-Tribune* was typical: "There is no excuse for a draft law that contains as many inequities as the one under which young Americans are now being called to military duty." 8 March 1968, p. 4.
8. Edward M. Kennedy, "Random Selection: An Alternative to Selective Service," *Current History*, August 1968, p. 93.
9. *Washington Evening Star*, 15 September 1968, p. 16.
10. The Nixon proposal to substitute a youngest-first for the oldest-first order of induction did not create undue controversy in Congress. The move had been recommended by various groups and authorities, including the Marshall Commission and the Clark Panel.
11. Frederick Taylor, "Luck of the Draw," *Wall Street Journal*, 9 December 1966, p. 1.
12. On 1 December 1969, the first national lottery drawing since 1942 was held in Washington, D.C. The drawing assigned a random sequence number (order of induction) to each birth-

date of the year. In subsequent years, new drawings were held for the age group becoming eligible for induction.

13. U.S. Congress, House of Representatives, Committee on Armed Services, Hearings, *Review of the Administration and Operation of the Selective Service System*, 22 June–30 August 1966, p. 9647.

14. Kenneth Boulding, et al., *The Draft?* (New York, Hill and Wang, 1968), p. 51.

15. Representative John V. Lindsay, *Congressional Record*, 21 April 1964, p. 8576.

16. President Nixon relieved General Hershey of his duties as Director of Selective Service by promoting him to full general and adding him to the White House staff in a new position of "Manpower Advisor" (which was terminated upon Hershey's eventual retirement). General Hershey's administration of the draft had been subject to increasing criticism during the Vietnam War years. Although the President had previously expressed his complete confidence in Hershey, his decision to replace him at the sensitive post was widely regarded as a concession to anti-draft and anti-war opinion.

17. In 1970 men with deferments for college studies were the largest group of deferees remaining in Selective Service files. Only 78,000 college students were deferred in 1951, but the number grew progressively, and by 1969 more than 1.75 million men held such deferments. Although many of these men entered the armed forces upon the completion of their studies, many others were able to avoid service by obtaining further deferment, passing their prime period of eligibility for induction, or failing the induction medical examination. The elimination of deferments for graduate studies and occupations, of course, had significantly reduced the number of college graduates or dropouts who obtained further deferment.

18. Theodore H. White, *The Making of the President 1972* (New York, Atheneum, 1973), p. 42.

19. Several indications of this trend were apparent in late 1978 and early 1979. For example, the chairman of the joint chiefs of staff, the secretary of the army, and the two armed services committees called for the restoration of a peacetime draft registration program. In addition, the Fiscal Year 1980 budget proposal, submitted to Congress by President Jimmy Carter in early 1979, contained considerably higher funding for the armed forces than in other post-Vietnam War years.

20. Morris Janowitz, "The Decline of the Mass Army," *Military Review*, February 1972, p. 13.

Chapter III

Political Reality:
The Abandonment of
Selective Service

When, in 1959, the House Armed Services Committee called the Selective Service System "vital to the preservation of the American way of life," few critics questioned its conclusion.[1] Yet with the commitment of American ground forces to Vietnam in 1965 and the corollary decision to build the army force level through inductions rather than mobilizing the reserves, the question of whether to support armed forces with conscripts or with volunteers became a major national issue.

The unpopularity of the war, of course, forced the emergence of this long dormant debate. But peacetime conscription had also been necessary in the years before Vietnam, and the prospect of returning to it after the war disturbed many citizens. Largely this was due to the bitterness of the Vietnam experience, but it also reflected the fact that the idea of a *voluntary* peacetime standing army—citizen soldiers—is deeply rooted among most Americans, a belief derived from the Anglo-American heritage of individual freedom and democratic political processes.[2] In fact, as of 1971, conscription of men into the armed forces had been approved for only thirty-three of the almost two hundred years of national existence. And in almost all of these thirty-three years, the United States had been involved in an armed conflict.

Thus the question of whether inductions were necessary during periods of peace was at the heart of the draft-AVF debate, though the issue could never be completely isolated from the Cold War. For example, the reinstitution of the peacetime draft in 1948 was prompted by developing Cold War tensions, highlighted by the

Berlin crisis and sustained by the Korean War. Thereafter, the maintenance of a large standing armed force was repeatedly justified on the ground of communist threats. Even the advent of more sophisticated nuclear weapons failed to convince Administration and congressional leaders that major changes could be made in U.S. military policy.

By the late 1960's, however, traditional justifications for strong armed forces were being seriously challenged by an increasing number of influential leaders. Armed with knowledge of waning support for the armed forces, and with growing anti-draft and anti-war sentiment among U.S. citizens, the leaders of the anti-draft forces recognized the trend which had been occurring in other Western democracies in the postwar years toward reduced strategic commitments supported by smaller active forces and much reduced reserve components.[3] In their view, the abandonment of conscription in the U.S. was only a matter of time.

Early Attempts to End Conscription

While Congress in 1965–67 was primarily concerned with reforming rather than ending the draft, more and more leaders pressed for serious consideration of a totally volunteer army.[4] Although the Department of Defense succeeded in summarily dismissing their suggestions for doing away with the draft primarily on grounds of cost, the Department's position was challenged by several experts, including Milton Friedman and Walter Y. Oi, and the views of these noted economists were accepted by an ever-wider audience.[5]

Friedman and Oi first presented their arguments for an AVF in 1966. Modified and repeated over the next few years, their economic justification formed the basis for the eventual adoption of pay increases and other benefits which made all-volunteer recruiting a viable alternative. During the years of the Vietnam conflict, however, such arguments were academic, for even the most optimistic proponents of the AVF concept did not envision that the nation could support an AVF during wartime. Yet, as the withdrawal of U.S. forces from Vietnam became a reality, the achievement of a peacetime armed force manned by volunteers became a realistic objective.

President Nixon and the AVF

If any one man was most responsible for the abandonment of conscription, it was Richard M. Nixon. He correctly recognized that by late 1968 the Vietnam War and the draft had so
soured American voters that a political position which pledged
an end to interventionist capability and the conscription system
needed to sustain that capability would bring victory in the forth-
coming presidential election. Nixon's challenge of the 2½ war
capability and peacetime conscription provoked enthusiastic support, and his comments—which were interpreted as a pledge to
reduce the role of the armed forces and to end the draft—were
repeated throughout the last weeks of the 1968 campaign.

All presidential candidates make promises, so one may ask
whether Nixon's promise to end the draft was a serious commitment? After all, the war was still raging, and the promise to implement AVF recruiting measures for the peacetime army need not
have been honored until at least several years thereafter.[6] Nixon
apparently was sincere, however, in exploring the matter. His ap-
pointment of the Gates Commission in 1969 was a major step in
this direction. Officially called the President's Commission on an
All-Volunteer Armed Force, and chaired by former Secretary of
Defense Thomas Gates, the group was asked to recommend actions necessary to support the armed forces totally with volunteers.

Although the Commission was charged with exploring the
adoption of an AVF, it was clear that the basic decision had already
been made and that the Commission's efforts would be directed
toward developing ways and means to implement it. Consequently, few people were surprised when, less than a year later, the
Commission recommended that conscription be ended.[7] In order to
accomplish this, the Commission suggested three policy changes.
First, basic pay for recruits would have to be increased by 75 per
cent. Second, comprehensive improvements would be needed in
recruiting programs and in conditions of military life. Third, a
standby draft system would have to be established to be activated
by joint resolution of Congress upon request of the President.

The focus of the Commission's effort was on the economic incentives required to attract an adequate number of additional
volunteers. Consideration of the impact of an AVF on U.S. strategic

capabilities was quite limited. In its deliberations, the Commission simply assumed that the peacetime level of the armed forces after completion of the withdrawal from Vietnam would be between 2.0 and 2.5 million. It also ignored recruiting problems which could be anticipated under an AVF concept in the reserve forces. In short, the Commission's research concentrated on the steps necessary to support a peacetime active force level somewhat below that of previous peacetime years. The report presented persuasive arguments and evidence, but its failure to analyze the probable impact of an AVF decision on strategic capabilities and, most particularly, on the reserve forces was a glaring omission. Nonetheless, the Commission report, based on a series of research studies which "disproved" a list of anti-AVF claims, prompted an immediate endorsement from President Nixon and a pledge to submit specific implementing legislative proposals to Congress at an appropriate time (when the United States was closer to complete withdrawal from Vietnam).

As expected, the report and the President's endorsement had a mixed reaction from Congress. While an impressive coalition of liberals and conservatives from all sections of the country praised the findings (with some members urging immediate implementation), others, including key members of the Armed Services Committee, were not so sure.

Despite this opposition, there were several premature attempts to legislate the pay increases recommended by the Commission and to set a final date for Selective Service inductions. The leader of this effort was long-term draft foe Senator Mark Hatfield, who obtained fourteen co-sponsors for his "implementation" bill, including Senators George McGovern (soon to be the 1972 Democratic presidential candidate) and Barry Goldwater.

Other measures, such as House Resolution No. 232 of 20 February 1969, signed by fifty-four Representatives, simply endorsed the President's decision to pursue the volunteer army concept. A corollary resolution (House Resolution No. 13379 of 16 March 1970), sponsored by twenty-nine members, urged the elimination of the draft by 1 July 1971. Still other proposals in Congress called for legislation to preclude the assignment of draftees to Vietnam.[8] While all these efforts were opposed by the Pentagon and White House as "premature," the support for congressional action was mounting, and it was clear that sooner or later Congress would seriously test the political acceptability of the AVF concept.

In a capital where the number of commissions, special study groups, and other investigative bodies are legion, why was so much credence given to the findings of the Gates Commission? The members of the Commission were distinguished Americans, including several former military commanders and business executives, but there were no manpower specialists. While staff and contract researchers were capable if not noted scholars, their views were weighted heavily in favor of the AVF concept (Walter Oi, for example, served as one of the key staff aides). And the limited time available to the Commission and its staff severely limited the thoroughness of its work. In short, its report normally would have provided the basis for further analyses, investigations, and hearings. Instead, it was accepted by many without question, and its findings were repeatedly cited by AVF advocates as "proof" that the AVF concept would work.

The reasons for this phenomenon were many. First and foremost, the unpopularity of the war and the draft had reached such a level among lawmakers and citizens that dispassionate, objective discussion of the Gates findings was no longer possible. Second, the report contained the first quasi-official justification of the AVF concept.[9] Third, those who opposed the conclusions of the report failed to offer solid and well-reasoned arguments. The pro-draft forces tended to criticize the AVF concept in general rather than rebut the arguments presented by the Commission. Finally, the weariness of the citizenry with peacetime conscription policies and seemingly endless interventions in foreign lands had to have a numbing effect on objectivity.

Congressional Decisions

Despite the early failure of Senators Hatfield, Goldwater, and others to gain legislative approval of the Gates Commission recommendations, support for their position was mounting. There was no doubt that the critical test of the AVF concept in Congress would come in 1971.

Congress was divided into three major positions on the issue.

Among supporters of the AVF, there were differences between the Hatfield-Goldwater bloc and the President on the speed with which the draft should be abandoned.[10] Competing against these positions was a second, led by Senator Edward Kennedy, who explicitly rejected the idea of an AVF and advocated a two-year extension of the draft with extensive reforms and a statutory ceiling of 150,000 inductees a year.

On the other side of the political spectrum, the two chairmen of the Armed Services Committees, as well as many other congressional supporters of a strong national defense posture, remained highly skeptical of or openly hostile to the AVF concept.[11] This Old Guard opposition had to be overcome if AVF advocates were to be successful.

In pursuing their objective, the advocates faced several interrelated problems. First, they needed approval of the pay and benefits package recommended by the Gates Commission to bring salaries and working environments of service personnel to the level of their civilian counterparts.

The second and biggest issue facing AVF advocates concerned the ending of inductions. In requesting the AVF funding package, President Nixon had reiterated that the draft could not be ended until the armed forces were completely withdrawn from Vietnam and were at a peacetime manning level. Nixon's goal for "zero draft calls" was 1973. In line with this, he had requested a two-year extension of the draft-induction authority until June 1973.

The third issue facing the AVF advocates concerned the status of Selective Service in the AVF era. Both the President and the Gates Commission had recommended a strong standby draft with the machinery to resume inductions in the event of a national emergency or the failure of the AVF. But would the authority to resume inductions remain with the President or be placed in the hands of Congress? In the view of many in Congress, the draft was the tool that had allowed the President to pursue the Vietnam War without popular consent and they were wary of what Richard Wilson called "the *de facto* power of the Chief Executive to initiate and wage war."[12]

Of the three main issues, increased expenditures for pay and benefits was the least controversial. Legislative steps had already been taken to link the pay of most servicemen to civil service pay rates, and the AVF proposal would simply complete this process for lower pay grades. Consequently, the argument was that the expenditures were necessary in order to provide equitable treatment for all service personnel. This view prevailed, and the measure was quickly passed.

The issue of the standby Selective Service also proved to be an easy victory for pro-AVF forces. Not only was a requirement for such a system legislated into the draft law, the President was precluded from resuming inductions without the consent of Congress.

The issue which caused the most emotional and lengthy debate concerned the extension of draft-induction authority. When the President requested that the induction authority be extended for only two years, there was almost no support—even among the Old Guard—for the more customary four-year extension. But the anti-draft bloc used the hearings on the two-year extension to challenge the idea of extending the system's induction authority at all.

Opposition to draft reform efforts had been successful only two years before, but the rising wave of anti-draft feelings in the country, in the media, and within Congress itself by 1971 overwhelmed the pro-draft advocates. Indeed, the Old Guard and other supporters of Selective Service were hard pressed to counter the "abolish now" moves of the anti-draft forces. Again and again, these forces tried to win congressional approval of an end to induction, or of an extension of the induction authority for less than the requested two years. When these efforts failed (some only by narrow margins), the anti-draft forces attempted to impose restrictions both on the numbers of men who could be inducted without specific congressional approval and on the assignment of inductees to Vietnam. These efforts also failed, though the margins again were very close.

After passage of the 1971 legislation, the draft induction authority was in fact used sparingly, and about one year later, President Nixon announced that his goal of zero draft calls would soon be achieved. Nixon chose the first week of his 1972 re-election campaign to unveil his plans. According to the President, the last draft calls would be issued in December 1972, some six months before the expiration of the induction authority. There was little doubt that Nixon's announcement was politically inspired. Yet the induction authority had only a few more months to run, and there was no sympathy whatsoever for further extension. Whether Nixon would receive political credit or not, inductions would be ending.[13]

Critical Issues in the Draft-AVF Debate

The decision to abandon conscription was a quick—and to many an unexpected—action. It was more the consequence of an overwhelming reaction to the war and the draft than of a positive endorsement of the AVF concept.

Criticism of the anti-draft forces was particularly evident among the Old Guard members of Congress who for so long had successfully defended the need for a draft. They had beaten down several attempts throughout the postwar years to legislate an end to the draft; by 1971, however, pressures for its abandonment had reached such proportions that even the vigorous efforts of the Old Guard could not block the change. In fact, the major role of the Old Guard had become one of protecting the President's request for a final two-year extension of the draft induction authority. The survival of Selective Service inductions was no longer an issue. The only question being seriously debated was when draft calls would end.

The Old Guard's loss of control and power over military manpower procurement matters during the early 1970's was the most striking indication of the strength of anti-draft and anti-war forces in the country. For to overthrow conscription in the face of Old Guard opposition would have been impossible without an unprecedented level of public dissatisfaction.

While arguments against the draft were often heard in varying forms and forums, arguments against the AVF were often limited to a few sentences and were neither as long nor as reasoned as those supporting the concept. Consequently, there never were any classic debates between the two forces. Instead, discussion tended to include a variety of attacks on and charges against the draft, some limited arguments for an AVF, and very little in defense of conscription policies. Nevertheless, during the four years or more when the merits of the draft and the AVF were being discussed and analyzed, several major issues emerged.

The first group of issues concerned human values, philosophy of government, citizen responsibilities, and the power of government. Within this group of issues, perhaps the fundamental difference between the two camps concerned their views on the obligation of citizens to perform military service. In the opinion of the pro-draft forces, the continuing survival of the United States required that all its citizens accept an obligation to serve the nation, and that failure to require this obligation would endanger the democratic heritage with its concept of the citizen-soldier. Although not all would be required to serve, it was essential that all citizens willingly accept a service obligation, thereby creating what B. H. Liddell Hart called "a necessary discipline and a spirit of service to the community."[14]

Opponents of this position argued that the willingness of the citizenry voluntarily to support the armed forces was a barometer of support for the nation's policies; thus the leadership could be expected to adopt policies which met with citizen support. In this way, the nation would be stronger than under a system of conscription, which pro-AVF advocates believed was a form of involuntary servitude, alien to American society.[15]

A second issue separating the two camps concerned the impact of the military recruiting system on the President's ability to wage war. Advocates stressed that an AVF would offer the best form of protest—nonparticipation—against an irresponsible foreign policy, and that the draft would allow the President to augment the armed forces for foreign ventures without the consent of Congress or the people (as had been done in Vietnam). Supporters of the draft countered that a President with a large standing AVF would be more inclined toward foreign adventures because severe demands upon the nonvolunteering citizenry would not be required; further, discontent among civilian draftees would create pressure to extricate the nation from unpopular wars.

Yet another objection advanced by opponents was that the AVF would eventually isolate the armed forces from the mainstream of American society. The military would become increasingly alienated and self-serving, a force of mercenaries. To this charge, supporters of the AVF argued that professional officers and NCO's had always controlled the military, and that the addition of a few thousand more volunteers to the ranks of the many thousands of enlistees would not change the character or patriotism of the forces, AVF advocates also stressed the traditionally strong civilian control over the U.S. military.

The issue of equity in the draft also frequently arose during the debates. The AVF forces charged that no draft could be fair (because relatively few would be required to serve), and that the draft penalized inductees by forcing them to serve at wages considerably below what they could earn as civilians. Rebutting the charges, the draft defenders pointed out that draft reforms had eliminated most inequities and that still more reforms would prevent the affluent and well-educated (who would not be enlisting in the AVF) from avoiding military service.

These and other lesser issues prompted almost endless discussions. As there were no right or wrong viewpoints, there seldom was agreement or compromise.[16]

Conclusion

The decision to abandon conscription was the final step in the reorientation of America's military manpower policies which resulted from the revolt of youth and other citizens against the involvement of U.S. combat forces in Vietnam. No doubt the decision should have been seen as a restriction on the ability of the armed forces to respond to all types of contingencies. Yet, during the debates, that issue was never fully addressed. The need for a draft in the event of emergency was recognized, but the ability of AVF forces to maintain the quality and quantity of personnel required to support U.S. strategic objectives was not seriously questioned. Lawmakers generally agreed that the ability of the armed forces to intervene in "foreign wars" ought to be reduced. They also agreed on the need to sustain the ability of the armed forces to meet all possible European contingencies. Thus both pro- and anti-draft forces assumed that the ability of the services to provide the personnel necessary to support NATO would be maintained. As the following chapters document, however, this was an erroneous assumption, the importance of which was not fully recognized until well after the decision had been made to support the forces with volunteers.

Notes

1. One of the exceptions was M. R. D. Foot, who argued that the ideal system of procuring men for the armed forces would be all-volunteer recruiting. According to Foot, volunteers would fight the best and would be better prepared to fight. See M. R. D. Foo, *Men in Uniform* (London, Weidenfeld and Nicolson, 1961), pp. 152–153.

2. For the first time in American history, lawmakers in 1940 gave serious consideration to a peacetime draft. Even during these troubled times, however, there was widespread opposition to the proposal. Although a clear military threat was developing, many lawmakers and other opinion leaders believed that the use of a draft during peacetime violated one of America's fundamental individual rights. A draft law was finally passed, but a necessary extension authorization passed the House of Representatives in August 1941 by only one vote, 203–202.

3. Morris Janowitz was the first of several observers to conclude that the trend in Western democracies toward smaller armies would affect U.S. strategic policy. See Janowitz, "The Decline of the Mass Army." Also see Janowitz, *U.S. Forces and the Zero Draft*, Adelphi Papers No. 94 (London, International Institute for Strategic Studies, 1973).

4. The draft had become an issue during the 1956 presidential campaign when the Democratic nominee, Adlai Stevenson, raised the question of its eventual abolition. While many rallied to the cause of ending conscription, the issue was not a paramount one in the election campaign. Since Stevenson's margin of defeat was so wide, it is impossible to isolate one issue that might have been the major cause of his unsuccessful bid for office. But the fact that he was debating with General Eisenhower, a man of outstanding military reputation and a strong supporter of the draft, assuredly contributed to the negative public reaction.

    The ending of the draft also was pledged by the Republican presidential candidate Barry Goldwater in 1964. "Republicans will end the draft together," he promised in his opening campaign speech, "and as soon as possible." See *New York Times*, 7 February 1964, p. 16; 4 September 1964, p. 1. Goldwater's promise went almost unnoticed and quickly dropped out of the campaign.

5. In Friedman's view, the real cost of drafting a man who did not enter service voluntarily was not his pay and upkeep, but the level of pay and other benefits that would have been necessary

for him to volunteer. Thus Friedman argued that the conscript himself was actually paying the difference in the form of a "hidden tax," and that these taxes had to be added to the budget costs of the armed forces in order to determine the actual costs to society of the military services. For a collection of Friedman's articles and papers on this subject, see *Congressional Record*, 18 August 1970, pp. S-13613–S-13616. The writings of Walter Oi bolstered the argument presented by Friedman with hard data analysis.

6. Four years later, during the 1972 campaign, President Nixon also pledged to end the draft. This "repeat" promise prompted the following editorial comment: "President Nixon's pledge to eliminate the draft, if reelected, may go down in history— along with his pledge to end the Vietnam War—as the twentieth century's most ingenious contribution to the art of electioneering: the 'two campaign promise.'" See *New York Times*, 3 September 1972, p. E-12.

7. President's Commission on an All-Volunteer Armed Force, *Report* (Washington, D.C., GPO, 1970).

8. The use of draftees as combat replacements in Vietnam angered many members of Congress. During 1969 draftees comprised 88 per cent of infantry riflemen in Vietnam. Draftees also were suffering a disproportionate share of casualties, with inductees being killed at nearly double the rate of nondrafted enlisted men. The reason for these differences was that men who enlisted for three or more years (draftees served for two years) could elect their areas of specialization and often the location of their first tour of duty. As a result, very few regular army enlistees chose the infantry or Vietnam assignments. For greater details, see Andrew J. Glass, "Defense Report/Draftees shoulder Burden of Fighting and Dying in Vietnam," *National Journal*, 15 August 1970.

9. Neither of the two major studies on the draft conducted in 1967 (Marshall Commission and Clark Panel) recommended the adoption of an AVF. The Marshall Commission report stated (p. 12): "An exclusively volunteer system would be expensive—although the Department of Defense gives no solid estimates of how much such a system would cost. And some members of the Commission see unfortunate social consequences in an all-volunteer military force sustained only by financial incentive. Such an establishment, motivated not by the concept of service, but by the lure of greater reward than the members' skills could command elsewhere, could easily—it is feared—be-

come a mercenary force unrepresentative of the nation."
10. Peter Barnes described this coalition as a mixture of ideological
    conservatives concerned with infringement of individual
    liberties, middle-class pragmatists who would like to quell stu-
    dent dissent, and liberals who maintain that no one should be
    compelled to fight an undeclared war. See Peter Barnes, "All
    Voluntary Army?," *New Republic*, May 1970.
11. For example, Senator John Stennis said that while he did not in
    principle oppose the goal of zero draft calls and a volunteer
    armed force, "It is a flight from reality and will be impossible
    to achieve." See *Washington Post*, 12 January 1971, p. 2.
    In the House, the new chairman, F. Edward Hebert of
    Louisiana (L. Mendel Rivers had died), told reporters that a
    volunteer army was "impractical, infeasible and too costly."
    See John L. Moore, "Defense Report/Draft, Volunteer Army
    Proposals Head for Showdown in Congress," *National Jour-
    nal*, 6 March 1971, p. 492.
12. Richard Wilson, "Problems of Ending the Draft and Waging
    War," *Washington Evening Star*, 3 February 1969, p. A-9.
13. Nixon's announcement prompted an unusual amount of editorial
    comment. The reaction covered the spectrum from bravos to
    guarded optimism to cynicism. For example: "A souring, con-
    tentious, divisive element will be gone from American life if
    military conscription is indeed ended," (*Cleveland Plain
    Dealer*, 30 August 1972). "An all-professional military force,
    without the leavening effect of civilian soldiers, could become
    a powerful political force in itself, and anti-civilian. Civilian
    soldiers, and civilian direction of the military, are what kept
    the Army responsive to the people," (*Knickerbocker News*,
    1 September 1972). "In fact, we'd like to see him take a
    second look at the whole all-volunteer concept which, realities
    aside, strikes us as an idea of dubious merit," (*New York
    News*, 5 September 1972). "Whatever historians make of the
    Vietnam War and its effect on this nation, the military draft
    that fed it manpower must go down as one of the most
    divisive elements of the times," (Robert Kotzbauer in the
    Philadelphia Evening Bulletin, 31 August 1972).
14. Liddell Hart, *Defence of the West*, p. 333.
15. Robert Evans, Jr., went so far as to call the draft a forced-labor sys-
    tem exhibiting most of the characteristics, save length of service,
    of those in Stalinist Rusia, Nazi Germany, and American Negro
    slavery. See "The Military Draft as a Slave System: An Econom-
    ic View," *Social Science Quarterly*, December 1969, p. 543.

16. The original legislative request for ending the draft had been the subject of sixty-four proposed amendments 454 prepared speeches, and hours upon hours of extemporaneous debate, delaying maneuvers, and filibusters. See *Washington Evening Star*, 21 September 1971, p. 1.

Chapter IV

The Changing Composition
of the AVF

On 30 June 1973, the last of the 1.7 million men drafted into the armed forces of the United States during the Vietnam War era entered the army.[1] Whereas the draft had allowed the armed forces to maintain pre-determined levels of quality recruits, the AVF decision forced the services to compete for recruits with schools and civilian employers in the open marketplace. As a result, the composition of the forces differed greatly from that of the draft era. Many of these changes were positive; but overall the results of AVF recruiting and retention policies from 1973 to 1978 were at best mixed, at worst alarming, with warnings of serious problems for maintaining effective forces and strategic capabilities.

Women

Perhaps the most dramatic—certainly the most positive—change to occur during the AVF years was in the numbers of women recruited for service and in the scope of their utilization. Even so, by the end of fiscal year 1978, the number of women in the armed forces was still very low. Nevertheless, their increased numbers were crucial to the attainment of AVF force levels because of difficulties in enlisting adequate numbers of males. Whereas the number of military women in 1964 was the lowest since immediately after World War II (only 1.1 per cent of total military strength), recruitment during the first five AVF years brought the figure up to 6.2 per cent (almost 130,000 women on active duty in 1978).[2]

Between 1971 and 1978, the army led the way among the services by far, increasing its proportion of women more than fourfold. During these same years, the proportion increased less than threefold in the navy and air force, while the proportion of women in the marine corps increased only slightly.

Participation of women in the reserve forces also increased, even more rapidly than in the active forces. Only some 3,700 women could be found in the entire reserve program in 1971 (.4 per cent of total reserve forces strength), but by 1978 there were more than 44,000 (about 5.4 per cent of all reserve billets). Within the reserves, the greatest change occurred in the army reserve, which increased its number of women some 26 times between 1971 and 1978.

The numbers of women entering the armed forces during the AVF years were too great to be absorbed in "traditional" fields of administration, supply, and medical/dental. The army thus expanded the career fields to which they could be assigned, opening 94 per cent of its jobs (as compared to 39 per cent previously). The navy increased its open occupations to 80 per cent, and the marine corps to 70 per cent. The air force led the way, and by the end of 1978 women were being assigned to all but 3 per cent of its career fields.

Yet, in 1978, women still were excluded from combat duties. While the army had opened a large number of new career fields to women, they were not permitted to serve in the infantry, armor, or artillery, though some women in 1978 were being assigned to combat support units, the result of several Army decisions in 1975–77 to broaden further service opportunities for women.[3] Yet the new trends were clear. Whereas more than 90 per cent of servicewomen in the draft years had served in medical, dental, and administrative fields, policy changes during the first five AVF years prompted major shifts in assignment patterns. By 1978 only 55 per cent of women were serving in the three traditional career areas.

The decisions to increase the numbers of servicewomen and to broaden their distribution into many previously restricted career fields had their roots in several trends of the 1960's. First was the increased demand for personnel for the Vietnam War. Although planned increases in the force size (up to a level of 3.5 million) were met by high draft calls for males, pre-Vietnam quality standards for recruits were not maintained. As the services continued to reject women volunteers who were better qualified than the male conscripts, the Pentagon began seriously to consider whether the use of women by the four services might be expanded.

Second was a growing realization that the draft would be abandoned and that the services would face severe problems in meeting male volunteer quotas.[4] As a result, a five-year plan was developed for the expanded use of women, calling for a 4 per cent level of women in the services by 1977.[5]

Third was the growing realization among military leaders that women could perform as well or better than men in certain support jobs.

Finally, there were indications that women were somewhat less costly to maintain than men because of differences in loss rates, involuntary separations, training problems, discipline, and so forth.

With these realizations in mind, military leaders allowed a major expansion in the number of women in the services and in their distribution patterns among career fields. But the services did not "open the door" for women as wide as they could have in the marketplace for volunteers. Indeed, during the first five AVF years, the numbers of women allowed to enlist were controlled by administrative quotas, the result of Pentagon decisions to limit them to predetermined percentages of the total force. Thus in 1978 there were both real and perceived barriers to full equality. For example, because higher numbers of women would have enlisted if they had been allowed to do so, the administrative quotas for women recruits called for higher education and intelligence standards than those applied to men. And there were legal constraints against combat flying and the assignment of women to ships which affected women in the air force and navy.[6]

Another barrier to greater utilization of women was not peculiar to the military services—it was the general male perception of women which prevails in society. Traditionally, women have been viewed principally as homemakers and mothers. While many men have changed their views of woman's role as a result of the feminist movement and other social changes of the 1960's and 1970's, the image persists. Many men still see women as objects of reverence or as fragile beings. Thus some male military leaders perceived women's safety as more important than that of their male counterparts, and consequently they viewed the assignment of women as a restriction on mission capability.

The problem of sex stereotyping also tended to influence men's perception of women's capabilities. Since women in the armed forces had traditionally performed administrative and clerical jobs, many military men doubted their ability to function in other more physically demanding roles.

By 1978 many of these traditional barriers had weakened; probably some of them will be removed altogether by the early 1980's. Yet due to the unique and often highly physical demands of service in the armed forces, it is unlikely that the armed forces will become a mirror of American society on the matter of women's rights.

As a result of major increases in the numbers of women volunteers and in the career fields open to them during the first five AVF years, at least two major issues emerged. The first concerns the reserve forces. During 1973–78 the reserves recruited large numbers of women without specific plans for their utilization. One must ask whether all of these women were appropriate candidates for the jobs to be filled, or whether the reserve forces, unable to recruit a sufficient number of males, were simply trying to meet their quotas. While the recruitment of women for administrative, supply, and other support organizations cannot be seriously challenged, much of the recruiting took place in combat-support units. There is serious doubt that these units were ready for such an influx of women and that the women themselves were fully aware of and qualified for some of the more physically demanding jobs to which they were assigned.

The second and more important issue concerns the impact of more women on the combat effectiveness of the active force, particularly since women have been allowed to volunteer for service with units whose support functions are directly related to combat operations. Without the experience of actual conflict, it is doubtful that the issue will ever be fully resolved. The army has nonetheless tried to answer the question through research evaluations of women in combat support units in simulated conflict situations.

One such study is called "Women Content in the Army (WITA)." As part of this evaluation, in 1976 the army conducted major tests on the impact of female participation in company-size units. Units were tested in three-day field exercises; the results showed no poorer unit performance as a result of assigned women. As a second test, similar units were evaluated in 1977 as part of the NATO exercise, REFORGER–77. This test, called REFWAC, confirmed the earlier results.[7]

Another research effort was conducted in 1975 by the Defense Manpower Commission. In a survey of unit commanders, the Commission determined that more than 85 per cent of the commanders who had women assigned to their units believed that these women had had no impact, or a positive one, on their unit's effectiveness.[8]

When most of the combat-support assignments were first made available to women in 1976–78, their response to the new opportunities was modest. In fact, as Cecile Landrum noted in a 1978 article, most women who entered the services during this period sought traditional jobs and job security and resisted assignment to nontraditional positions. In Landrum's view, this was largely due to male domination and intimidation in such job areas.[9] This theme has also been touched upon by Charles C. Moskos, Jr., who postulated that the army has been reluctant to open more traditional fields to women because women have not sought positions in the combat arms and combat support units. In Moskos's view, "they also serve" seems to be their motto.[10]

Regardless of the numbers of women who elect to serve in such nontraditional roles, certain characteristics associated with servicewomen could adversely impact on unit effectiveness. For example, more women in the services has, almost inevitably, meant more pregnant servicewomen, a condition which at least temporarily limits mobility and job performance. According to Pentagon sources, about one-third of all enlisted women during 1978 were married, many to servicemen, and many of these marriages led to pregnancy.[11] As Landrum noted, while healthy servicewomen in traditional jobs have continued their normal physical activity during pregnancy, problems relating to size, balance, and environmental hazards have precluded some servicewomen in nontraditional jobs—such as those who are heavy equipment mechanics—from performing all their required tasks.[12] Further, some of the pregnant servicewomen have been unmarried, and in those cases where the women have continued in the service, they have encountered severe mobility problems.

In analyzing the probable impact of servicewomen on combat

effectiveness, an examination of the use of women in the Israeli Defense Forces (IDF) may be useful. In 1978 Israel was the only other modern state utilizing large numbers of women in the armed forces. Both men and women are subject to conscription in Israel, although differences in periods of service and exemption policies limit the number of women in the IDF to about 20 per cent of the force level.[13] Women are not generally assigned to combat units; rather, they perform administrative, supply, and other support functions. In some infantry battalions and other combat units, a few women serve in headquarters, but they would be reassigned to support units in the event of hostilities.[14]

Israel developed its military service policies in order to counter an ever-present danger of sudden attack. It has also faced a numerically superior foe and has been forced to utilize all available resources. Thus it is not surprising that women have played such a major role in meeting IDF personnel needs. Even with the continuing threat of attack and the ability to conscript women, however, Israeli military leaders have limited the numbers of women in the IDF and have precluded their assignment to combat roles. Consequently, if the Israeli experience is to be used as a model for the U.S., a restriction on combat unit assignments and a limit of 20 per cent of force levels for women could be viewed as long-term planning goals. Conversely, because of tactical and structural differences between Israeli and U.S. forces, Pentagon plans to increase the number of women in the U.S. forces to about 10 per cent of the force level by the mid-1980's, and to continue the assignment of women to combat support units, cannot be unduly criticized.

Education, Intelligence, and Other Quality Indicators

One of the fears expressed by critics of the AVF concept was that new recruiting policies would result in an overall lowering of recruit quality. If this occurred, the critics argued, serious problems in leadership and discipline and in meeting the ever-increasing demands of modern weapons systems would arise, and the national defense capabilities of the services would be diminished.

Among many methods available for measurement of recruit quality, the Pentagon focused on two major tools: the proportion of high school diploma graduates among recruit groups, and the scores achieved by enlistment applicants on pen-and-pencil entry tests.

The Pentagon has determined that high school diploma graduates are twice as likely to succeed in the services as nongraduates.[15] Thus the services during the AVF years concentrated on enlisting such diploma graduates, though their goals of 65 to 70 per cent of all recruits were more of a target in the volunteer marketplace than an ideal level.[16] Nevertheless, these goals have generally been met, though above average educational levels for women and air force recruits have counterbalanced below-average levels for male enlistees in the army, navy, and marine corps. And as a consequence of this phenomenon, the educational level of male enlistees in the AVF years—with the exception of the air force—has been lower than the equivalent civilian population and the level of both draftees and volunteers in 1964. This has been particularly apparent in the army, where rising educational achievements among black recruits have been offset by lower educational levels of more numerous white recruits. Concerning the army's record overall, as Moskos has noted, "While the national trend has been toward improving high school graduation rates, army accessions have been going the other way."[17]

The active forces also set recruitment goals in terms of intelligence test scores. Such scores are derived from a battery of tests administered to all potential recruits as part of the pre-enlistment screening process.[18] Although the test scores are also used to match recruits with specific service occupational fields and technical schools, their prime use to the evaluators of AVF policies is in their reflection of the relative success of the recruitment programs in attracting average to above-average young men and women.[19]

Candidates for enlistment are ranked in Mental Group I to Mental Group V, from highest to lowest, and Mental Group V personnel (the lowest 10 per cent) are excluded by law from enlistment. In the AVF years, the services have tried to limit the number of Category IV personnel (lower 10 to 30 per cent) in each enlistment group. In 1970 about one of every five active forces recruits was ranked in Mental Group IV. During the AVF years, this percentage was steadily reduced to the one in twenty level of 1978.

While the services justifiably cite this achievement as a mark of improved recruit quality, there is at least one detracting statistic: a marked increase in the proportion of Mental Group III-B enlistees (those youth whose scores placed them in the bottom half of Mental Group III). For example, in the army the proportion of III-B's increased from 33 per cent in 1974 to 50 per cent in 1977. It appears that reductions in Mental Group IV recruits were offset by increases in the Mental Group III-B recruits, which raises some doubt about the accuracy of the testing procedures in light of heavy pressures on recruiters to meet quotas.

Furthermore, the exclusion of some Mental Group IV enlistees may actually have damaged service effectiveness, for there is a large number of less-demanding jobs to be done, especially in some support units.[20] Indeed, the Pentagon told Congress in 1974 that the army needed about 19 per cent Mental Group IV personnel in order to achieve maximum effectiveness.[21] Despite this declaration, however, the army and other services have made every effort to reduce their proportions of Mental Group IV recruits to 5 per cent or lower. They justify this partly by pointing to the growing sophistication of new weapons systems and the resulting demands for better personnel. But the deliberate restrictions on the recruiting of Mental Group IV men and women has not been justified through extensive research.

An examination of Armed Forces Qualification Test (AFQT) scores for 1971 and 1977 also offers insights into the relative success of AVF recruiting programs. Although changes in service tests and testing procedures have precluded exact comparisons, scores for the two years indicate a slight improvement in mean AFQT scores from 1971 to 1977, with the major advances occurring in the marine corps and the air force.

For the active forces, then, various quality measurements of AVF recruit groups indicate a range of change from the draft years, from somewhat worse to somewhat better. Clearly, fundamental changes in recruit quality did not occur. But the reserve forces was another story. In terms of diploma high school graduates, the reserves showed a marked decrease, from a proportion of 94 per cent in 1970 to 39 per cent in 1978 (high school diploma graduates made up about 75 per cent of each cohort group in the gen-

eral population). A corresponding decrease occurred in the proportion of Mental Group I-III youths recruited by the reserves.
Whereas only 4 per cent of their recruits in 1970 were ranked in
Mental Group IV, the proportion climbed to 28 per cent in 1974
and then leveled off at 12 to 13 per cent for 1977–78.

The changes in the quality of reserve recruits during 1973–78
probably impaired the ability of the reserves to carry out their
assigned missions, but we have no evidence of this. Regardless,
it may be argued that reservists should have the same educational
and intelligence skills as their active forces counterparts. Indeed,
as William R. King has noted, the reservist, unlike his active
forces peer, cannot spend large blocks of time to learn and practice new skills. He must learn rapidly in his short drill or camp
experiences, and he must retain these skills, without the opportunity for practice, while he goes about his unrelated civilian
activities.[22] Recognizing these greater demands, a strong case may
be made for the need to enforce even higher intelligence and
educational standards for the reserves than for the active forces.
Obviously, the realities of the volunteer recruiting marketplace
have made this impossible, and there is little doubt that the lower
quality of reserve recruits has affected personnel and unit effectiveness.

Yet two factors have helped to ameliorate this impact: (1) the
numbers of recruits without prior service has declined, and (2)
the large proportion of college-trained, draft-motivated enlistees
of the Vietnam era had provided too many over-qualified recruits.
Indeed, many observers of armed forces manpower policies during the Vietnam War years were highly critical of reserve efforts
to recruit college-trained youth, and these same critics welcomed
at least some of the changes that occurred in recruit educational
levels during the AVF years.

Adding to the problems created by recruits with less education
and lower test scores were a recognizable number of recruits who
were clearly less qualified than their records indicated. Many of
these substandard youths were recruited by the reserve forces
through "processing irregularities" prompted by heavy pressures
to meet quotas.[23]

In relation to the many recruits who met all standards, the number of men who were irregularly enlisted was quite small; thus,
their impact on mission effectiveness was negligible. Furthermore,

such irregularities were not unique to the AVF; they also existed before 1973, albeit at lower levels.[24]

Unexpectedly high levels of attrition and reading difficulties also have emerged as problems during the AVF years, and each portends far greater dangers to force effectiveness than the numbers of recruiting irregularities.

During the first five AVF years, the services experienced large increases in attrition rates—the proportion of enlistees who fail to complete their terms of service. For example, men who enlisted in the army in 1971 had a 25 per cent attrition rate for their first three years of service. For those who enlisted in 1974, however, the three-year attrition rate had climbed to 40 per cent (two of five army enlistees had failed to complete their three-year enlistment terms).[25]

The reasons for this major increase in attrition were varied. For one, attitudes among NCO's and officers toward marginal recruits had changed. Instead of helping them develop into suitable servicemen, some began quickly discharging those who showed poor performance and commitment. At the same time, relaxations in policies toward administrative discharges made it easier for NCO's and officers to wash their hands of potential troublemakers.

Also contributing to the rise in attrition was the AVF concept itself. In a climate of volunteerism, it was much more difficult for the services to enforce enlistment contracts. Indeed, due to changes in discharge policies, most of the stigmas which historically were associated with discharge from the service prior to completion of the term of enlistment (Undesirable or Bad Conduct Discharges) were removed. Consequently, men and women enlistees who decided that they did not like service life were generally allowed to "resign" without major attempts to change their minds.

The second problem area, reading difficulties, was not fully recognized by military leaders until 1977 or thereabouts. By 1978 little definitive data had been collected or analyzed. But there was a growing realization among service personnel that recruits had greater reading problems and resulting difficulties in coping with training programs, particularly those of a more technical nature. Nor was the problem limited to other than high school graduates.

Although reading tests were not given to entering recruits, Pentagon analysts in 1978 could make reasonable estimates from existing test data about the reading skills of recruits during the AVF years. First, the reading abilities of service recruits were somewhat better than those of the population they were drawn from; and, second, an imbalance existed among the services, with the largest share of poor readers among army recruits.

In terms of reading grade levels, the Pentagon estimated that 31 per cent of army recruits in 1977 could read at the eleventh-grade level, but that some 25 per cent could read at only the sixth-grade level or lower. In contrast, 53 per cent of air force recruits in 1977 could read at the eleventh-grade level, while only 8 per cent had a sixth-grade reading level or lower.

As the services have acquired more and more sophisticated equipment during the AVF years, the need for recruits with reasonable reading skills has become critical. Indeed, the army's high attrition has been disproportionately high among those recruits with low test scores and less-than-average education. It may be argued that the inability of these personnel to master the complex skills of various weapons systems contributed to the high attrition rates.

During the AVF years, as during the draft era, it has been army practice to assign less-qualified recruits to combat arms. This practice has continued despite the advent of new infantry, artillery, and armor weapons and systems which require training and skills far beyond those needed by combat arms personnel in earlier years. If the smaller AVF is to be a truly professional force, the standards for assignment to combat arms will have to be raised at least to the level of most technical specialties. In order to do so, however, it will be necessary for the army to recruit a much higher proportion of men with higher reading skills. And in the face of continuing declines in overall reading abilities within the general population, this may be exceedingly difficult. The services may be forced to adopt widespread remedial reading programs as part of the recruit training process. This would add significant costs to armed forces training and would require force level adjustments in order to counter an increased proportion of personnel in a training status.

One final point should be added to this somewhat bleak forecast. By necessity, the various quality measurements discussed in this section have been limited to broad observations of service-wide trends and achievements. Looking more specifically at males and females and at combat and noncombat assignments, other bothersome facts become apparent. Foremost among these is that the quality of male personnel assigned to combat arms has been significantly below overall service statistics. As the ability of the services to fight depends in large measure on the competence of personnel in combat arms, changes in these components during the AVF years portend greater difficulties in 1979 and later years.

An Army of the Poor?

"What kind of society excuses its most privileged members from defending it?"[26] This question posed by Charles Moskos, was echoed by many observers during the early AVF years. Such an army is morally wrong, some critics charged; others cited the probability that Congress and the public would withdraw funds and support; yet others worried about disproportionate casualties in the event of war, while some even worried about the reliability of volunteer troops in domestic contingencies.[27]

During the draft years, the army was essentially a cross-section of American society, though a larger proportion of young men from families with above-average incomes used the Selective Service deferment and exemption schemes to avoid military duty.[28] As a result, there was a somewhat smaller share of recruits from this segment of society than from the middle class, whose members could not so readily take advantage of deferment and exemption schemes. Meanwhile, many sons and daughters of poor parents also served, but the substandard education and health care often received by children in such families precluded a representative segment from qualifying for enlistment or induction. Even in the years of high inductions during the Vietnam War, entry standards were maintained at a reasonably high level.[29]

With the end of the draft, manpower experts expected the decline in enlistments that occurred among young men whose families were in the upper economic brackets. Most of these youth attend college or receive job opportunities after high school and for this group the incentives offered by the AVF are not sufficient to prompt many enlistments. Conversely, youths who do not attend college or attain worthwhile civilian employment are the prime targets of AVF recruitment programs. And during the initial AVF years, service leaders were concerned that a sufficient number of qualified youths from this segment of society would step forth. For if the response to the AVF was less than required to sustain force levels, enlistment standards would have to be lowered, allowing more marginally qualified youths to enter. Thus at least one legitimate concern over a "poor man's army" was that many men and women who could not meet traditional standards would be allowed to enter the services because of recruiting difficulties. If this occurred, a serious problem would arise over the quality of the recruits and their ability to perform their service roles. Except for a brief period during the initial months of AVF recruiting, however, service manpower managers have not lowered either physical or mental minimum standards. Indeed, the opposite has been true. Department of Defense data show that some 17 per cent of the youth who qualified for entry into the service in 1972 would not have met the tightened entry standards of 1978.[30]

Since the advent of the AVF, several researchers have analyzed the economic status of recruits' parents, and the data supports the general conclusion that a disproportionately few sons and daughters of wealthy or poor families are enlisting. As a result, a higher than average number of recruits are coming from families in the broad middle economic segment of American society.[31]

Faced with limited employment opportunities, many of these youths considered enlistment as the only available option. Of course, higher pay rates and other incentives made the services competitive with civilian employers, and the continuing theme of AVF advertising and recruitment literature was that the armed forces offered skill training, advancement opportunities, and other rewards of employment. So it is not surprising that many AVF recruits were attracted primarily on these grounds, particularly during those years when youth unemployment was so abnormally high.[32] For example, a 1977 survey of new military enlistees determined that 26 per cent were unemployed when they decided to enlist and a similar percentage were still in school but facing probable unemployment in the near future.[33]

In regard to force effectiveness, we may reasonably doubt the willingness of recruits to sacrifice life or limb if their motives for joining have been monetary, skill training, or employability rewards. The little research that exists on this subject suggests that the emphasis in recruitment on nonpatriotic and monetary gains is having an adverse impact on the services.[34]

Geographical Representation

Critics of the AVF decision also expressed concern over what they believed would be a less representative force geographically. Such a situation, it was assumed, would weaken congressional support for the services and limit their ability to deal effectively with domestic disturbances.

During the draft years, Selective Service provided a geographically well-balanced pattern of accessions. Each state had its quota for inductees, and this quota was related to the state's proportion of the draft-eligible population. Due to variations in regional educational standards, volunteerism rates, health conditions, and so forth, some differences in induction patterns existed between areas of the country, but they were not significant.

The first five AVF years witnessed a slight movement away from the pattern of the draft era. Yet the most populous states still provided the bulk of recruits as well as the bulk of those in above-average Mental Groups; regional preferences for one service over another remained; and the Midwest generally was a better recruiting ground than other regions of the country. The proportion of AVF recruits from different areas generally paralleled their share of the population, though enlistments from the northeastern states were somewhat below, and from the southern and western states somewhat above. Department of Defense analyses also determined that the services were getting a somewhat higher proportion of their recruits from rural rather than urban areas, but the differences were not large.

Several assignment and recruitment options, however, created disproportionate representation within certain units and at certain bases. For example, the army's "unit of choice" and "station of choice" enlistment schemes allowed some popular units and bases —such as the 197th Infantry Brigade at Fort Benning, Georgia— to recruit almost entirely from nearby areas. Although units with such clustering policies are likely to have more personnel off post on evenings and weekends, and would thus have problems in responding to emergencies, this is balanced by reductions in family problems, a generally higher morale among participating personnel, and some cost savings. Furthermore, the policies have been a highly effective recruiting tool, and it is doubtful whether the army would have been able to meet its recruit quotas without them.

While changes in geographical representation during the AVF years have not been great, two trends have emerged which are cause for concern. First, greater rural representation has brought an increase in the number of poor rural whites, most of whom have ranked in the bottom quarter in terms of education and test scores. In addition, these men have generally been assigned to combat arms, where there also has been an overconcentration of blacks from inner-city areas. This combination within the vital combat arms portends human relations and effectiveness problems for the future.

Second, concerning the input of new officers, there has been a marked movement away from a representative officer corps toward a group with more rural, isolated, and less sophisticated backgrounds. At the same time a trend may be seen toward "self-recruiting" of the sons and daughters of military personnel, and higher inputs from the South and Southwest where military traditions are strongest. It is too early to identify the ramifications of these trends, but the potential appears to exist for an officer corps somewhat isolated from—or at least with quite specialized and narrow ties to—the civilian society, and with its own set of beliefs about civil-military relations.

An Army of the Black?

A major issue—many would say the only issue—in the socio-economic composition of the AVF is whether more black enlistments and officer appointments during the first five AVF years have adversely affected the nation's defense capability. Behind this issue are the perceptions of many whites that black soldiers are less willing and able to meet responsibilities than their white counterparts.

Many other reasons may also be cited for the uneasiness felt by some national leaders and critics of the AVF over the racial composition of the forces. For example, three "senior army officers" were reported as believing that the large numbers of blacks joining the AVF would make the army too isolated and could reduce necessary support from the white community.[35] The Secretary of the Army in 1974 expressed a commonly held concern over disproportionate casualties in times of war, a view shared by sociologist Morris Janowitz and at least one black newspaper.[36]

What actually occured in racial composition during the first five AVF years? Whereas blacks comprised 7.5 per cent of recruits for the active forces in 1949 (and less than 1 per cent of new officers), the proportion reached 9.2 per cent at the beginning of the Vietnam War. Thereafter, until the advent of the AVF, blacks comprised 9 to 10 per cent of enlisted accessions. Far fewer blacks were recruited in the reserves. At the end of 1969, only 1 per cent of army national guard and army reserve personnel were black (black youth ages seventeen to twenty-two represented about 12 per cent of the total youth population).[37]

The abandonment of the draft, however, caused significant changes in black enlistment rates. In 1978 blacks comprised about 20 per cent of enlistments in the active forces, including 28 per cent of army accessions. The AVF "high" was reached in 1974, when 21 per cent of accessions were black, including 28 per cent of army enlistees. The percentage of black officer appointments also increased. Whereas all four services still were appointing only about 1 per cent black officers in 1969, the proportion rose to about 7 per cent by 1978.

There were several reasons for these shifts. First, in the open marketplace of volunteer recruiting, many more blacks than whites were to be found in the ranks of the unemployed or underemployed, and these men and women were receptive to service opportunities. Second, within the context of continuing fears and suspicions between the races in most segments of U.S. society, the armed forces have been in the forefront of those institutions making progress toward eliminating the remaining vestiges of racial bias. Also contributing to the rise in black enlistments was a major increase in the numbers of blacks eligible for military service, a consequence, cited by Richard V. L. Cooper, of the increasing number of black high school graduates.[38] In fact, since the end of the draft, the proportion of black high school graduates entering the army has exceeded that of whites by 60 per cent to 40 per cent. This phenomenon, according to Moskos, has resulted in the only major arena in American society where black educational levels surpass those of whites, and by a significant margin.[39]

Greater numbers of blacks entering the active forces also prompted increases in the proportion of blacks in the services. For example, in 1969, army enlisted personnel were 11 per cent black; by 1978 almost 25 per cent were black. On the other hand, there was little change in the navy, which increased its black representation from 5 per cent in the late 1960's to 8 per cent in the AVF years.

The most dramatic change in the proportion of blacks in accession groups and in on-board strength occurred in the reserve components. Denied draft-motivated enlistees from 1973 on, the national guard and the reserves opened the door for blacks with phenomenal results. From less than 2 per cent of accessions in 1971, the black proportion steadily rose to a high of almost 28 per cent in 1977. The most spectacular change occurred in the army reserve, where the percentage of black recruits rose from 1.3 per cent in 1971 to almost 40 per cent in 1976, before falling off to 30 per cent in 1978.

With these changes have come shifts in occupational assignment patterns for black enlistees. As during the draft years, disproportionately high numbers of blacks are assigned to the infantry, armor, artillery, and other combat arms, as well as to administrative specialist and clerk positions. And a disproportionately low number of blacks is assigned to the more technical specialties, such as electronics equipment repair and other occupational areas which provide skill training and experience transferable to the civilian job market. Some improvements, however, have occurred in these assignment patterns during the AVF years. Consequently, the distribution of blacks among the various specialties was more equitable in 1978 than in the previous AVF and draft years.

The problem is that fewer blacks have qualified for more technical assignments because of higher entry test score and educational requirements. Also, the concentration of blacks in combat arms has been heightened by various enlistment options which allow recruits to select their units, stations, or regions of service.

As a result, there are disparities between units. For example, the army's readiest division, the 82nd Airborne, contains approximately 26 per cent blacks, while the Second Infantry Division, recruited in the Pacific Northwest, has an almost totally white composition.

Concentration of blacks in front-line units has also occurred within brigade- and division-sized organizations. Thus almost 40 per cent of the men in the Second Marine Division's infantry battalions were found to be black, with disproportionately fewer in headquarters and support elements.

These concentrations have provoked an undercurrent of uneasiness among some senior officers, as well as a reluctance to consider committing these units in all possible contingencies. Various criticisms from the academic community have supported these views. Morris Janowitz and Charles Moskos believe that the services will experience a "tipping effect" when the proportion of blacks becomes so high that large numbers of whites will no longer volunteer.[40]

In past years, of course, the services have had many units in which there were disproportionate numbers of blacks and whites, with no serious racial problems and outstanding combat achievements. Furthermore, fears of problems in the AVF have not been realized, either through research or experience. Thus it may be argued that the fears are misguided or based on bias, and that the ability of the armed forces to meet their various strategic commitments has not been damaged. Most observers agree that there has been much greater interest in the issue in academic, political, and higher military circles than at operational levels, whether of regiments, battalions, or other combat units.[41] Most black and white personnel in the lower enlisted and officer ranks see themselves primarily as "soldiers," "sailors," "marines," or "airmen," not as "whites" or "blacks." Commanders of units with high percentages of blacks have been universal in denouncing racially inspired fears.[42] Finally, these concerns appear to discount such traditional service strengths as leadership, training, and morale.

At least two developing racial trends are nonetheless worth noting, each of which could cause severe human relations problems and diminished public support in the future. The first trend concerns the increasing proportion of blacks in the armed forces.

While more black recruits during the 1973–78 period has been discounted as a problem, the total forces are becoming progressively blacker, and this phenomenon could prompt an adverse public and political reaction.

The second trend concerns black officers. Whereas the proportion of black officers entering the services during the AVF years also has increased, the gains have not been nearly as large as those of blacks in the enlisted force. Therefore, the army in particular is becoming an increasingly black enlisted force supervised by a much whiter officer corps. Because of academic and mental qualifications, the proportion of black officers is not likely to increase.

These potential problems have caused some military leaders to urge the adoption of a formal representational policy under which the services would be given the tools to control the racial composition of recruit groups and their distribution throughout occupational areas and units.[43] Although such a policy has not been formally adopted, the issuance of statistical reports which discuss representation, the publishing of monographs on representation, and various public statements from civilian leaders support the conclusion that representation in the armed forces is a basic policy objective.[44]

Alvin J. Schexnider and John Sibley Butler, among others, have been critical of this stance. Pointing to the almost total absence of research into the question of race and military effectiveness, they assert that efforts to implement a representational policy beg the true issue of deciding appropriate quality criteria for enlistment.[45] Yet others see the discussion of representation as a smokescreen for the issue of black troop reliability or loyalty in domestic and international conflict.

Recognizing the role of the army in keeping peace in some racially inspired domestic disturbance, some whites fear that black troops may have greater loyalty to other blacks than to their sworn duty. This rationale is also used to question the use of heavily black units in possible interventions in the Middle East or in Africa, particularly in situations involving majority-minority group conflicts. Such charges are, of course, reprehensible to black soldiers and many others. Nevertheless, in the absence of research, and as long as some white leaders, including senior officers, indicate a reluctance to commit heavily black units to domestic or overseas contingencies, the ability of these forces to meet their strategic commitments has been diminished.

Conclusion

The changes discussed herein which occurred in the various categories of force composition measurements should not be viewed as separate and isolated. Rather, they should be seen as interrelated factors. Thus, an AVF recruit with high or low entry test scores could be male or female, poor or rich, from an urban or rural area, and black or white. The complexities of these mixes and the uncertain impact of some changes on strategic capabilities make it impossible to determine which changes have created a more or less effective force. For example, one of the most positive achievements of the services during the AVF years has been the reduction in the proportion of Mental Group IV's in recruit accession groups. Yet even this apparent success must be weighed against the views of many that more Mental Group IV personnel are needed for less-demanding jobs.

Clearly, the sum total of the changes has created more problems than existed in the draft era. Nonetheless, there have been several accomplishments, including the recruitment of more highly qualified women and their assignment to previously restricted career fields, and the improvement in measured entry test scores of active forces recruits.

The negative side of the ledger, however, is far weightier. First, an unanswered question exists concerning the impact on combat effectiveness of women in combat support units. Recruit quality in the reserve forces has fallen off significantly in all the services. As a result of AVF policies, the services face an overconcentration of personnel from the middle economic segment of society, and potential for serious human relations problems in combat arms as a result of the assignment to these units of more urban blacks and poor rural whites. Finally, the growing blackness of the forces portends the possibility of diminished public support and confidence.

As a consequence of these changes, there is little doubt that the AVF of 1978 was less able to meet strategic objectives than the draft-volunteer force of the pre-Vietnam years, particularly in terms of a mobilization of all total force elements in response to a conventional attack by Warsaw Pact forces in Central Europe. If doubts of this judgment remain, it need only be added that the changes in the composition of the forces have occurred within the context of major reductions in force levels, a shifting of responsibilities to the less-ready reserves, and an overall lowering of mobilization capabilities. In the following chapter, these subjects are addressed.

Notes

1. With the exception of 1947–48, men were drafted into the armed forces from 1940 onward. During these thirty-one years of conscription, 14,915,105 men were inducted.
2. By 1984 the number of military women is programed to reach 199,000. See Department of Defense, *Annual Report, Fiscal Year 1979* (Washington, D.C., Department of Defense, 1977), p. 238. A 1977 Brookings Institution study, however, estimated that without major changes in assignment policies, close to a quarter of all military personnel (up to 500,000 in the active forces) could be women. See Martin Binkin and Shirley J. Bach, *Women and the Military* (Washington, D.C., Brookings Institution, 1977), p. 105.
3. The army policy in effect in 1978 stated: "Women are authorized to serve in any officer or enlisted specialty, except some selected specialties, in any organizational level, and in any unit of the Army except infantry, armor, cannon field artillery, combat engineer, and low altitude air defense artillery units of battalion/squadron or smaller size." See Deputy Chief of Staff for Personnel, Department of the Army, "Memorandum for DAPE-MPE–SS," 7 December 1977. Following the issuance of this directive, women were assigned to brigade-level headquarters, Hawk and Hercules Missile Air Defense units, missile and field artillery elements such as lance units, signal battalions, and wheel and track vehicle maintenance battalions.
4. For an excellent summary of the evolution of armed forces policy on women, see Delores Battle, "Women in the Defense Establishment," *Defense Manpower Commission Staff Studies and Supporting Papers,* Volume IV (Washington, D.C., GPO, 1976).

5. Central All-Volunteer Task Force, Office of the Assistant Secretary of Defense (M & RA), *Utilization of Military Women* (Washington, D.C., Department of Defense, 1972), p. 45.

6. Section 6015, 10 U.S. Code, 10 August 1956; Section 8549, 10 U.S. Code, 19 August 1956. During 1977 and 1978 the Department of Defense called for the repeal of both laws.

7. Office of the Assistant Secretary of Defense, (Manpower, Reserve Affairs and Logistics), *America's Volunteers: A Report on the All-Volunteer Armed Forces* (Washington, D.C., Department of Defense, 1978), pp. 75-77. Also see *Women Content in Units Force Development Test,* U.S. Army Research Institute for the Behavioral and Social Sciences, October 1977; and *Women Content in the Army: Reforger 77,* U.S. Army Research Institute for the Behavioral and Social Sciences, March 1977.

8. A survey of 154 commanders in all services was conducted. See Kenneth J. Coffey, Edward Scarborough, Frederick J. Reeg, Audrey J. Page, and James W. Abellera, "The Impact of Socio-Economic Composition in the All-Volunteer Force," *Defense Manpower Commission Staff Studies and Supporting Papers,* Volume III (Washington, D.C., GPO, 1976).

9. Cecile Landrum, "Policy Dimensions of an Integrated Force," *Armed Forces and Society,* August 1978, pp. 693–694.

10. Charles C. Moskos, Jr., "The Enlisted Ranks in the All-Volunteer Army," in John Keeley, ed., *The Military in American Society* (Charlottesville, University of Virginia Press, 1978), p. 69.

11. There also have been marked increases during the first five AVF years in the numbers of servicemen with dependents. Overall, by mid-1977, slightly more than half of all enlisted personnel in the four services had dependents. The greatest overall increase in the proportion of enlisted personnel with dependents was in the army, whose proportion of enlisted personnel with dependents increased by 30 per cent between 1971 and 1977. During this same period the proportion of E-4's and E-5's (sergeants) with dependents increased more than 60 per cent.

12. Landrum, "Policy Dimensions," p. 693.

13. Israel, Ministry of Defense, *Chen* (Tel Aviv, I.D.F. Spokesman, 1969), pp. 6–7. Confirmed by embassy in 1978.

14. See Sgan Aluf Shanl Ramati, *Israel Today: The Israel Defense Forces* (Jerusalem, Israel Digest, 1966), p. 28.

15. In addition to lower attrition rates, high school diploma graduates also exhibit higher productivity and lower disciplinary rates. The acquisition of a high school diploma therefore appears to

reflect the acquisition of those social traits (work habits, punc-
tuality, self-discipline) which make for a more successful service experience. Whereas the services in the early AVF years
included holders of General Education Certificates (GED's)
in their quotas and statistics for high school graduates, examination of their performance by various service research efforts
determined that the desired traits associated with high school
diploma graduates were not evident in men and women with
GED's. Accordingly, the services adopted the use of the
diploma high school graduate definition which excludes
GED holders from recruiting quotas and high school graduates
recruiting statistics.

16. Dr. John P. White, Statement of the Assistant Secretary of Defense
   (Manpower, Reserve Affairs and Logistics), *Hearings Before
   the Task Force on National Security,* House Budget Committee, 13 July 1977, p. 9.

17. Moskos, "The Enlisted Ranks," pp. 41–42.

18. The armed forces began using the Armed Forces Qualification
   Test (AFQT) in 1950. For more than twenty years it was the
   only common test administered by all four services. The AFQT
   was designed to predict suitability for general military service.
   It contained four areas: word knowledge, arithmetic reasoning,
   spatial perception, and knowledge of tool functions. In January
   1976 all four services began using the Armed Services Vocational Aptitude Battery (ASVAB) in lieu of the AFQT. The
   new test, however, also features item components of the
   AFQT so that classification of candidates by Mental Groups
   has continued.

19. Each service occupation and technical school assignment has specific test score requirements. Thus a potential recruit may meet
   the minimum standards for enlistment (and assignment to occupational fields with low test score requirements, such as the
   infantry) but not meet the standards for assignment to his desired occupational field.

20. The Secretary of Defense in 1973 pointed out that if the overall
   proportion of Mental Group IV personnel fell below 15 per
   cent, some brighter recruits would be underchallenged by their
   job assignments. See Elliot L. Richardson, secretary of defense, *The All-Volunteer Force and the End of the Draft*
   (Washington, D.C., Department of Defense, 1973), p. 13.

21. The army's stated requirement for Mental Group IV recruits for
   the combat arms was 28 per cent. See Department of Defense,
   Defense Manpower Quality Requirements, Report to the Sen-

ate Armed Service Committee, as required by Report No. 93-385, January 1974.

22. William R. King, "The All-Volunteer Armed Forces and National Service: Alternatives for the Nation," in *Senior Conference on National Compulsory Service* (West Point, U.S. Military Academy, 1977), p. 67.

23. For a detailed analysis of recruiting irregularities during the initial AVF years, see Kenneth J. Coffey and Frederick J. Reeg, "Recruit Processing Controls," *Defense Manpower Commission Staff Studies and Supporting Papers*, Volume III (Washington, D.C., GPO, 1976).

24. See Eli Ginzberg, James K. Anderson, Sol W. Ginsburg, and John L. Herman, *The Lost Division* (New York, Columbia University Press, 1959).

25. The attrition rates for the other services changed less dramatically during the three-year period. Among men entering the navy in 1971, 28 per cent were discharged within three years; in 1974, 38 per cent were discharged within three years. In the marine corps, the attrition rate for the two groups increased from 21 to 37 per cent, while the rates in the air force increased from 21 to 31 per cent. During 1979 and later years, the services hope to reduce their attrition rates by tightening discharge procedures.

26. As quoted in Bruce Bliven, Jr., *Volunteers, One and All* (New York, Reader's Digest Press, 1976), p. 126.

27. The Defense Manpower Commission staff discovered that a perceived prejudgment was being made for individuals who were thought to come from families at the lower end of the socio-economic scale. Many of the officers and senior NCO's (particularly at the basic training centers) felt that accessions coming from poor families were problem-oriented underachievers, not good leadership material, and would fail at a higher rate than individuals who came from families above the poverty level. Most had no specific data but "just knew it." See Coffey, et al., "The Impact of Socio-Economic Composition in the All-Volunteer Force."

28. In research conducted at the University of Wisconsin, Neil D. Fligstein related socio-economic factors to military service in the period from World War II through Vietnam. According to his conclusions, blacks, farmers, and the higher educated were less likely to have served, but overall the selection of youth for military service was not strongly related to statification vari-

ables. See "Who Served in the Military, 1940–1973?," unpublished monograph, July 1976.

29. During the Vietnam War years the services were able to set different minimum entry standards for high school and non-high school graduates and to place various restrictions on the enlistment and induction of Mental Group IV personnel. Although the army demanded the most recruits, the large surplus of manpower available through the draft allowed the army to reject more than half of induction candidates. See *Semi-annual Report of the Director of Selective Service, January 1, 1974– June 30, 1974* (Washington, D.C., GPO, 1974), p. 67.

30. See *Interim Report, Study of the All-Volunteer Force* (Washington, D.C., Department of Defense, 1978), p. 21.

31. The research relied on information provided by recruits and on data on earnings by postal Zip Code zones for enlistees' home areas, and this methodology produced only general conclusions. Furthermore, the research did not focus on the differences in economic status between recruits for technical fields and those for combat arms. It appears there is a major difference between these two groups. See Office of the Assistant Secretary of Defense (Manpower and Reserve Affairs), *Representational Monograph*, 28 November 1975, and subsequent updates. Similar analyses also have been published in other Defense Department reports. Also see Richard V. L. Cooper, *Military Manpower and the All-Volunteer Force* (Santa Monica, Rand, 1977), pp. 223–229.

32. The unemployment rate of teenagers sixteen to nineteen in 1976 was 19 per cent, or almost three times that of persons twenty years and over. Furthermore, the unemployment rate for black teenagers was more than twice that of their white peers, reaching more than 40 per cent in central city areas. See Diane N. Westcott, "The Nation's Youth: An Employment Perspective," *Worklife*, Department of Labor, June 1977, pp. 13–18.

33. Cited in Congressional Budget Office, "National Service Study Outline," unpublished staff working paper, 6 September 1977, p. 14.

34. Research by Jerry L. Reed in 1978 confirmed this observation. Based on interviews with more than five hundred army personnel in the U.S. and in Germany, Reed's study reported that the army is becoming more of an employer and less of a disciplined profession, and that army recruiters believe most new enlistees have joined the AVF because of underemployment or

unemployment. See Jerry L. Reed, *The Beard Study: An Analysis and Evaluation of the U.S. Army,* a report prepared for the office of Congressman Robin Beard, April 1978, pp. 9, 162.

35. Commenting on the rising number of black enlistments, "one of the army's highest-ranking generals" said privately: "It will be the beginning of the kind of army which would not be an acceptable army for the American people." None of the generals cited were identified by name. See Michael Getler, "Heavy Black Enlistment Worries U.S. Army," *Washington Post,* 14 August 1973, pp. 1, 18.

36. Secretary Howard Callaway's views were reported by General Paul Phillips, Deputy Assistant Secretary of the Army (Manpower and Reserve Affairs), in an interview, 10 December 1974. Janowitz stated his position in testimony before the Defense Manpower Commission on 17 July 1975. For the black newspaper "voicing alarm at the prospect of disproportionate black casualties in time of war," see *Chicago Defender,* 8 May 1975, p. 7.

37. Statistics on black accessions and representation provided by the Office of the Assistant Secretary of Defense (Equal Opportunity). Other data from *The Negro in the Armed Forces: Statistical Fact Book* (Washington, D.C., Department of Defense, 1971), supplemented by *Blacks in the Armed Forces,* unpublished 1973, 1974, and 1978 updates.

38. Cooper, *Military Manpower,* pp. 209–216.

39. Moskos, "The Enlisted Ranks," p. 46.

40. The two critics also stated explicitly that in the event of war the U.S. would not permit either blacks or whites to bear a disproportionate share of combat and casualties. See Morris Janowitz and Charles Moskos, Jr., "Racial Composition of the All-Volunteer Force," *Armed Forces and Society,* Fall 1974, pp. 109–110, 113.

41. Interviews with officers and NCO's of the heavily black 197th Infantry Brigade on 13–14 March 1975 revealed an absence of serious racial problems within the unit, despite stated beliefs of "outsiders" to the contrary. Among those cited as worrying about the racial composition of the 197th were senior Pentagon officials.

42. In the early 1960's the army's 82nd Airborne Division was ordered by "high political authority" to remove black soldiers from certain units committed to civil rights-related riot control duty. In the view of officers in the division in 1975, the decision had been based on the erroneous judgment that the black troopers

could have perceived a greater loyalty to the rioters than to
the army.

43. Perhaps the closest the services ever came to a truly representative force was in the closing months of World War II, when
73.1 per cent of all nineteen- to twenty-five-year-old males
were in service. The remainder, about one man in every four,
was disqualified or excused. See *Fourth Report of the Director
of the Selective Service* (Washington, D.C., GPO, 1946),
p. 481.

44. For example, the Assistant Secretary of the Army had this to say:
"Equally important as having a quality and professional Army
is having an Army which is generally representative of the
American people. I mean representative in the racial, geo-
graphic, and socioeconomic senses." See Statement of Assistant
Secretary of the Army (Manpower and Reserve Affairs) Donald G. Brotzman before the Defense Manpower Commission,
17 July 1975.

45. Alvin J. Schexnider and John Sibley Butler, "Race and the All-Volunteer System," *Armed Forces and Society*, Spring 1976,
p. 423.

Chapter V

The AVF and the Capability
for Total Force Mobilization

Within the context of worldwide U.S. strategic commitments, the decision to abandon conscription has no doubt had its greatest impact on the ability of army ground forces to respond to the challenges of a major conventional war in Europe between the forces of NATO and the Warsaw Pact. The manifestation of this impact has been the implementation of the total force policy and resulting reductions in the strengths of active and reserve forces, the shifting of some responsibilities for combat and support to the reserves, and the increasing inability of these elements to meet their mobilization commitments.

The total force policy was developed by the Department of Defense in 1970–72 when it became clear that the draft would be ended and that AVF policies would not secure sufficient personnel to sustain the pre-Vietnam force structure. The policy calls for reservists, rather than draftees or volunteers, to be the primary source of personnel for the augmentation of the active forces in all military emergencies.[1] Although this policy may appear to be the same as existed in the years before the Vietnam War, two fundamental changes have been made. First, reductions in the manning levels of the active forces during the initial AVF years have been justified on the ground that the reserves can provide combat-ready units and individuals on short notice. Second, because of the reduced size of the active forces, the army reserve forces (army national guard and army reserve) have assumed a major contingency role for meeting a Warsaw Pact attack on NATO in Central Europe, with commitments for deployment that are nearly as demanding as those of the "forces-in-being."

The Most Likely Scenario

The military contingency used by the Pentagon as the basis for planning total force policy—and the contingency that would make the greatest demands on the army's mobilization resources—is a sudden massive attack upon NATO forces in Central Europe. Such a confrontation probably would involve an intense conflict on land and might develop with only a brief warning (as opposed to the many weeks or even months of warning before previous major wars). It might last only a few weeks, or combat might be very intense for the first few months and then drop off to a lingering war of attrition. In either case, the need for mobilization would be paramount. As explained in 1976 by Secretary of Defense Donald Rumsfeld: "The force balance (between NATO and the Warsaw Pact) reaches an acceptable level of risk with the arrival of U.S. reinforcements, but only after a very critical period in the first few days when the force ratio could reach dangerously high levels. This clearly demonstrates both the necessity for U.S. reinforcements and the rapidity with which they must be able to deploy once the Pact's actions are known."[2]

Pentagon plans for providing these reinforcements call for the full participation of total force units and individuals. In short, as an important Defense Department official explained to Congress, "The first months of intensive combat would have to be fought with the Active and Reserve component force structures that existed before the war started."[3] In Pentagon plans, this capability would require some 1,525,000 combat-ready troops, plus 200,000 replacements for casualties, during the first 120 days after mobilization.[4]

Whereas the strength of the active and reserve forces in the draft years was sufficient to provide these 1,725,000 personnel, changes in all elements of the total force since the adoption of AVF have prompted major mobilization problems.

Force Level Reductions

Reductions in the manning levels of the active and reserve forces during the initial AVF years have impacted more than any other AVF-related changes on U.S. strategic capabilities. In assessing the extent of the changes, the buildup in U.S. forces for the Vietnam War must be discounted. The strength and composition of the armed forces at the end of fiscal year 1964 may be used as a benchmark for comparison. Although there were some advisers in Vietnam in 1964, increases in the size of forces following President Johnson's decision to commit ground combat troops did not occur until 1965 and later. Thus fiscal year 1964 may be considered as the last year of peace and of stable, peacetime-level armed forces. In that year, some 2.68 million men and women were on active duty, including more than 972,000 in the army. These active forces were supported by a selected reserve of more than 950,000, including 650,000 in the army reserve forces and a pool of individual ready reservists (IRR) of more than 845,000, most of whom were in the army IRR. In addition, the nation's mobilization resources included some 483,000 standby reservists.

Fourteen years later, in 1978, the size of the active and reserve forces was substantially smaller.[5] In the active forces there were slightly more than two million men and women, including 767,000 in the army. These forces were supported by a selected reserve of about 788,000, including less than 526,000 in the army reserve forces; a pool of individual ready reservists of only 356,000, of whom 177,000 were in the army IRR; and a standby reserve of 183,000. Thus in the transition from a conscript-supported force to an AVF, the active forces were reduced by about 600,000, or 22 per cent of their 1964 level. The selected reserve had been reduced by 162,000 (about 20 per cent), while both the IRR and the standby reserve had been reduced in strength by about 60 per cent.

As these data illustrate, the reductions were particularly evident in the army total force elements, which at the end of fiscal year 1978 were more than 700,000 below FY 1964 strength levels. Furthermore, during this fourteen-year interval, the number of civilians employed by the army had been cut by more than forty thousand.

Considering overall Department of Defense strength, because the bulk of the manpower cuts were made in the mission support and central support areas, the impact on the mission forces—strategic, ground, tactical air, naval, and mobility—was disproportionately low, though some 216,000 personnel spaces were removed from these elements. Nor was there much change in the strategic forces (intercontinental nuclear missiles and aircraft), where the technological advances of new weapons systems easily offset the small personnel losses which occurred.

In terms of land forces, the initial AVF years witnessed a reduction in strength of about 25 per cent, due primarily to the cut in active army divisions from sixteen to thirteen. By 1978, however, most of the pre-Vietnam land forces strength had been restored, though a heavier proportion of the units were in the reserve, whose readiness and capabilities were significantly less than the active forces. Albeit the level of total force infantry and tank battalions in 1978 was slightly above the 1964 level, the ability of the ground forces in 1978 quickly to respond to crisis situations was clearly reduced.

In tactical air strength, a 25 per cent increase in personnel occurred, though there was a reduction overall of some 850 aircraft and a shift of about 250 planes from the active to the reserve forces. Because of weapons developments, however, the combat capability of the tactical air elements in 1978 was substantially higher than in FY 1964. In contrast, the navy suffered major reductions. Together with manpower cuts of some 130,000 personnel, the number of ships was reduced by 360 (about 40 per cent), only partially compensated for by adding larger and more modern ships.

The number of total force personnel assigned to mobility forces (air and sealift) also decreased slightly. Airlift capacity, however, doubled, the result of larger transports, while sealift capability was dramatically decreased, with a reduction in the number of navy or controlled charter ships available for transport of men and equipment from 101 in FY 1964 to only twenty-seven in 1978.

The Impact on the Active Army

The overall impact of these reductions on the initial combat capability of the active army was relatively modest. A combination of reductions in the mission forces, the shifting of more combat responsibilities to the reserves, and disproportionate manpower reductions in mission support and central support areas, however, caused a fundamental weakening of sustained war capabilities.[6] For example, whereas the increase in active army divisions from thirteen to sixteen, which took place in 1975–77, appeared to restore pre-Vietnam combat power, a detailed examination of the army's manpower requirements for sustaining these divisions in combat identifies two problem areas.

First, a large share of nondivisional combat and tactical support requirements was assigned to the reserves. Second, in the event of war, the eleven active army divisions in the United States would have to make substantial use of reserve force components to round out their combat force units. Indeed, in 1978 four of the active army divisions consisted of two active brigades and one reserve brigade, while five other divisions contained one to three reserve battalions integrated among their active force brigades. In total, during 1978 twenty-six reserve maneuver battalions were used to flesh out nine of the eleven army divisions in the United States. To the extent that these reserve units are adequately trained and available, they contribute to the army's deployment capability. But because of deficiencies in reserve manning and equipment levels and training, there is no doubt that the active army divisions are really much weaker than overall total force indices would indicate.

The restoration of the army's sixteen-division structure also appeared to have been achieved at the expense of a fundamental weakening in the support structure. Even upon full mobilization of the total force, in 1978, the army would have been some 250,000 tactical support personnel under strength.[7] This phenomenon was especially evident in the armed forces in Europe (see Chapter VII). And despite planned conversions of additional administrative elements into the division force equivalent structures during 1979 and 1980, by 1981 the army's support units would still be under strength by some 220,000 personnel if a mobilization were to occur.[8] Thus, while the restoration of sixteen divisions gave the army more short-term combat power, this capability was bought at the price of reductions in tactical support personnel and combat staying power.

In terms of the NATO contingency, then, the active army of 1978 was considerably smaller than the forces of 1964, though the level of initial combat power had been generally sustained at the expense of disproportionate reductions in support elements. Nevertheless, against the unchanging if not growing requirement for personnel to meet the demands of the "worst case" contingency, the proportion of the load borne by the active army has been significantly reduced.[9] In 1964, the 972,000 personnel of the active army would have provided more than 56 per cent of the 1,725,000 troops needed for a conventional conflict in Central Europe. By 1978, however, the 767,000 men and women in the active army would have provided only 44 per cent. Thus during the AVF years the major share of the army's mobilization responsibilities shifted from active to reserve forces. The army's ability to meet its strategic objectives will therefore depend largely on the strength and readiness of the army national guard and the army reserve.[10] These units form the so-called selected reserve. They are the army's readiest resource for augmenting the active forces in the event of a NATO-Warsaw Pact conventional conflict.

The Army Selected Reserve in the AVF Years

The vital role of the selected reserve in the event of a conflict in Europe can be seen by examining the proportion of the army's deployed forces which would be units of the army national guard or reserve. Whereas some 52 per cent of infantry and armor battalions in Europe in the event of full deployment would be from these two components, they also would provide some 57 per cent of field artillery, 65 per cent of combat engineers, and 65 per cent of all tactical support units.[11]

In order to provide these forces upon mobilization, the army selected reserve forces would require a mobilized strength of 430,000 personnel in the national guard and 276,000 men and women in the army reserve.[12] In total, these 706,000 individuals would provide some 41 per cent of all personnel required by the army. Yet units of both the national guard and reserve are not maintained at mobilization strength level during peacetime. Rather, each year Congress authorizes peacetime manning levels. Thus, in the event of mobilization, the units would have to be brought up to wartime strength by the assignment of "filler" personnel from the individual reserve pools.

Even though peacetime manning levels for the army selected reserve have been considerably lower than their wartime manning levels, the ability of the units to maintain their strength has been severely curtailed by recruiting difficulties during the AVF years. The recruiting failures were particularly evident in 1976–78. For example, the army national guard started fiscal year 1976 with 395,000 personnel; by the end of FY 1978 its size had shrunk to 341,000, 49,000 below the minimum peacetime authorized size of 390,000.[13]

The same recruiting problems occurred in the army reserve. Despite the fact that its peacetime strength authorization was gradually reduced during the AVF years from 261,000 in 1973 to 212,400 in 1978, the army reserve still was unable to achieve its desired strength. Recruiting shortfalls were most evident in fiscal year 1976 when 29,000 more men and women were discharged than enlisted. As a result, the year-end strength of the army reserve was 196,000. As of October 1978 the strength had further eroded to 186,000, some 26,000 below the minimum authorized level.

In addition to these shortfalls, the Department of Defense in 1976 projected an additional shortfall in 1979 and 1980 of some 37,000.[14] If such additional recruiting difficulties occur, the army selected reserve would be some 112,000 below its desired peacetime strength level.

Although these statistics portray the inability of the selected reserve to meet peacetime manning levels, a more relevant contrast is that of actual manning levels with wartime manning requirements. For example, although the 1978 shortfalls were reduced by lowering the required peacetime size of the national guard from 400,000 to 390,000, and of the army reserve from 219,000 to 212,400, the level of strength required for mobilization has remained unchanged. Furthermore, some 5 per cent of army national guard and army reserve unit members are not expected to be available in the event of mobilization. Thus "fillers" would be needed both to replace these expected mobilization losses and to bring unit strengths up to mobilization levels. At the beginning of fiscal year 1976, the national guard would have required 55,000 personnel from the individual reserve pools to reach mobilization strength. At the end of fiscal year 1978, 105,000 fillers would have been needed.

The requirements for filler personnel for the army reserve are just as large. At the beginning of fiscal year 1976, the army reserve would have needed 63,000 fillers in order to reach mobilization strength. By the end of FY 1978, almost 100,000 would have been needed. Although it would not have been difficult to augment the national guard and army reserve from the individual reserve pools when the draft was still in effect, the decision to support the armed forces with volunteers has caused major shortfalls in the pools. Thus the increasing demands for filler personnel for the selected reserve units has compounded what was already a serious manpower deficit in the individual reserve pools.

Mobilization Role of the
Individual Reserve Pools

The decision to abandon conscription and the resulting reductions in the force levels of the active army and the army selected reserve placed a much greater share of the mobilization burden on the individual reserve pools (individual ready reserve [IRR] and standby reserve). In the draft year of 1964, all but 134,000 of the 1,725,000 personnel needed by the army within 120 days of mobilization would have been provided by the active army, the army national guard, and the army reserve, and only about one-sixth of the almost 670,000 men in the IRR and standby reserve would have been called to duty.

By the end of FY 1978, however, the strength on mobilization of the active army and the army selected reserve would have been only 1,268,000. And due to these strength reductions, the requirements for personnel from the individual reserve pools would have increased from 134,000 in 1964 to 457,000, or fully 25 per cent of the overall army requirement 120 days after mobilization. If those individuals who are sick, in transit, or in longterm training are excluded from the tabulation of combat-ready personnel in the active army, the need for fillers is even higher.

For example, in early 1976 Assistant Secretary of Defense (Manpower and Reserve Affairs) William K. Brehm told Congress that the demand for individual reservists would be approximately 51,000 for the active forces, a minimum of 120,000 for the selected reserve, and some 100,000 individual reservists to staff currently unmanned units that would be needed for the NATO contingency force structure. If the forces were deployed in the kind of intense combat expected in a NATO-Warsaw Pact confrontation, about 200,000 additional men would be needed to replace casualties during the four to five months before the army could train volunteers or draftees and assign them to combat units. In total, then, the Pentagon saw the need for some 471,000 trained fillers to supplement and support the total force structure.[15]

Since then, growing shortfalls in selected reserve units have increased the need for filler personnel. By July 1976, only four to five months after the Pentagon's requirements were presented to Congress, the need for personnel to augment the selected reserve units had increased from a "minimum of 120,000" to 176,000; by the end of FY 1978, it was more than 200,000. When the numbers needed to fill out the active forces, staff currently unmanned units, and provide casualty replacements are added, the total army requirement for filler personnel reaches about 550,000, a number compatible with the initial determination of a 471,000 requirement, plus an allowance for those members of the active army who would be excluded from a tabulation of combat-ready personnel.

Whether the requirement in FY 1978 was 471,000 or 550,000, it is clear that available manpower pools were woefully unable to provide the needed personnel. And how many could have been provided by the individual reserve pools? The answer is not easy to determine because of the absence of a recent large-scale call-up. Nevertheless, an examination of mobilization yield rates developed by the Department of Defense, and the mid-1978 strengths of the individual reserve pools, provide a basis for a reasonable estimate. For example, in FY 1978 there were some 177,000 men in the army's IRR pool. Given the Pentagon's 70 per cent yield factor, a pool of this size would have produced some 124,000 personnel upon mobilization.[16] The standby reserve would have increased the number of available personnel by 42,000. Thus the combined returns from both individual reserve pools would have been some 166,000, or about one-third of even the more optimistic estimate of the army's requirement.

In 1980 the situation is not likely to improve. On the one hand, the projected decline in army selected reserve strength would add to the requirement; on the other hand, several internal army policy changes, designed to increase the strength of the IRR (they are discussed below), could offset the added requirements.[17]

In determining the strength of the problem, the expected loss factor upon mobilization must also be taken into consideration. The army expects some 70 per cent of the IRR to report; thus the size of the IRR must be some 30 per cent higher than actual mobilization requirements. This means that an IRR pool of almost 800,000 must be maintained in order to provide the army upon mobilization with up to 550,000 "fillers" (an IRR of 800,000 would eliminate the need to call up less available standby reservists or other individuals). At the end of FY 1978, the army's IRR and standby reserve pools contained only some 260,000 men, or some 540,000 personnel less than the manning level goal for the pools.

Reductions in the size of individual reserve pools during the AVF years can be directly attributed to the decision to support the armed forces totally with volunteers.[18] In determining these numbers, several factors affecting the flow of manpower into the active forces must be considered. These include length of enlistment terms, attrition rates, numbers of women enlistees (because women have not had reserve service obligations), re-enlistment rates, and the number of veterans who sign up for service with selected reserve units after completion of active duty.

With a somewhat smaller active force size, and with the trend toward longer enlistment terms, fewer men have been entering the army, and each year fewer of them have been completing their initial term of service. As more women have enlisted, the number of men has declined even further. In addition, because of higher attrition rates and because more men completing their first term of service have been re-enlisting, the number of men leaving active service at the end of their enlistment term has diminished. Furthermore, because more veterans have been signing up for duty with selected reserve units, even fewer men have been available for assignment to the IRR pool.[19] For example, in fiscal year 1976 the army enlisted some 195,000 personnel, 16,000 of whom were women. Of the 179,000 men, approximately two-thirds (or 120,000) are expected to complete their initial tours of duty. Some 30 per cent of the 120,000, or 36,000, are expected to re-enlist. The remainder, 84,000 men, should be released from active duty in 1979 and 1980.

Each year, however, the army national guard and the army reserve recruit about 100,000 veterans. Unless dramatic changes are made in these flow patterns, most of the 84,000 men leaving active service in 1979 and 1980 will be recruited by selected reserve units, and the number of men entering the IRR pool will be negligible.

Army Initiatives to Eliminate or
Reduce the Shortfalls

Pentagon programs aimed at resolving these mobilization shortfall problems have been directed toward increasing the supply of pretrained individuals who would be available for assignment to operating units within 120 days of mobilization. Thus military leaders have discounted the value of newly trained volunteers and conscripts in meeting the initial requirements for filling active army and reserve units and providing casualty replacements. And through a series of management improvement actions and policy changes, the army expects to reduce the projected shortfalls by significant amounts. For example, in 1977 the Pentagon took steps to amend the appropriate legislation in order to extend the six-year service obligation to women who previously had not been subject to recall. Unfortunately, the move will not diminish projected shortfalls in the IRR until women enlisting in 1978 and beyond complete their initial tours of active duty. Since women normally enlist for four-year terms, the first large segment of women should enter the IRR in 1982.

Several other programs initiated by the army in 1977–78 will have an immediate impact on the size of the deficit. First, the army, through administrative action, has stopped the automatic transfer of IRR members to the standby reserve at the completion of five years of service. Because of higher yield rates from the IRR (and avoidance of the requirement that the Selective Service System screen the reservists for availability), the move should produce additional mobilization resources.

The army also is selecting certain men from those who are discharged before the completion of their initial terms of service for transfer to the IRR. Before 1978, although all dischargees retained a six-year service obligation, the army and the other services did not require these personnel to serve in the reserve. In 1979 and later years, however, those men and women discharged on other than adverse conditions will be required to complete their six-year terms of total obligated service in the IRR.

Finally, the army has obtained permission to experiment with several enlistment schemes which should eventually result in an increase in IRR size, and to experiment with programs to obtain extensions in the IRR from those who would be legally eligible for transfer to the standby reserve or for discharge. Collectively, these measures should not significantly reduce the army's possible maximum shortfall of 540,000. Nevertheless, if the measures are fully implemented, the manning level deficit in the IRR could be cut by 25,000 in FY 1980 and by up to 100,000 in later years.

A much larger source of additional pretrained personnel is the pool of military retirees and those active army personnel who are serving in positions that could be occupied by civilians.

Concerning retirees, by late 1978 the army was developing plans to recall significant numbers upon mobilization.[20] The most readily available of the various categories of retirees are retired enlisted regulars who have not reached their thirtieth service anniversaries. These men and women can be recalled by the President without legal restrictions and without the need for a declaration of war or national emergency. Not all of these personnel would be available or of use to the services upon mobilization, however. Many would be disqualified or granted deferments or exemptions. While the army has not prepared detailed plans, a 1978 study estimated that 90 per cent of those who had retired within one year, 85 per cent of those who had retired within two years, and so forth, would be available. Overall, for the prime group, this logic results in a yield rate of about 70 per cent. Thus the army could expect to reduce its mobilization shortfall in pretrained individuals by calling some 56,000 retirees.[21] More retirees also would be available if the army decided to utilize those men and women who had passed their thirtieth service anniversaries.

The civilianization of some support positions immediately following mobilization also would reduce the projected shortfall. Again, however, as of late 1978 no specific plans had been developed, though army planners have discussed a rate of some ten thousand conversions per month. It is unlikely that this rate could be achieved in the early months following a mobilization, however, because of the need to make major increases in the civilian work force unrelated to relieving military personnel.

The implementation of both of these options would allow the army to make substantial reductions in its projected mobilization manpower shortfalls. But major deficits still would exist. In order to reduce these shortfalls even further, the army in 1978 was seriously considering asking Congress for two fundamental changes in AVF personnel policies. These changes concern the length of the military service obligation assumed by all new enlistees, and the use upon mobilization of those veterans who no longer have a recall obligation.

As conceived by Army planners, the proposal to extend the military service obligation (MSO) would be effective only for those who enter the armed forces after the date of congressional approval. Thus, at best, this action would increase the size of the IRR in 1985 and later years. At the same time, however, it would establish an inequity of service among youth and would very likely have a negative impact on recruiting programs. Consequently, the proposal is highly controversial, and if the Administration approves the scheme for submission to Congress, the resulting debate will be heated and probably indecisive.

The army also is exploring the possibility of gaining approval for the emergency recall of veterans, those men who have completed their six-year periods of obligated service. In a crisis, the prime group of veterans would be those who have successfully completed their initial terms of active duty, are not members of reserve units, and are under the age of thirty. Within this definition in 1977 were almost 600,000 personnel, of which 25 per cent were trained in combat skills and another 5 per cent were medics. The numbers of veterans who could be utilized in a full mobilization, however, have not been determined, nor have any decisions been made concerning exemptions, such as excusing those with Vietnam combat experience. Nonetheless, if the army gains legislative authority and prepares detailed utilization plans, the

recall of veterans in an emergency could reduce or even eliminate projected manpower shortfalls.

If such a policy were approved by Congress, it would amount
to an involuntary extension of the MSO. As such, it would
prompt strong opposition from those who object to any form of
conscription, even though the opposition to involuntary service
policies increasingly diminished during the 1973–78 period.[22]

Collectively, the various policy changes which the army initiated in 1977 and 1978, together with proposed major policy adjustments, could eliminate projected full mobilization manpower
shortfalls, at least in numerical terms. But each of the proposals
is fraught with political and emotional overtones. If approval
finally is obtained, it is likely to come only after a period of extended congressional and public debate.

Relationship of the AVF Decision to Strength Reductions

Strength reductions, the greater mobilization responsibilities of the reserves, and the decline in the number of available
individual reservists have clearly resulted in a weakened national
defense capability, especially in sustaining a high deterrent
against a non-nuclear attack on NATO by Warsaw Pact forces in
Central Europe.

Many observers consider a return to the draft the easiest way
to correct the deficiencies, but it is important to note that not all
manpower problems have been caused by the abandonment of
conscription. For example, an argument can be made that about
one-third of the strength reductions in the active forces during
the AVF years were related to the new realistic deterrence strategy and the corollary reduction in planning goals from a 2½ war
capability to a 1½ war capability.

In this regard, in 1969 the Pentagon discussed a peacetime
force for the post-Vietnam War years of 2.68 million men and
women, the level which had been maintained before the Vietnam
build-up.[23] But when Secretary of Defense Melvin R. Laird presented the military aspects of the new Nixon foreign policy to
Congress in 1971, he spoke of a peacetime force made up of "no

more than 2.5 million men and women who are volunteers"—
some 200,000 fewer than envisioned by military leaders before
the development of Nixon's new strategy.[24] The services' requests
to Congress for a strength authorization of 2.5 million at the end
of fiscal year 1972 confirmed Laird's position.[25]

It appears, therefore, that about one-third of about 600,000
positions removed from the active forces structure were directly
related to the new strategy. What prompted the additional cuts?
Three factors can be identified. First, the army and the other
services were under pressure to modernize their forces and would
not have been able to pay for equipment without offsetting reductions in personnel costs. Second, the higher per-man costs of
the AVF era created pressures to cut personnel in order to hold
manpower costs near their pre-AVF levels. Third, as outlined by
a former high army official, service leaders were under political
pressure to accept an end to the draft and to adopt AVF recruitment policies, an impossible move without substantial reductions
in yearly recruiting goals.[26]

Reductions in the selected reserve, however, were caused entirely by the AVF decision. For despite congressional mandates to
retain pre-Vietnam strength, the inability of the army national
guard and army reserve units to recruit and retain enough qualified personel made the reductions inevitable. The AVF decision
may also be blamed for reductions in the individual reserve pools.

Conclusion

Whatever the causes, the reductions in key elements of
the army total force during the first AVF years have had a marked
impact on U.S. strategic capabilities, especially as they relate to
a full mobilization in support of a NATO defense in Central Europe. On the one hand, the strength of the active army and army
selected reserve has dwindled by 329,000 personnel. On the other
hand, pools of individual reservists needed to bring units up to
their wartime strength levels have shrunk well below the levels
necessary to meet mobilization needs.

Beyond these apparent numerical shortfalls are a myriad of
other issues and problems resulting from the AVF decision. High
among these is imbalance between combat and combat-support

resources which has resulted from the army's efforts to retain initial combat power within an overall reduced force structure.

Many other problems involve the call-up of various categories of personnel in the event of full mobilization. Foremost among these is the high uncertainty of the various yield rates used by the army to predict mobilization strength gains. Whereas the loss of 5 per cent from the selected reserve can be supported by both historical experience and various mobilization exercises in the late 1970's, the loss factors for the other manpower groups are progressively less certain. The fact is that the true availability of these mobilization resources cannot be determined. On the one hand, in total, there are more than enough personnel in the IRR, standby reserve, and retired reserve to meet the army's needs. On the other hand, if estimated losses from these sources upon mobilization are understated, the army's problems would be even greater than 1978 projections.

Another major problem concerns the matching of the army's specific needs with available mobilization personnel. The army estimates that some 70 per cent of the IRR would report upon mobilization, but little attention has been paid to whether these personnel could perform useful functions. For example, approximately 75 per cent of the army's filler and replacement needs would be in combat arms or medical, combat engineer, and direct support fields. Yet only about 25 per cent of the personnel in the IRR in 1978 possessed these skills. An overabundance of officers in the IRR compounds this problem.

Next, a serious question arises whether the manpower available upon mobilization would be ready in time to play a useful role in the critical early weeks.

The army has concentrated on matching sources of supplementary pretrained manpower with its projected shortfalls—but it has ignored deployment problems. The manpower requirements of the services upon mobilization do not increase steadily; most of the personnel needed to boost the force to peak level is needed in the first few weeks. During this period, units of the active and reserve forces would be filled to their wartime complements. Thereafter replacements would be needed, but their numbers would be less than those needed in the initial weeks.

Nor would personnel from the supplementary pools be immediately available for deployment. Initial ordering, administrative processing, and pre-reporting leave would take time. Many of these personnel would require refresher training before they were able to resume old specialties. And those assigned to new specialties would require even longer periods of training. Thus, although supplementary sources of manpower might eliminate the peak manpower shortfalls, they would not likely satisfy needs immediately after mobilization, when trained personnel are needed to fill deploying units.

Finally, even if the army manages to resolve its projected shortfall problems, the deployed forces would be far less combat ready than the forces of the pre-Vietnam War years. This conclusion is based on the fact that personnel of the active army are readier than personnel of the selected reserve, and that men and women in both of these groups are readier than members of the individual reserve pools or retirees or veterans. Although the army conceivably could field a mobilized force as large as that of 1964 it would not have as many trained active and selected reserve personnel.

Reductions in U.S. forces also should be related to changes in Soviet strength. Though a defensible comparative analysis of NATO-Warsaw Pact forces and capabilities would require analysis of all the national forces involved, a comparison of the two major superpowers nevertheless offers insights into the relative impact of the U.S. force structure changes. Whereas U.S. forces have never matched Moscow's massive army, Soviet personnel strength in 1978 was about 2.5 times that of U.S. forces. U.S. divisions were outnumbered about seven to one, though the larger size and more sophisticated equipment of the U.S. units somewhat offset the Soviet edge. The military superiority of the Soviet forces overall cannot be seriously questioned. Furthermore, during the period when U.S. forces were being cut, the Soviets continued a general program of force expansion. As the Library of Congress notes, the Soviet manpower advantage of more than 850,000 in 1965 had more than tripled by the late 1970's.[27]

This widening gap, coupled with the various problems of and unanswered questions about mobilization of the army total force, portends an ominous future for the deterrent value of the army's conventional warfare capabilities. This is part of the price being paid for the AVF.

Notes

1. In Pentagon plans, the concept of total national mobilization (as in 1940–45) has been replaced by a much reduced call-up objective. Thus, in this paper, the term "mobilization" refers to augmenting the active forces with all members and units of the reserve forces and then sustaining this larger active force by a continuing flow of new enlistees or draftees.
2. Department of Defense, Office of the Secretary of Defense, *A Report to Congress on U.S. Conventional Reinforcements for NATO* (Washington, D.C., Department of Defense, 1976), p. VII-1.
3. Statement of William K. Brehm, Assistant Secretary of Defense (Manpower and Reserve Affairs) before the U.S. Congress, House of Representatives, Committee on Armed Services, Subcommittee on Investigations, *Hearing on the Selective Service System*, 21–26 January 1976, p. 3.
4. *A Report to Congress on U.S. Conventional Reinforcements for NATO*, p. IX-3.
5. Data on 1964 and 1978 contrasts are contained in *Department of Defense Manpower, FY 1964–FY 1977, The Components of Change*, a report prepared by the Department for the Defense Manpower Commission in April 1975, and in supplementary materials provided by the Office of the Assistant Secretary of Defense (Manpower, Reserve Affairs, and Logistics).
6. Perhaps the greatest weakness which has developed in the army's war-sustaining capabilities is its inability to provide the personnel fillers and casualty replacements which could be needed in the early weeks of a conflict. This weakness is due to major falloffs in the strengths of the individual reserve pools.
7. The army's determination of a support shortfall is based on its traditional structure of support. This is the division force equivalent, consisting of some 48,000 personnel: a combat division of sixteen thousand soldiers supported by twelve thousand soldiers in corps-level combat units (additional artillery, engineers, aviation, air defense, etc.), and some twenty thousand personnel in tactical support functions (supply, maintenance, medical, transportation and so forth). As the full division force equivalent was devised to provide extended support for the division in combat, not all of the support elements would be needed in the critical early weeks of a war. For this reason, the army's projected support shortfall is not

a major cause of concern among military and civilian leaders.

8. Congressional Budget Office, *U.S. Army Force Design: Alternatives for Fiscal Years 1977–1981* (Washington, D.C., U.S. Congress, 1976), p. 24.

9. Although the requirements for the mobilization force structures have not changed significantly since 1964, increases have been made in combat replacement needs primarily because of the high casualty rates of the 1973 Middle East war.

10. The army reserve forces reached their 1978 configuration only after several reorganizations within the previous fifteen years. The first efforts were made by Secretary of Defense Robert S. McNamara in the early 1960's. Rather than maintaining a larger number of undermanned, undertrained, and under-equipped reserve combat divisions (twenty-seven in the national guard and ten in the army reserve), McNamara sought a smaller number of more responsive units for which more equipment and other resources would be available. In 1963 he was able to eliminate four national guard and four army reserve divisions. This was followed in 1965 by the elimination of the remaining six army reserve combat divisions. The final major reorganization occurred in the late 1960's when the records of the few small reserve forces units which had been called to active duty in 1968 convinced Congress that fewer and smaller units would be more appropriate for future contingencies. As a result, the army national guard combat divisions were reduced from twenty-three to eight, and many smaller units were created.

Despite these structural improvements, the failure of the Johnson Administration to call up the reserve forces en masse in 1965 and beyond threatened their credibility. Equipment was taken from them and sent to Vietnam, and additional equipment they were scheduled to receive was withdrawn or diverted. As few persons during the post-1965 Vietnam years believed that the reserve forces would be mobilized, most of their enlistees signed on to avoid the draft and possible assignment to Vietnam. Thus by 1969, when the newly-elected Nixon Administration began to assess the practicabilities of supporting the armed forces with volunteers, the reserve forces had been subject to almost continuing reorganization and questioning of their value and future usefulness. To those in the reserve forces, the development of the total force policy re-established their legitimate role as the prime

source for augmentation of the active forces. For a more
thorough discussion of the state of the army reserve forces
during the Vietnam War period, see *Annual Report of the
Secretary of Defense on Reserve Forces, Fiscal Year 1972*
(Washington, D.C., Department of Defense, 1973).

11. Statement of Robert L. Nelson, Assistant Secretary of the Army,
Before the Committee on Armed Service, Senate, Hearings,
*Department of Defense Authorization for Appropriations for
FY 1979*, 15 March 1978, p. 2119.

12. The army national guard is oriented toward combat involvement
and is composed of one mechanized, two armored, and five
infantry divisions; twenty-one combat forces brigades or regiments; and assorted support units. The army reserve is oriented toward support and training. It is composed of the cadres
of twelve training divisions, eight combat support brigades
and a variety of smaller units. For a detailed discussion of reserve forces organization, see Department of Defense, *Reserve
Forces Manpower Requirements Report, FY 1976* (Washington, D.C., Department of Defense, 1975), Appendices A & B.

13. Department of Defense, Office of Deputy Assistant Secretary of
Defense (Reserve Affairs), "Reserve Forces Manpower
Charts," 30 September 1978.

14. Department of Defense, Office of the Assistant Secretary of Defense (Manpower and Reserve Affairs), *The All-Volunteer
Force: Current Status and Prospects* (Washington, D.C., Department of Defense, 1976), p. 13.

15. U.S. Congress, House of Representatives, Committee on Armed
Services, *Hearings on the Selective Service System*, 27–29
January, 2–3 February 1976, pp. 168–169.

16. The numbers of reservists reporting quickly upon mobilization is
not expected to be 100 per cent. Planners within the Pentagon
have estimated reporting percentages from the various categories. These were based on evaluations of the mobilizations
of 1940, 1950, 1961, and 1968, with allowances for better
management and control. Despite the fact that standby and
retired reserves have never been activated and that the U.S.
has not fully mobilized since 1940, the Pentagon estimates that
95 per cent of the selected reserve unit members, 70 per cent
of the IRR, and 50 per cent of the standby reserve would respond to a mobilization call. Both the percentages for the selected reserve and IRR are higher than historical precedents.
See Department of Defense, Secretary of Defense, *The Guard*

and Reserve in the Total Force, unclassified portions of Secret document (Washington, D.C., Department of Defense, 1975), p. 11.

17. The strength of the army IRR at the end of FY 1972 (the last year of conscription) was 1,059,000. Before the new army programs, the strength level of the army IRR was expected to be only 119,000 in FY 1982, or some 11 per cent of the FY 1972 strength. If the new army programs prove successful, however, the strength of the army IRR could be increased by as much as 100,000 by FY 1982.

18. Before the report of the Defense Manpower Commission in 1976, the Pentagon erroneously relied on draft-era data which grossly overstated the expected size of the IRR pool during AVF years. See Defense Manpower Commission, *Defense Manpower: The Keystone of National Security* (Washington, D.C., GPO, 1976), p. 421.

19. Men who enlist in the active forces assume a six-year service obligation. The final or sixth year normally is spent in the standby reserve. Thus the IRR is composed of those who have completed three- or four-year active duty enlistments, do not opt for affiliation with a selected reserve unit, and have not yet completed five years of military service. Other members of the IRR include reservists who can no longer meet the commitments of service with the selected reserve, and men who volunteer to stay in the IRR beyond their statutory commitment.

20. In mid-1977 the army began to collect minimum essential data on retiring army personnel. Additional resources have been provided to construct data on persons who retired before mid-1977. By mid-1979 the army expects to have a usable data base on the approximately 110,000 individuals who retired since mid-1974. At the same time, the army has initiated a research effort to identify those mobilization positions which could be filled by retirees.

21. Study by Linton and Co. for Office of Assistant Secretary of Defense (Manpower, Reserve Affairs and Logistics), "Military Retirees as Mobilization Assets," 26 April 1978, pp. V-3 and V-4.

22. Public support for the draft, which had reached an all-time low in 1972, began to climb during the AVF years. In 1977 a poll determined that 36 per cent of those surveyed favored a return to the draft. And by December 1978 another poll determined that 53 per cent favored a return to the draft.

See *The Gallup Poll—Public Opinion 1972–77* (Wilmington, Scholarly Resources, 1978), pp. 991–992. Also see Louis Harris, "ABC News, Harris Survey," 6 December 1978.

23. See briefing by Vice Admiral William Mack, Acting Assistant Secretary of Defense (Manpower and Reserve Affairs) on "Project Volunteer," at news conference of Secretary of Defense Melvin Laird, 18 February 1969.

24. *Hearings Before and Special Reports Made by Committee on Armed Services, House of Representatives, on Subjects Affecting the Naval and Military Establishments* (Washington, D.C., GPO, 1971), p. 2326.

25. *Ibid.*, pp. 2318–2319.

26. Interview with General Bruce Palmer, Jr., U.S.A. (Ret.), who, during the early years of the AVF, served as Vice Chief of Staff and Acting Chief of Staff of the U.S. Army.

27. Congessional Research Service, Library of Congress, *United States/Soviet Military Balance: A Frame of Reference for Congress* (Washington, D.C., GPO, 1976), p. 16.

Chapter VI

Mobilization and New Recruits: The Hedge Against a Protracted Conflict

U.S. mobilization plans for the "worst case" scenario of a conventional conflict in Central Europe call for new recruits to enter training in the weeks and months after mobilization of the total force. They would not be ready for assignment to operating units for at least three to four months, and thus would be unavailable to fill units of the active or reserve forces or replace casualty losses during the initial weeks following the outbreak of hostilities.

Yet if the conflict were to continue for an extended period, the newly trained personnel would be available for use not only as individual replacements but also as the basis for the formation of new units within a general expansion of the total force structure. Furthermore, if the decision to increase the input of new recruits preceded the outbreak of hostilities by several weeks or more, some recruits would likely complete their training during the first ninety days of the war. They could help fill manpower vacancies in the deployed units. Of course, if hostilities erupted after only a brief political warning and lasted for only a few weeks, newly trained personnel would have no role in the outcome. But the capability to provide operating units with a large and steady flow of newly trained personnel three to four months after mobilization would provide a hedge against a protracted conflict. In addition, such a capability would strengthen the deterrent value of the armed forces.

During the years of peace which preceded the Vietnam War,

the Selective Service System guaranteed the army that a sudden need for major increases in monthly recruit totals could be met. Since the advent of the AVF, however, Selective Service has stopped all activities other than contingency planning. Consequently, by 1978 the value of the system in meeting sudden demands for new manpower was negligible.

Post-Mobilization Training Requirements

During the peacetime years of the AVF, approximately eighty thousand recruits at any one time are enrolled in army initial training programs, on leave following completion of their training, or on their way to their first assignments with operating units. In order to sustain this flow of new recruits, the army must enlist about twenty thousand youths each month, including about 4,500 for the reserve forces (reserve recruits are trained with active force recruits). In the event of mobilization, the army's need for new recruits would significantly increase. As the training base capacity also would have to be expanded, the greater numbers of new recruits would have to be phased over the initial months following the mobilization decision. Nevertheless, by sixty days after mobilization the army would have to increase the monthly flow of new recruits from twenty thousand to 100,000 or more per month.

Volunteers for Service

In the event of a major conventional military threat to NATO by the Warsaw Pact, a large number of American youths would volunteer for military service. Whether their numbers would be adequate to meet the greatly increased need for new trainees, however, would largely depend on the public's perception of the danger to U.S. nationals or the American way of life. For example, if the mobilization decision were made in a period of mounting political tensions, major increases in recruiting totals would be doubtful. Indeed, if such a mobilization decision were not enthusiastically supported by the nation's moral and political leaders, as well as the media, even peacetime recruiting levels might not be maintained.

In the event of a direct military attack in Central Europe on U.S. and other NATO forces, however, there can be little doubt that vastly increased numbers of youth would volunteer for service. One only has to explore the reaction of American youth to the attack on Pearl Harbor in 1941 to recognize that they could respond to an emergency at a level far beyond the ability of the services to enlist and train them. But the army cannot count on this, and since the deterrent value of mobilization would depend upon the military posture during the first critical days and weeks, it is vital that the army have a guaranteed flow of new trainees to support a full mobilization. To achieve this goal, sources in addition to the uncertain numbers of volunteers must be developed.

One such source is the Delayed Entry Pool (DEP). These young men and women have already enlisted, but their initial reporting for active duty has been delayed so that they may finish civilian schooling or meet the scheduling demands of service technical training courses. Such youths are subject to call-up in the event of an emergency. While this action would disrupt service training programs in later months, the army by 1978 was increasingly committed to the use of DEP personnel to meet its demand for new trainees during the initial weeks following mobilization. At any one time, an average of some 35,000 youths may be found in the army DEP, with another 65,000 or so youths in the DEP's of the other services. The size of the pools, however, fluctuates widely. And many DEP members are high school students who would likely be excused from the call-up. If this assumption is correct, most of the army DEP's during the months between September and July would be unavailable.[1]

The continuation of volunteer recruiting programs and the call-up of DEP members would provide the army with an initial surge in recruit totals during the weeks immediately following mobilization. Severe shortages in new trainees would nonetheless exist, and they could be met only if the Selective Service System could quickly resume inductions. The ability of the draft to meet emergency manpower demands has thus been the subject of increasing attention and debate.

Requirements for a Standby Draft

The requirement for a standby draft, established by Congress in 1971, was based upon recommendations of the Gates Commission and Administration officials.[2] The key phrases of the legislative mandate are: "The Selective Service System . . . shall . . . be maintained as an active standby organization, with (1) a complete registration and classification structure capable of immediate operation in the event of a national emergency, and (2) personnel adequate to reinstitute immediately the full operations of the System."[3]

Specific mobilization delivery requirements for the standby draft were first defined in 1972–73, when a National Security Council task force made recommendations based on the assumption that inductees would be needed in the event that a conventional conflict between the forces of NATO and the Warsaw Pact in Central Europe should last more than 120 to 150 days.

Utilizing the NATO conventional war scenario and the total force concept (call-up of selected reserve units, IRR, standby reserve, and retired reserve before beginning inductions), the Pentagon's Total Force Study Group in 1974–75 again determined that a need for inductees would exist immediately following mobilization. As a result, the secretary of defense stated that the standby draft mechanism should be able to begin inductions within thirty days after mobilization and to deliver a total of up to 500,000 men within 180 days.[4] In January 1977 this requirement was raised to 650,000.[5] At the same time the joint chiefs of staff stated their need for 100,000 trained inductees within 150 days of mobilization.[6] This requirement means that the standby draft must be able to deliver 100,000 inductees within thirty to sixty days after the decision to mobilize.

These requirements were based on "full" mobilization, that is, the call-up and support on active duty of the total force structure. They did not take into account the possibility of a larger or "total" mobilization, in which the role of Selective Service would be considerably greater. Not only would the draft be responsible for inducting additional numbers of men (and women?), but various deferment and exemption policies designed to aid critical industries would no doubt need to be reinstituted. In the views of military planners, however, a "total" mobilization is highly unlikely, due both to the changed nature of warfare and the inability of the industrial base to provide equipment and supplies in sufficient quantities and in sufficiently short time periods. Thus, in the context of mobilization planning in 1978, the paramount role for the Selective Service System is the fast provision of new recruits required to sustain the total force structure in combat beyond a period of three to four months.

Reductions in Standby Draft Delivery Capabilities

The standby Selective Service System was able to meet the Pentagon's mobilization requirements during the first two years of the AVF. Indeed, with the end of monthly induction calls in December 1972, the system remained an active agency of the federal government with several continuing statutory duties, including the registration of young men for possible induction, and their classification and examination "as soon as practicable" following registration.[7]

A new concept of operations, scheduled for implementation in 1976, would have further cut funding for the system, local board processing, and administrative support, and would have registered eighteen-year-olds once a year instead of on their birthdays. Even with these changes, the system would have been able to maintain its delivery capability. Unfortunately, resistance to once-a-year registration developed on political grounds, and the executive orders to implement the program were not issued. Since the old form of registration had been stopped in early 1975 in anticipation of the once-a-year program, the failure to authorize the new form resulted in the end of all ongoing registration activities.[8] And as the end of registration removed most processing from local draft boards, funds for the standby Selective Service System were cut to a level that required closing the local boards and their administrative offices. As a result of these actions, the delivery capability of the system was substantially reduced. In 1973–75, it could have begun inductions within thirty days; in 1978 it would have required somewhere between 70 and

135 days—up to 105 more than the delivery schedule requested by the Pentagon.[9]

Restoring the System's Delivery Capability

At the time of the last draft calls in December 1972, Selective Service maintained some three thousand local draft boards, administered by 626 area offices, fifty-six state headquarters, and the national office. More than forty thousand volunteers were involved in system operations, plus more than six thousand paid employees. By 1978 the decision to place the system in "deep standby" had resulted in the elimination of most of these functions and personnel. Local boards had been disbanded, area offices had been closed, state headquarters had been reduced to one-man (unpaid) staffs, and registration and classification activities had been suspended. During FY 1978 only ninety-eight full-time employees, plus some seven hundred part-time national guard and army reserve officers in paid drill status, remained on the system's rolls, and their activities were limited to contingency planning.

During the AVF years, Selective Service developed the Emergency Military Manpower Processing System (EMMPS) which would allow emergency induction processing for most young men without the involvement of the state headquarters or the local draft board. Nevertheless, the local boards would have to be reconstituted quickly in an emergency in order to handle deferment and exemption requests, postponements, and requests for information. The magnitude of this task can be appreciated when one examines the reconstitution goals.

As the system's director noted in 1976, the objective of the agency upon mobilization would be to restore the structure and employment level of September 1974, when there were fifty-six state headquarters (with 562 supervisory and management personnel); 626 area offices (with 1,587 personnel); offices at each of the sixty-six armed forces entrance and examining stations (with 198 personnel); and 3,014 local or appeal boards (manned by some fifteen thousand volunteer members).[10] In addition, a registration program would require another 100,000 volunteers and some fifty thousand sites for a one- to two-day registration effort.[11]

In order to be able to induct up to 650,000 youth within 180 days, Selective Service officials maintain that an initial registration of two complete male year-of-birth groups (some 3.8 million men) would be required. The system's calculations, however, have been based on Vietnam-era experience, and it is doubtful that the kind of draft opposition present then would be repeated in the event of a mobilization prompted by a crisis in Europe.[12] Nevertheless, system officials believe that the use of Vietnam-era data provides a necessary hedge against miscalculation.

In addition to initial registration, the reactivated system also would have to process registrants. In 1977 and 1978 officials maintained that the registration-to-induction cycle could be accomplished in somewhat less time than the 110 days stipulated by the director in 1976. But a 1978 examination of the system's contingency planning and preparations raised a modicum of doubt about its ability to improve this delivery schedule without fundamental changes in processing, a return to peacetime registration, or much higher peacetime funding levels. This judgment was based on several observations.

First, specific planning for the reconstitution of the Selective Service had not proceeded beyond the state headquarters level. While each state has developed state reconstitution and registration plans (based on starting inductions 110 days after mobilization), the information in these plans about local boards, area offices, and employees for the most part simply lists names associated with the system in 1974–75, the last period of active operations. Since 1975 there have been no contacts whatsoever with past volunteers, employees, or site landlords.

Second, the system's seven hundred or so national guard and reserve officers—its major mobilization resource—have been involved primarily in training for state headquarters operations and in preparation of state registration and reconstitution plans. Little specific planning for the re-establishment of area offices and local boards has occurred.

Third, because of concern expressed by the White House, the officers have made no local area contacts, even though they would be responsible for the emergency reconstitution of area offices, local and appeal boards, and staffs.[13] In addition, because of staffing limits on the size of the system's national guard and reserve units, some reservists have responsibility for more than one area. In some large metropolitan areas, such as New York, one Selective Service reservist would have to establish up to forty local draft boards and their supporting offices and staffs.

Prospects for Improvements in the System's Delivery Capability

Can Selective Service ever achieve a capability to resume inductions within thirty days of mobilization, deliver 100,000 inductees within sixty days and 650,000 within 180 days? Or should the Department of Defense re-evaluate its plans concerning the role of inductees in a mobilization? These are difficult questions to answer, at least within the constraints of funding restrictions, the inability to conduct a peacetime registration, and the unwillingness of Selective Service officials and Congress to consider major efficiency-related changes in the system's structure and operations.

Several conclusions, however, may be drawn. First, unless major changes are made in system funding and operations, it probably cannot meet the army's requirement. Second, even with major funding and staffing increases, the enormity of the registration and reconstitution tasks is such that serious doubts would remain about the ability of the system to meet the initial delivery requirement. Third, as the implementation of the system's new processing program, EMMPS, depends upon Congress not only for additional funds but also for several amendments to the system's operating guidelines, a fundamental change in the congressional attitude toward Selective Service would have to occur.[14]

If such actions were taken, Congress would be removing the authority of local boards to initiate deferment and exemption requests.[15] For under the EMMPS concept, authority for initiating requests for deferment or exemption would be transferred to the individual registrants. Thus no consideration would be given to a youth who did not request such status. Critics concede that this change would allow much faster processing in an emergency. They argue, however, that the local boards should retain their responsibilities to their communities and to the families of registrants, and that this would be possible only if they retained authority to initiate classification actions.

At the root of this controversy lies political power. Few discretionary judgments may now be made by local draft boards under the limitations on deferments and exemptions, but the situation was vastly different in the two world wars and even during the Korean and Vietnam conflicts when the boards made many such judgments and had real local political power. Many of those who oppose reducing the responsibilities of local draft boards believe that a major national emergency will require the restoration of many categories of deferment and exemption and thus a return of political power to the local boards.

For these reasons, the willingness of Congress to implement EMMPS by quickly stripping the local boards of their remaining powers should be viewed with some skepticism, unless the emergency is a direct military threat to the United States.

Conclusion

An influx of new recruits in the weeks following mobilization would have an undetermined impact on the outcome of a conventional confrontation in Central Europe. Indeed, if military planners could be sure that such a conflict would be resolved within four months, the pretrained personnel assigned to the training base could be better utilized in operating units. Without such a guarantee, U.S. war plans must include the training of new personnel to sustain the manning levels of operating units in the period beyond the initial deployment of the total force.

In this regard, it would be folly to assume that a mobilization anticipating an attack by the Warsaw Pact in Central Europe would prompt the kind of response from volunteers that would meet the army's need for new trainees, even if opportunities for enlistment were extended to a much larger audience by lowering standards and by equalizing entry standards for women with those for men.[16] The major burden for providing the army with new personnel during the weeks immediately following mobilization would have to be assumed by the Selective Service System. And in order to do its job under the Pentagon's mobilization planning assumptions, the system would have to overcome two major barriers: (1) its inability in the event of crisis quickly to obtain and process a list of eligible registrants, and (2) its inability quickly to reconstitute its offices, staffs, and boards.

Suggestions have been made by the Congressional Budget Office, among others, to simplify the system's plans by using existing computerized lists of young men, or by assigning the registration responsibility to another federal agency, such as the Social Security Administration, the Postal Service, or the armed forces recruiting commands, with inplace sites and personnel.[17] The system, however, has opposed such suggestions, claiming that registrants would not be able to obtain adequate information and that the registrant lists would be less complete than those compiled by traditional methods. Despite these assertions, there is no doubt that either of the recommended changes would provide a greater guarantee to the army that Selective Service would be able to meet its post-mobilization delivery schedule.

A return to peacetime registration, of course, would provide a delivery guarantee beyond that offered by other registration schemes. Peacetime registration has been required by the Military Selective Service Act since the end of active inductions, though the White House allowed the program to lapse in 1975. It could be reactivated by presidential Executive Order.[18]

Obtaining registrant data, particularly if the program were combined with improvements in the system's computer facilities, would allow the system to begin inductions almost immediately after mobilization and the congressional restoration of the induction authority, even though the structure of the system still would have to be restored to avoid court-ordered restrictions on the induction flow, prompted by claims of unfairness. Thus if the structure of the system were maintained in peacetime and some classification actions were taken, virtually all doubts about the ability of the system quickly to respond to the army's needs in an emergency would vanish. An ongoing registration program would also keep the military service obligation of young men in the public eye and would prompt some service enlistments.

As failure to register is a violation of the law, an ongoing registration program would require the Administration to prosecute some youths for draft offenses—not a politically acceptable reaction in the AVF years. For this reason, political leaders have resisted the restoration of a peacetime registration program. Nor have they seriously considered possible alternatives, such as a voluntary program, though Selective Service experience with peacetime registration during 1973–75 indicates that such a concept would be feasible.

The second major barrier which the Selective Service System would have to overcome concerns the magnitude of its reconstitution chores. Although recommendations for change have been submitted by, among others, the President's Reorganization Project, by early 1979 no recommendations had been implemented.[19] If a reduction could be made in the historic number of Selective Service offices and boards during the early months of a "full" mobilization, while the system retained the ability to expand the number if the workload dictated, the army would be more likely to receive conscripts on schedule.

Two final points should be made regarding the delivery capability of Selective Service. First, this discussion has been based on the army's stated need for new recruits during the weeks just after mobilization, and has ignored the possibility that new recruits would also be needed to fill units of the active and reserve forces structure because of the army's inability to correct its projected shortfalls in pretrained reservists. The army maintains that such fillers would be required before newly trained recruits are available, but recruits may be the only personnel available. Thus, unless shortfall problems in the individual reserve pools are corrected, the ability of the draft quickly to deliver new trainees must be considered an important element in the army's ability to meet its initial wartime staffing and casualty replacement needs.

Second, this discussion also has assumed a minimum political warning prior to mobilization. Yet, as Chapter VIII discusses, an extended warning period would be likely. If so, and if a decision could be made to reactivate the system during the warning period, the delivery capability of the system would be greater than that reflected in Pentagon and Selective Service statements. Consequently, even with its 1978 delivery capability, the system could play a vital role in the army's mobilization and efforts to sustain war.

Notes

1. In September 1978 the army's DEP contained some 34,000 individuals. Of these, however, the army estimated that some 22,000, or two thirds, were enrolled in high school and could not be considered as immediately available mobilization assets.
2. The Gates Commission recommended five guidelines for a standby draft system (1) a register of all males who might be conscripted when essential for national security; (2) a system for selection of inductees; (3) specific procedures for the notification, examination, and induction of those to be conscripted; (4) an organization to maintain the register and administer the procedures for induction; and (5) a standby draft system to be activated only by resolution of Congress at the request of the President. See President's Commission on an All-Volunteer Armed Force, *Report*, p. 119.
3. Section 10 (h) of *The Military Selective Service Act of 1967* (Public Law 40, 90th Congress), as amended by *The 1971 Amendments to the Military Selective Service Act* (Public Law 129, 92nd Congress).
4. *The Guard and Reserve in the Total Force*, p. 32.
5. U.S. Congress, House of Representatives, Committee on Armed Services, *Hearings on Military Posture and H.R. 5068*, 23 February–16 March 1977, p. 10.
6. Statement of Dr. John P. White, Assistant Secretary of Defense (Manpower, Reserve Affairs and Logistics), *Hearings Before the Task Force on National Security*, House Budget Committee, 13 July 1977, Tab R-5, "Standby Draft."
7. *The Military Selective Service Act* has not been repealed; rather, Section 17(c), which is the induction authority, was allowed to expire. As a result, Section 10(a) still requires the maintenance of a Selective Service organizational structure; Section 3 requires the registration of young men; Section 4(a) requires classification and examination. The system also is responsible for determining the availability of members of the standby reserve following their ordering to active duty in a national emergency (Title 10, U.S. Code, Section 672(a) (2).
8. The failure of the Selective Service system to conduct either an ongoing or a once-a-year registration would seem to be in violation of Section 3 of the *Military Selective Service Act*. For the law to be enforced, however, "injured" parties would have to bring suit in federal court, a very unlikely possibility.

9. The range of estimates were made by Selective Service Director Byron Pepitone and Acting Director Robert E. Shuck. Appearing before Congress in 1976, Pepitone estimated that the system could begin inductions at 110 days following mobilization if men were inducted as part of the examination process; at 135 days if they were given traditional leave and travel time following their examination and before their actual induction. In Pepitone's view, the system would need 150 days in which to deliver 100,000 inductees to army training centers. See Committee on Armed Services, Subcommittee on Investigations, *Hearings on the Selective Service System*, p. 28. Shuck made his estimate of seventy days in his FY 1979 budget submission. In Shuck's view, the seventy-day delivery capability (with 100,000 inductees delivered by 115 days) could be achieved through administrative processing shortcuts. See Robert E. Shuck, Acting Director, Selective Service System, "Budget Estimates, F.Y. 79," 1 September 1977.

10. Committee on Armed Services, *Hearings on the Selective Service System*, p. 41.

11. Selective Service also must be able to "determine the availability" of standby reservists upon mobilization. Requirements now call for the processing of some 67,000 army standby reservists in thirty to forty-five days, and an additional 70,000 standby reservists for the other services in sixty days. In 1976 Selective Service Director Byron V. Pepitone estimated that it would take about seventy days for the screening of the standby reservists to be completed and that another thirty days or so would then be required for their pre-reporting leave.

12. Selective Service has conducted several analyses of the actual induction experience during 1971–72 by Random Sequence Number (RSN). These studies determined that approximately six registrations were needed to prompt one service accession.

13. Under Selective Service concepts, national guard officers will be responsible for the reconstitution and staffing of state headquarters, while reserve officers will be responsible for reconstituting area offices and local boards.

14. The EMMPS is designed to move a flow of candidates for induction into processing stations without the involvement of the local draft boards. To implement this system, however, a change will have to be made in the *Military Selective Service Act* to allow the Director of Selective Service, rather than local draft boards, to issue induction orders. At present, such orders would have to be issued by the local boards. Thus in an emer-

gency the local boards would have to be reconstituted and functioning before induction orders could be issued.

15. Section 10(b) (3) of the *Military Selective Service Act* reads as follows: "Local boards ... have the power within the respective jurisdictions of such local boards to hear and determine, subject to the right of appeal to the appeal board herein authorized, all questions or claims with respect to inclusion for, exemption or deferment from, training and service under this title, of all individuals within the jurisdiction of such local boards."

16. Physical standards can be lowered to a "mobilization" level at the discretion of the service secretaries. If such decisions were taken, men and women with physical conditions such as missing limbs and poor eyesight would be accepted for limited duty assignments. Concerning mental minimum entry standards, the Secretary of Defense has the authority to designate entry standards, except that Mental Group V personnel are precluded by law from enlistment or induction.

17. Congressional Budget Office, *The Selective Service System: Mobilization Capabilities and Options for Improvement* (Washington, D.C., U.S. Congress, 1978), pp. 39–53.

18. The chairman of the joint chiefs of staff, the secretary of the army and the four service chiefs in early 1979 openly urged Congress to restore peacetime registration. Despite their testimony and the approval by the armed services committees of several proposed legislative changes which would require Selective Service to resume registration, the outlook for congressional approval in 1979 was bleak.

19. See President's Reorganization Project of the Office of Management and Budget, "Selective Service System Reorganization Study, Final Report," August 1978.

Chapter VII

The Conventional Defense
of Central Europe

The centerpiece of U.S. military strategy, according to the Secretary of Defense, is the provision of the general purpose forces necessary to establish and maintain a forward defense in Central Europe.[1] Thus the possibility of a major conventional confrontation between the forces of NATO and the Warsaw Pact is the driving force behind all military policy decisions, and the standard against which changes in capabilities resulting from the AVF decision should be measured.

The balance of ground forces in Central Europe justifies this focus of attention for both political and military reasons. The major share of both NATO's and the Pact's military resources are directed toward this area. And ground forces, more often than air or naval forces, are determinants of political boundaries. Furthermore, U.S. general-purpose land forces are clearly planned primarily for this NATO contingency. This is also viewed as the most demanding scenario for the U.S.: if its forces can successfully meet a major attack by the Warsaw Pact, they will be adequate for other contingencies as well, including a simultaneous military involvement in a minor conflict which could require the services of up to five or more combat divisions.

Years of Neglect and
a Renewed Commitment

Despite the apparent commitment of the United States to support NATO objectives, a decade of neglect existed between

1964 and 1974. Among the reasons were the U.S. preoccupation with Vietnam and Southeast Asia and the resulting public weariness with all things military; a euphoria induced by apparently improving relations between East and West; and various crises over the availability of oil, situations which not only diverted public attention from NATO but also constrained possible military activities.

U.S. neglect of its NATO responsibilities was mirrored by European members of the alliance, though their inattention was not as severe as that of the United States. As these nations would provide some 77 per cent of NATO's mobilization manpower and 82 per cent of its combat aircraft, and, on a NATO-wide basis, could commit forty-eight division equivalents, the combined impact of U.S. and European neglect portended grave consequences.[2]

By the mid-1970's NATO and national defense officials recognized that NATO defensive weaknesses had reached serious proportions and that the survival of NATO's conventional deterrent depended on corrective actions by the United States and other NATO members. The major impetus for actions came from President Jimmy Carter, who not only reaffirmed the priority of NATO preparedness within U.S. strategic goals but also convinced the NATO ministers at the 1977 London Summit to join with the U.S. in a program to strengthen NATO's conventional forces. The key element in this long-term defense program was the pledge by all NATO governments to increase their NATO-oriented defense spending by 3 per cent a year, after adjustment for inflation.

Since the London agreement, European NATO members generally have met their commitments for increased support. Whether the U.S. will do so remains open to conjecture. President Carter requested the additional funds in his budget for FY 1979, submitted in early 1978. Due to congressional changes and the President's veto in August 1978 of the defense weapons authorization bill, however, the budget finally approved by Congress in late 1978 did not contain the extra funds. Pentagon leaders hoped that a supplemental budget request which was submitted to Congress in early 1979 would restore the President's programs.

The Budget for FY 1980, submitted by the President to Congress in early 1979, also contained a request for the additional defense monies. And despite increasing calls from civilian and military leaders for the strengthening of NATO forces, 1980 budget reductions in domestic social and educational programs are bound to create a "guns and butter" conflict in congressional debate over the budget. Consequently, the fate of the President's pledge to increase defense spending remained unclear.

The Army's On-Site Forces in Europe

The United States has maintained a strong commitment to NATO since its inception.[3] The major feature of this commitment has been the presence of large army ground forces (and nuclear weapons) in Europe. Yet, as a consequence of the Vietnam War and the adoption of AVF recruiting policies, the combat power and war-sustaining capabilities of these forces have been reduced.

The commitment of army ground forces to the defense of Western Europe remained essentially unchanged from 1950 through the mid-1960's. During these years the army maintained the equivalent of six divisions, consisting of two infantry and two armored divisions positioned east of the Rhine, one infantry division west of the Rhine, a reconnaissance screen of armored cavalry regiments along the border between East and West Germany, and a brigade in Berlin. These units, which formed the cutting edge of U.S. forces in Europe, were augmented by various units and staffs adequate to fully support the combat commitment of the six-division force. Altogether, approximately 235,000 army personnel were stationed in Europe, though this Seventh Army command was temporarily increased by more than forty thousand during the 1961–65 period as a consequence of the Berlin crisis.[4]

When the Vietnam War began, the assignment of personnel to Southeast Asia became the highest priority, causing periods of major personnel shortfalls within European-based units. The shortages were particularly high among junior officers and senior NCO's.

In 1967 the Administration, with congressional support, decided on a permanent reduction. Although the affected units—two-thirds of a division—would remain under the command of U.S. Army, Europe, they were returned to bases in the United

States. Under the army's dual-basing concept, the units maintain pre-positioned equipment in Europe, periodically return to Europe on deployment exercises, and would be the first reinforcements for Seventh Army forces in the event of an emergency. This tactical move reduced the number of Seventh Army personnel by about 35,000.[5]

Paramount among the reasons for the cutback in on-site forces was the increasing balance-of-payments problem. Too, the Vietnam War had reached its highest level of combat and was draining U.S. forces.

The army, of course, maintained that the dual-basing concept and the retention of command of the returned units by the Seventh Army would result in few changes in the combat power of European forces.[6] Yet, as Hanson W. Baldwin has noted, "Dual-basing is no substitute for troops on the scene ready to fight instantly."[7] And while the dual-basing concept provides an assurance of additional combat units in relatively short order, the decision clearly weakened the Seventh Army's initial ground combat capabilities.

With the end of the Vietnam War, some of the justification for the dual-basing program was eliminated. But the nation was then involved in non-military priorities, and the existing force level in Europe became the standard force size objective for the immediate post-Vietnam War years.

As a result of the 1977 London commitments, however, several actions have been or will be taken to improve the combat capabilities of the Seventh Army. For example, during 1978 and into 1979, more personnel will be added in Europe. The increases will include some 8,200 personnel in 155mm and 8-inch artillery battalions.[8] In addition, the manning levels of front-line combat units will be raised to 105 per cent. By the end of 1979 the strength of the army will rise from a Vietnam-era low of some 176,000 to more than 205,000.

More manpower also will be assigned to NATO-oriented stateside divisions. The combat elements of the three heavy divisions which have brigades deployed in Europe will be brought to 105 per cent manning, while two additional NATO-oriented divisions will be brought to 100 per cent levels.

Even with these improvement programs, the Seventh Army will still be somewhat under strength, and the remaining ten thousand or so unfilled billets could significantly affect the combat effectiveness of the forces in the early days of a conflict. And because these unit shortfalls are primarily in the medical, engineering, and other support fields, skills which also are in short supply in army units in the continental United States, it would be difficult to bring the European forces up to their wartime strength levels in the critical early weeks of a war.

The shortages of support personnel have been created by major structural changes in the composition of the Seventh Army. These changes were caused by the so-called Nunn Amendment of 1975 which required that the army eliminate some eighteen thousand support positions in Europe or convert them to combat billets. The result of this new congressional mandate was that two additional combat brigades were added to the forces in Germany.

At issue in the Nunn Amendment actions was the self-sufficiency of Seventh Army units in Germany. Before the Nunn conversions, army forces would have been able to sustain operations for a reasonable period. Since 1976, however, sustaining the units in combat would require the priority return to Europe of support personnel. And as a former commander of the Seventh Army pointed out, the movement and preparatory requirements of such support units would be greater than those for combat units.[9] The overall result of the Nunn Amendment actions, therefore, has been an increase in the combat power of on-site forces—at the expense of a major increase in reinforcement burdens, an area already fraught with major transportation, equipment, and resupply problems.

The changes in size and structure of the on-site forces also should be viewed in the context of the strength of forces of other NATO countries and those of the Soviet Union. While conflicting estimates exist, there is no disagreement over the fact that the ground forces of the two principal protagonists, the United States and the Soviet Union, are grossly disproportionate in the crucial central front area. There five U.S. divisions and 200,000 army personnel are outnumbered two and three to one. Even when the forces of other NATO countries and the remaining members of the Warsaw Pact are considered, the ratios remain essentially the same. Thus, the results of the dual-basing and Nunn Amendment actions and the 1977–79 programs to improve the Seventh

Army's combat capabilities have not significantly changed the relative balance of forces, though the changes have placed a greater priority on the ability of the army to quickly and effectively reinforce Seventh Army units.

The Scenario for a NATO-Warsaw Pact Conventional Conflict

Within the NATO defense effort, U.S. forces would be counted on to perform at least two and probably three basic roles. First, the on-site forces would be responsible for defending their assigned sectors. Second, U.S. forces stationed in the United States would be the major source of NATO's strategic reserve and would be available for deployment where reinforcements are needed. Third, because of greater U.S. stockpiles of equipment and war reserves, the United States probably would provide supplies as needed to other NATO forces.

In the event of hostilities, the United States would likely be called upon to fulfill all three of these roles, for as Laurence Martin has pointed out, most analysts now believe that if aggression takes place on the central front, it would take the form of a pre-emptive full-scale attack, and that successful defense against such an attack would require the commitment of all available NATO resources.[10]

What is known of Warsaw Pact doctrine and capabilities suggest that if such an attack occurred, Soviet and Pact forces would attempt to break through, encircle, and destroy NATO's armies as quickly as possible, perhaps in just two weeks. If this is correct, only a part of U.S. army forces would participate in the early phase of such a conflict. But planners expect that such a short, intense conflict could become a lingering, long-term holding action, in which case the army's reinforcement capability would become a key factor in sustaining combat.

Regardless of mobilization capability, the initial brunt of the U.S. share of combat would be borne by the Seventh Army. This command, but for a brigade in northern Germany, is deployed along the border in southern Germany.[11] The Seventh Army is comprised of two corps, Fifth and Seventh, and together with two West German corps and a Canadian battle group it makes up NATO's Central Army Group, normally led by the command-ing general of the Seventh Army. One of two army groups in the Central Region of NATO, the Central Army Group is responsible for the conventional defense of southern Germany. Its forces are concentrated to stop Warsaw Pact attacks through the Fulda Gap and Hof Corridor.

In a military emergency, American forces would be rapidly augmented by dual-based units that serve in both Europe and the United States, and by other units which have stockpiles of equipment and supplies in West Germany. In 1978 such stock-piles were sufficient for an augmented force of about 2.3 divi-sions, the personnel of which would be airlifted to Europe in case of potential or actual conflict.[12] These initial reinforcements would be supplemented by other airlifted or sealifted divisions and support troops, including active army units (augmented by reserve fillers), and army national guard and army reserve com-bat and support units. While Secretary of Defense James Schle-singer could note in 1975 that some twelve or thirteen divisions would be deployed, indications since then, such as the planned conversion of the 2nd Infantry Division to a NATO-oriented mech-anized infantry division, are that even more divisions would be committed to the conflict.[13]

Because the deployment schedule would allow little time to send crucial reinforcements, most of the early transported units would be from the active army, with national guard and army reserve forces serving as a first echelon of reinforcements and as replacements for active army units involved in initial combat. No doubt, however, the bulk of the army national guard units, as well as the vast majority of combat support units in the army reserve, would be deployed to Europe in an extended conflict. Under current planning decisions, the first reserve units to de-ploy would be those maneuver battalions needed to round out active army divisions. Such units would depart within thirty days of the mobilization decision. At the same time certain sup-port elements needed to augment supply and maintenance func-tions in Europe also would be deployed. Shortly thereafter, ad-ditional reserve combat units and support elements would be embarked. Finally, the eight national guard divisions would be committed. In total, planners expect that the full deployment of designated active army, army national guard, and army reserve units could be completed in somewhat more than a hundred days, though the Pentagon has established a deployment goal for all of the reserve forces of ninety days or less.[14]

The European NATO members could of course augment their forces much sooner. For example, West Germany could activate reinforcements almost immediately in numbers large enough to bring its regular army units up to wartime strength and provide additional home guard formations. Regular army personnel and reserves from the United Kingdom, Belgium, the Netherlands, and perhaps France also could be quickly added to on-site forces in order to bring them up to full battle order.[15] The initial wave of units airlifted from the United States would be in a position for combat within a few days after the decision to mobilize.

Many uncertainties nonetheless remain concerning the employment of conventional forces by NATO and the Warsaw Pact countries in a European conflict. For example, little is known about the need for Soviet troops for internal security in satellite states. Nor is the reliability or availability of all Warsaw Pact and NATO forces certain, since some forces in the Soviet sphere might revolt, and France and other NATO countries might stay neutral. Because the ability of both sides to augment and mobilize their forces is untested, it is relatively unknown, as is the readiness of reserve forces, especially their training and equipment. Relatively unknown, too, is the impact of a large variety of different weapons systems and logistic demands.

Thus hypotheses, predictions, and specific scenarios are estimates at best. In determining strategy, tactics, and requirements for manpower, funding, and logistics, no amount of research can hide the fact that a large number of variables and unknowns remain.

The best contingency plan for NATO is therefore one which provides for the most likely possibilities. In this regard, if a conflict occurred, reinforcing units from the United States would most likely be required. While one cannot guarantee this situation, the ability of the U.S. army to provide massive reinforcements would provide a major bargaining asset in negotiations during times of crisis, an added deterrent to those forces already in Europe, and an actual military capability in times of armed conflict. Even greater benefits could be achieved if the need for reinforcements were eliminated by a major increase in the size of Seventh Army forces. Such a move, however, would be very expensive, would create massive balance-of-payments problems, and probably would not be possible under the limited manpower resources of the AVF. For these reasons, U.S. military and civilian leaders have supported a policy which places a significant burden on U.S.-based forces, albeit that such a policy may contain major and unsurmountable problems, which, in addition to manpower, concern limitations on transporting reinforcements to Europe and on supporting all of the active and reserve forces units in Europe with equipment, supplies and ammunition, fuel, and other essentials for sustained combat.

Strategic Mobility Limitations

The availability of trained reinforcements in the United States is but one of several conditions which must be met before U.S. forces can meet their strategic commitments in the defense of Central Europe. Another key factor is the availability of adequate air and sealift resources. If we cannot get the troops to Europe quickly, their availability will add little to NATO defensive efforts.

In 1978 the U.S. military air fleet was the world's best.[16] Although government policies supported its development since the early 1960's, however, U.S. strategic air transport still had shortcomings. The 304 aircraft in the U.S. military fleet, plus the resources of the Civil Reserve Air Fleet, (CRAF), are an imposing resource. But at any given moment many aircraft are grounded for maintenance and service, and the combined capacity of all available aircraft would be sufficient to transport only a small portion of the massive reinforcements needed for a conventional conflict in Europe. Estimates are that upon the outbreak of hostilities it would take about ten days to transport the first reinforcing division, if most of the unit's heavy equipment were already stockpiled in West Germany.[17] Transporting the 2.3 division equivalents that have stockpiled equipment waiting for them would therefore take three to four weeks. As Robert Fischer points out, however, a number of factors could further delay this schedule. Due to delays in training and in personnel and equipment augmentation, the first units scheduled for deployment might not be ready; cargo aircraft might be diverted during early mobilization to transport rear-area support equipment and personnel; or reception areas in Europe might be jammed. And if fighting has begun, it might be more difficult to use civilian passenger and cargo aircraft as well as civilian airfields.[18]

Despite these possibilities of delay, the Pentagon believes the airlift can be accomplished on schedule. For planning purposes it is assumed that a maximum of five additional American divisions could be in Europe within thirty-five days after mobilization. In order to realize this goal, however, two and two-thirds divisions plus their equipment would have to be moved via military airlift, while civilian passenger airliners and cargo carriers would be required to transport the men and supplies of the two and one-third division equivalents with pre-positioned equipment.[19]

If the Pentagon has its way, improvements will be made in the strategic airlift over the next decade to double the capacity of the 1978 fleet. This program would include modification of C-5's, lengthening the fuselage of C-141's, buying new mid-air refueling tankers, and modifying civilian airliners better to handle military cargo. In total, the program would cost about $4 billion. For this reason, and because of congressional opposition to providing funds to the civilian airlines, the full amount of funds requested for the program in FY 1979 was not appropriated. Consequently, unless there is a major change in attitude in the Congress toward the modification/purchase program, a vastly increased strategic airlift capacity cannot be expected.

Whether airlift capacity is enhanced or not, only a few active army divisions earmarked for Europe could be on the scene soon after the decision to deploy units from the United States. Indeed, to airlift even a small proportion of these units would be an immense task. One infantry division and its support weigh more than seventy thousand tons. It would take about fourteen days for the fleet to deliver a single division.[20] The air transport of a mechanized infantry division would be even more time-consuming. Such a division normally includes about 250 tanks; as the C-5 is the only aircraft capable of carrying tanks (and only one at a time), all seventy C-5's in the fleet would be required to make more than three round trips just to move the tanks. The time required to move the tanks of an armored division would be substantially higher, with more than nine round trips required.[21] Resupply requirements for the forces already in Europe would surely divert some aircraft from this task, while other aircraft would be grounded for maintenance or repair.

If all of the total force elements designated for transport to Europe are to be delivered there on schedule, then, a major share of the burden will have to be assumed by sealift resources. Yet the capability of the U.S. sealift also is seriously deficient. For example, the Military Sealift Command in 1978 maintained only twenty-seven dry cargo ships and thirty tankers, a fleet capable of moving not much more than one division.[22] Another 145 inactive "mothballed" dry cargo ships were controlled by the Maritime Administration; of these, eight were in the so-called ready reserve fleet and could be made available in five to ten days. It would take many weeks, however, to activate the remaining 137 ships. Their use in a mobilization would be negligible. To a large extent, then, the United States would have to rely on 291 U.S. flag dry cargo ships or on the cargo ships of the Eupean allies.[23] Although almost two hundred NATO ships had been identified by the end of 1978 for use in a NATO reinforcing effort, these ships and the U.S. flag dry cargo ships would be poorly suited for military use, or would not be readily available.

The success of limited U.S. transport resources also would depend on preserving reception facilities in Europe. Many of these facilities are quite close to the East German border and militarily vulnerable. Indeed, if Pact forces should manage to penetrate West German territory to any significant degree (and certainly if they should reach the Rhine in two to seven days, as some observers predict), airfields in West Germany that receive and unload the large American jet transports would be in enemy hands or under hostile fire.[24] The seaports where ships unload U.S. reinforcements and supplies (such as those in Belgium and the Netherlands, as well as the main port, Bremerhaven, in north Germany) also would be vulnerable, as would the 250-mile line of communication between the ports and Seventh Army units in southern Germany, although the line of communication to the U.S. brigade in northern Germany would be more secure.[25] Yet, because no reinforcing units from the United States could arrive by air in less than several days and by sea in less than several weeks, on-site NATO forces, together with quickly available reinforcements from West Germany and the other European NATO allies, would have to defend the reception airfields and seaports for a significant length of time. Alternative facilities might be located in France, away from the probable battle area, but there is no assurance that France would allow a landing of American troops, equipment, and supplies. In all probability, failure of the NATO on-site forces to hold the West German airfields and the designated seaports would cancel out most of the potential benefit of reinforcements from the United States.

In summary, although an exact determination of U.S. transport capabilities cannot be made because of classified information, the limitations and problems outlined in public hearings and published documents strongly support the contention that the United States cannot quickly move and then supply all army active and reserve units which have been designated for transport to Europe.[26]

Equipment Stockpiles and War Reserve Limitations

The size and comprehensiveness of equipment stockpiles and war reserves in Europe also would impact on U.S. capabilities. For if well-trained units of the total force can be transported to Europe but cannot be fully equipped upon arrival or sustained with ammunition, food, fuel, and other supplies, their availability on the battlefront would add little to the NATO defense.

The usefulness of early reinforcements in Germany following mobilization would depend upon the status of the pre-positioned equipment stockpiles. (The army's phrase for this equipment is POMCUS, an acronym for "pre-positioning of material configured to unit sets.")[27] As noted earlier, some two and one-third divisional sets of equipment are supposed to be maintained. Thus a matching of the U.S. reinforcing units with this equipment could be accomplished in a short time by use of military and commercial passenger-carrying aircraft, without using vital cargo-carrying C-5 aircraft.

Despite the need for such stockpiles, for some years they were in short supply and ill repair.[28] During the 1973 "Yom Kippur" war between Israel and the Arab states, the vast majority of the army's tanks and heavy weapons stockpiled in Germany were shipped to Israel as replacements for combat losses, and as late as 1976 the tanks and other heavy equipment had not been fully replaced.[29] Indeed, in 1977 the Defense Department was still lamenting that "the degraded condition of these stocks would not only slow down the deployment of units dependent upon these stocks but would also tax strategic mobility assets in the early critical days of mobilization."[30] Finally, by the end of 1978, the two and one-third division sets had been largely restored (90 per cent of their key equipment) compared with lows of 12 to 30 per cent of some key items at various times during 1969-75.[31]

Plans for Increasing POMCUS Divisional Sets

In the army's view, the limitations inherent in a reinforcement plan which requires the quick movement of men and material to Europe are such that European stockpiles should be enlarged so as to remove some strategic transportation burdens. In a major departure from previous policy, the Pentagon decided in 1977 to support a short-term goal of stockpiling three additional divisional sets of equipment in Europe by FY 1983, with a long-term goal of six additional sets by the late 1980's.

The short-term goal was endorsed by the NATO ministers at their spring 1978 meeting. If all goes according to plan, the first additional set will be largely in place by the end of FY 1980. This set, as well as the second and third additional sets, would be positioned in northern Germany rather than in the south where the existing two and one-third sets are located. If this plan is implemented, U.S. forces would be able to reinforce the U.S. brigade which is being deployed to northern Germany, and this three and one-third division force would then serve as the major support for the West German, British, and Dutch forces in combat on the north German plains.

The army hopes to achieve these stockpiling goals within its budget for FY 1979 and later years. Consequently, instead of being able to purchase most of the required equipment, the army will have to provide the bulk of the new sets from existing equipment sets or from new equipment already committed to replacement programs for active and reserve units.

The impact of this program on active and reserve forces in the

United States would be very great. With the exception of three and two-thirds divisions which would be shielded from the equipment drawn down (in order to maintain a ready force for small military contingencies), the remaining units would be stripped of most of their first-line equipment, reducing them to only 60 to 75 per cent of their authorized levels.

Ultimately there could be some eight and one-third divisional sets of equipment in Europe in addition to the five and two-thirds being utilized by units of the Seventh Army. Such a concentration of equipment in Europe would, of course, significantly increase the army's ability quickly to reinforce the Seventh Army. A myriad of problems would be associated with the program, however, including an adverse impact on the training, readiness, and morale of active army, army national guard, and army reserve units which would be stripped of most of their first-line equipment. In addition, storing additional tanks, armored personnel carriers, artillery, and other items is extremely costly, and more storage depots near the East German border could increase the possibilities of a surprise attack by Pact forces. Indeed, if all planned divisional sets were in place, their seizure would effectively end the combat capabilities of the army. The program also will require more U.S. soldiers to maintain the additional weapons in fighting order, operations and maintenance costs will increase, and additional funds will be needed to build new storage facilities, assuming of course that the West German government will be willing to provide the needed land. During 1978 some problems in this area developed, with Congress failing to appropriate the full amount requested by the army for POMCUS construction.[32]

Regardless of whether the goal of six divisional sets is achieved, the pre-positioning of even one additional set would improve U.S. reinforcement capabilities. And if three additional sets are pre-positioned by 1983, as planned, it would be reasonable to expect that the first three reinforcing divisions could be on the scene in about seven days, with the remaining two POMCUS-equipped divisions arriving shortly thereafter.[33]

Such improvements in equipping airlifted U.S. reinforcements with POMCUS would be of little value, however, unless war reserve stocks also were improved. These stocks are combat-essential items stockpiled for use as replacements for losses.[34]

Although all NATO members have formally agreed to develop war reserve stocks sufficient to sustain their forces in combat for identical time periods, each nation calculates its requirements differently. For example, in the mid-1970's the United States, alone among NATO allies, doubled its requirements.[35] This decision was based primarily on the very early but heavy losses of ammunition and other material in the 1973 Middle East war, as well as on the increasing weight of opinion that a war in Europe would be fought largely with the material on hand.[36]

Ammunition supplies are among the critical shortfall items, and this problem is compounded by a shortage of ammunition storage areas, port facilities with ammunition handling capabilities, and U.S. production limits. The army's ammunition stock objective for Europe is 1.3 million tons, but this goal will not be reached until the early 1980's. During 1978 some 210,000 tons were added to European stocks, bringing the total to about 700,000 tons, or slightly more than half the desired level.[37] If hostilities were to occur before completion of the war reserve stockpiling program, about one-quarter of the surface cargo heading for Europe would need to be ammunition. Despite these and other problems, however, there were more U.S. war reserve stocks in Europe in 1978 than at any other time in history.[38]

European NATO members also have made some increases in their reserves, and their efforts during 1979 and later years will be directed toward bringing their depleted stocks up to programmed levels. Indeed, much of the additional money appropriated for NATO improvements will be used for this purpose. Despite these gains, however, the war-sustaining capabilities of the European NATO members will remain well below the capabilities of U.S. forces. Indeed, a special subcommittee of the Committee on Armed Services of the House of Representatives concluded in early 1979 that the European forces will begin to run out of equipment and ammunition in a matter of days rather than weeks or months.[39] If this assessment is correct, the building of larger U.S. war reserve stocks becomes an even more critical issue, for the United States would likely provide support to its NATO allies in the event their reserves became exhausted in a protracted conflict.

In summary, the limitations on POMCUS and war reserve stocks in Germany raises serious doubts about the army's ability to equip and then support a large number of additional reinforcing units. The planned improvements in POMCUS stocks and war reserves, if fully implemented, will ease but not eliminate the problem. They would allow some reinforcements to be quickly added to the battlefield. Yet the bulk of U.S. forces, particularly those units required for an extended conflict, would still be faced with equipment and support problems. Combined with the limits on transport to Europe, the restrictions inherent in the 1978 and planned levels of POMCUS and war reserves also appear to diminish the army's ability to meet its strategic commitments for an extended conflict in Central Europe.

Conclusion

The problems of transporting, equipping, and supplying reinforcements for army units in Germany focus attention on the importance of maintaining on-site, combat-ready forces large enough to deter attack or, if a conflict develops, to fulfill the U.S. role in NATO defensive action.

Yet, in 1979, the ability of the Seventh Army to sustain combat operations for an extended period was doubtful. The net result of the dual-basing and Nunn Amendment decisions has been to maintain the front-line forces, to eliminate many supporting elements, and to compound the problems of augmenting the Seventh Army with additional divisions committed to the NATO defensive effort. Within the boundaries of smaller force levels during the AVF years and a reduced commitment to the maintenance of army forces in Europe, military leaders have chosen to emphasize both immediately available combat power and the capability to sustain combat operations for an extended period. As a consequence of limited resources, however, neither capability is adequate. The on-site forces of the Seventh Army would have severe problems in sustaining combat operations for the first several weeks of an intensive conventional war. At the same time, the army would have great difficulties in providing the reinforcements necessary for a prolonged conflict. In short, the army does not possess the manpower, transportation, equipment, and supply resources to support both a short-war and a long-war capability.

Notes

1. Donald H. Rumsfeld, secretary of defense, *Report to the Congress on the Fiscal Year 1977 Budget and Its Implications for the Fiscal Year 1978 Authorization Request and the Fiscal Year 1977–81 Defense Programs* (Washington, D.C., Department of Defense, 1976), p. 116.
2. Justin Galen, "Restoring the NATO-Warsaw Pact Balance: The Art of the Impossible," *Armed Forces Journal*, September 1978, p. 46.
3. At the time the NATO treaty was signed in 1949, intelligence estimates indicated that the dozen or so scattered, understrength Western divisions in Europe faced twenty-five fully armed Soviet divisions in Central Europe and, overall, at least 140 to 175 Soviet divisions at full battle strength (not even counting the numerous satellite divisions). In these early years of NATO, however, the nuclear superiority of the United States was considered clearly adequate to deter Soviet aggression.
4. General Earle Wheeler, army chief of staff, Statement Before the Committee on Armed Services, House of Representatives, *Hearings on Military Posture and H.R. 2440*, 6 February 1963, p. 691.
5. The move also resulted in a return to the U.S. of some 28,000 military dependents and a savings in 1968 of some $75 million in foreign exchange. See Statement of Secretary of Defense Robert S. McNamara Before the Committee on Armed Services, Senate, *Hearings on Authorization for Military Procurement, Research and Development, F.Y. 1969, and Reserve Strengths*, 2 February 1966, p. 103.
6. Defense Secretary McNamara had argued for a 75,000-man reduction against the opposition of the State Department and his own Joint Chiefs of Staff. The ultimate transfer of 35,000 troops back to the United States emerged in part as a compromise in this controversy. See *United States Security Agreements and Commitments Abroad: United States Forces in Europe*, Hearings Before the Subcommittee on United States Security Agreements and Commitments Abroad of the Committee on Foreign Relations, Senate, 1970, pp. 2061–2069.
7. Hanson W. Baldwin, *Strategy for Tomorrow* (New York, Harper and Row, 1970), p. 141.
8. The added units will provide roughly a 10 per cent increase in combat firepower for the Seventh Army. See Statement of

General Alexander M. Haig, Jr., Before the Committee on Armed Services, Senate, *Hearings on Department of Defense Authorization for Appropriations for Fiscal Year 1979*, 3 March 1978, p. 1891.

9. James H. Polk, "The New Short War Strategy," *Strategic Review*, Summer 1975.

10. Laurence Martin, *Arms and Strategy: The World Power Structure Today* (New York, McKay, 1973), p. 172.

11. NATO tacticians have long recognized the relative weaknesses of the NATO forces in the north German plains, an area much more suitable to modern tank warfare than the area of southern Germany occupied by the bulk of U.S. army forces. In an attempt to improve defenses in the north, a brigade of the 2nd Armored Division in 1978 began a permanent redeployment to a new base outside Bremen, where U.S. tankers will reinforce West German, British, and Dutch units. Some U.S. air force squadrons also have been moved to the north.

12. Originally there was pre-positioned equipment for three division equivalents, but some of this equipment has been used for the two combat brigades added to the Seventh Army as a result of the Nunn Amendment.

13. U.S. Congress, House of Representatives, Appropriations Committee, *Department of Defense Appropriations for 1976* (Washington, D.C., GPO, 1975), Part I, p. 105.

14. *Fiscal Year 1978 Authorization for Military Procurement, Research and Development, and Active Duty, Selected Reserve, and Civilian Personnel Strengths*, Hearings Before the Senate Committee on Armed Services, March–April 1977, p. 2436.

15. Many NATO military commanders believe that the true reserves of NATO would be the French regular army, whose two divisions in Germany and three in France could provide much needed, immediately available ground combat strength. For a discussion of this point, see *A Conventional Strategy for the Central Front in NATO*, A Report of a Seminar held at the RUSI on 23 October 1974 and 26 March 1975 (London, Royal United Services Institute, 1975). For a detailed discussion of the military potential of "surplus" reservists within the ranks of the NATO armed forces, see Kenneth Hunt, *The Alliance and Europe: Part II, Defence With Fewer Men*, Adelphi Papers No. 98 (London: International Institute for Strategic Studies, 1973), pp. 10, 31–33. Other analysts who urge the greater use of European reserves in a conventional conflict include Alain Enthoven, "U.S. Forces in Europe: How many?"

Doing What?," *Foreign Affairs,* April 1975, p. 520; and Richard D. Lawrence and Jeffrey Record, *U.S. Force Structure in NATO: An Alternative* (Washington, D.C., Brookings Institution, 1974), pp. 103–109.

16. According to Secretary of Defense Harold Brown, the airlift capacity is largely provided by seventy C-5 and 234 C-141 jet transports of the Military Airlift Command, and 227 commercial jet airliners which could be made available in an emergency through the Civil Reserve Air Fleet (CRAF). See Statement Before the Committee on Armed Services, House of Representatives, *Hearings on Military Posture and H.R. 10929,* 2 February 1978, p. 179.

17. Estimate made by Secretary of Defense Harold Brown, as quoted in "U.S. Ground Forces: Inappropriate Objectives, Unacceptable Costs," *Defense Monitor,* November 1978, p. 5. A more detailed analysis of the U.S. airlift capability was provided by the U.S. army to the Library of Congress and is cited in *United States/Soviet Military Balance: A Frame of Reference for Congress,* p. 30. The army estimate stated that the planned move of the 82nd Airborne Division to the Middle East in 1973 would have required one week if alert times had permitted prior preparation, longer if not. This move would have involved a somewhat smaller than normal U.S. division (about eleven thousand men), a basic load of ammunition, and five days' supply of rations and fuel. The one week time estimate for moving the first reinforcing division to Europe is repeated by authors of other works. See, for example, Leon Sloss, *NATO Reform: Prospects and Priorities,* Washington Papers of the Center for Strategic and International Studies (Beverly Hills, Sage, 1975), p. 40.

18. Robert Lucas Fischer, *Defending the Central Front: The Balance of Forces,* Adelphi Papers Number 127 (London, International Institute for Strategic Studies, 1977), p. 22.

19. Upon declaration of a national emergency, some ninety-one long-range passenger and 153 long-range cargo jets from commercial airlines will be made available to the Department of Defense within forty-eight hours. See *Hearings on the Posture of Military Aircraft,* Research and Development Subcommittee, Committee on Armed Services, House of Representatives, November 1975, p. 17.

20. *Hearings on the Posture of Military Aircraft,* p. 235.

21. John M. Collins, *Imbalance of Power* (San Rafael, Presidio Press, 1978), p. 200.

22. Secretary of Defense Harold Brown, Statement Before the Committee on Armed Services, House of Representatives, *Hearings on Military Posture and H.R. 10929*, 2 February 1978, p. 179. In 1970 the number of dry cargo ships totaled more than 190, or some seven times the 1978 totals. See Collins, *Imbalance of Power*, p. 207.

23. Sealifted reinforcements could begin to arrive in Europe about three weeks after mobilization. With certain improvements in the contingency planning and preparation phase, however, the Pentagon believes that up to four divisions could be sealifted to Europe within thirty days. See Department of Defense, *Navy Accelerated Sealift Study: Project Sea Express*, 25 July 1974, p. 43.

24. The main airfield reception area for C-5 transports in West Germany has been Frankfurt's Rhein/Main airport, which is only 178 miles from the East German border.

25. Instead of using the Bremerhaven LOC during wartime, army planners would like to relocate the LOC through ports in France or the Benelux countries. As of late 1978, however, no funding or personnel had been authorized for this plan, nor had political barriers to the use of French ports, railroads, and highways been eliminated.

26. Whereas army units could not arrive in Europe in large numbers until several weeks or more after mobilization, the U.S. air force could move a significant portion of its augmentation force to Europe in three days. These tactical air units could provide invaluable help in slowing a Warsaw Pact attack until ground forces in Europe were in position and reinforcements began to arrive. For a detailed discussion of the role of tactical air units in a NATO-Warsaw Pact confrontation, see Congressional Budget Office, *Planning U.S. General Purpose Forces: The Tactical Air Forces* (Washington, D.C., Congress of the United States, 1977).

27. The POMCUS equipment and supplies are located at eight sites, all east of the Rhine River and reasonably close to major airfields (and to the border with East Germany). Equipment is maintained in controlled humidity warehouses, covered storage, and some open storage facilities.

28. Secretary of Defense, *FY 1977 Defense Report* (Washington, D.C., GPO, 1976), p. 203.

29. General Michael S. Davison, who commanded the Seventh Army in Germany until his retirement in late 1975, has spoken about the U.S. capability for providing reinforcements to Europe after

having shipped stockpiled tanks and other heavy equipment to Israel. In General Davison's view, the lack of stockpiled tanks and heavy equipment in West Germany during 1973–75 would have negated the tactical usefulness of reinforcements airlifted from the United States and would have significantly reduced NATO's response capability in a conventional conflict. Also see *A Report to Congress on U.S. Conventional Forces for NATO*, p. VIII-1.

30. Department of Defense, "Deploying U.S. Forces to NATO," *Commanders Digest*, 20 January 1977, p. 7.

31. Galen, "Restoring the NATO-Warsaw Pact Balance," p. 43.

32. Despite strong objections from the Department of Defense, Congress in 1978 cut the army's request for funds to build additional POMCUS storage facilities by some 35 per cent.

33. According to Michael Getler, the increase in U.S. reinforcement capability would be "highly dependent" upon cooperation of the European allies who are supposed to provide reception facilities and equipment to move the additional troops into battle positions. See Michael Getler, "NATO Agrees on Plan to Speed U.S. Reinforcement," *Washington Post*, 19 May 1978, p. 13.

34. Pre-positioned war reserve stocks are a separate category of equipment from POMCUS, though many of the same items are contained in each. POMCUS equips dual-based units; war reserve stocks replace items such as ammunition and tanks that are likely to be expended once a conflict begins.

35. Richard Burt reported in 1978 that the United States' five-year defense plan calls for the provision of war reserve stocks for a ninety-day conflict. See "U.S. Analysis Doubts There Can Be Victor in Major Atomic War," *New York Times*, 6 January 1978, pp. A-1, A-4.

36. Total tank losses by the Arabs and the Israelis in the three weeks of the 1973 war were roughly double the total number of tanks maintained by army units in Germany in 1978.

37. Eric C. Ludvigsen, "Huskier NATO Heads '79 Defense Priorities," *Army*, March 1978, p. 16.

38. Congressional Budget Office, *U.S. Air and Ground Conventional Forces for NATO: Mobility and Logistics Issues* (Washington, D.C., U.S. Congress, 1978), p. 4.

39. *NATO Standardization, Interoperability and Readiness*, Report of the Special Subcommittee on NATO Standardization, Interoperability and Readiness, Committee on Armed Services, House of Representatives (Washington, D.C., GPO, 1979), p. 2.

Chapter VIII

The AVF and NATO Defense:

Implications and Conclusions

The military strategic goals of the United States for a conventional conflict in Central Europe between NATO and Warsaw Pact forces have not changed since the advent of the AVF. By maintaining a strong on-site force and a rapid, though limited, immediate reinforcement capability, and in concert with the forces of European NATO members, the U.S. hopes to deter aggressive action. Failing this, the readily available active force units, together with the available forces of other NATO members, would be expected to contain any Pact advances within West German territory long enough to equalize the balance of forces through reinforcement and to prevent the conflict from escalating into a tactical or general nuclear exchange.

In terms of these strategic goals, then, what are the implications of the changes in the army total force during the AVF years? In broad terms, they concern two fundamental policy concepts: the validity of the total force, and the viability in a time of limited resources of maintaining both a long-war and a short-war capability.

Validity of the Total Force Concept

The implementation of the total force concept in the early 1970's shifted a major portion of the national defense burden to the reserve forces, particularly in relation to providing the reinforcements needed to sustain combat in Europe beyond the initial weeks—or short-war phase—of the war. Prompted by the adoption of the realistic deterrence strategy, as well as pressures on the Defense Department to limit expenditures for the more-expensive AVF, the total force policy requires the national guard and army reserve to provide primary augmentation for the active forces in any military emergency.[1]

During the Vietnam War years, just before the adoption of the total force policy, army reserve forces were treated as a second-rate military resource while the active forces received the vast majority of attention and funding. In addition, since the President was unwilling to call major units to active service, the role of the guard and reserve was ill-defined.[2] Their effectiveness was marginal to poor because most of their modern equipment had been sent to Vietnam and their units were staffed with many young men who had enlisted in order to avoid the draft and Vietnam combat assignments.

The adoption of the total force policy has brought noticeable improvements in national guard and army reserve units. The concept has reinstituted a clear sense of mission among reservists; equipment inventories are being replenished and modernized; training is being intensified, and the draft-motivated enlistees of the Vietnam era are being replaced by volunteers. At the same time, as we have noted, manpower, transportation, equipment, and supply problems have surfaced, problems which the Administration and Congress have been unable or unwilling to resolve. The result has been a steady deterioration of the army's mobilization and war-sustaining capabilities, serious weaknesses which provide the basis for questioning the appropriateness of continuing the total force policy.

The army's experience in using reserve forces in crisis mobilization situations offers insights into this issue. An examination of the three limited call-ups that have occurred since 1950 supports the contention that the usefulness of the reservists who would be available—particularly the filler personnel—would be far below expectations; particularly in light of the very limited time which would be available between mobilization and deployment. For example, the call-ups of 1950–51 for the Korean War, which involved more than 139,000 members of the army national guard and 196,000 members of the army reserve, made only limited manpower immediately available for the active forces. Because of unexpected delays in readiness training and the need to receive and train large numbers of filler personnel, more than sixteen months elapsed before the first two national guard divisions were ready for duty. Some of this delay was due to the fact that many trained officers and NCO's were stripped from the divisions and sent to Korea as individual replacements. Nevertheless, much of the delay occurred because more training was needed for individual reservists, most of whom were World War II veterans and had received no training since their demobilization in 1945. Furthermore, as Herman Boland has pointed out, the army's records were not up to date, and many individual reservists were called with little or no warning.[3]

The second postwar mobilization occurred in response to the Berlin crisis. Men were called to active duty in the summer of 1961 and released some ten months later. More than 133,000 guardsmen and reservists were activated, including four army national guard combat divisions and one training division of the army reserve. As in 1950–51, the army's planners underestimated the time needed for these units to become operational. They had assumed that the reserves would be combat-ready in three to five months, but many of the units required five to six months beyond that. Although the Korean War had demonstrated that the key to fast combat availability for activated reserve units was a high level of unit training and a minimum requirement for filler personnel, units activated for the Berlin crisis were still unprepared and had large demands for fillers. I. Heymont and E. W. McGregor estimated that when allowances were made for undertrained members of the selected reserve units, no activated unit had more than 48 per cent of its billets filled with trained men who could be committed to combat on short notice.[4]

By 1968, the year of the very limited call-up for the Vietnam War, the leaders of the army's reserve forces had apparently learned some of the lessons of the Korean and Berlin mobilizations. They were maintaining units at manpower levels much nearer the strengths authorized for wartime. But only 82 per cent of the wartime quota for army reserve units reported when activated, and 89 per cent of the quota for national guard units. As a result, individuals still had to be called to duty and absorbed, actions which delayed the deployment of the units. Expected to be combat-ready after eight weeks of refresher training, the major units actually took some seven months, or more than three times the expected delay.[5]

Further improvements in the readiness of the army national guard and army reserve have been made since these Vietnam call-ups of 1968. But an examination of readiness indicators in 1978 adds weight to the argument that the guard and reserve units, especially those scheduled for early deployment, still would not be able to meet their mobilization commitments.

Under the army's evaluation reporting scheme, the readiness of the guard and reserve is reported in terms of "C-ratings" for each unit's personnel, equipment, and training, as well as a summary rating for each unit as a whole. There are four levels of ratings, ranging from "fully ready" (C-1) to "not ready" (C-4).

Although readiness for mobilization would require a C-1 rating, most units in the army reserve forces are rated "marginally ready" (C-3). A substantial number of units are rated "not ready." Most detailed data is classified, yet in 1976 the army informed Congress that 43 per cent of all army national guard units and 54 per cent of all army reserve units were rated "not ready."[6] Such evaluations were concentrated in units with late deployment schedules, but a substantial number of early deploying units were rated as only "marginally ready" or "not ready." These judgments did not reflect expected strength or equipment levels at time of deployment but rather at time of rating. Thus, allowing for men and women who would be excused from reporting or granted delays, and for equipment breakdowns, the mobilization capabilities of the units would be even lower than their C-ratings, though the units would be assigned additional personnel and equipment from stockpiles and the individual reserve pools in the immediate post-mobilization period.

Other indicators support this assessment.[7] For example, the army told Congress in 1977 that 36 per cent of its enlisted reservists were working outside the skills for which they were recruited and trained. The army also admitted that many of its key guard and reserve units still were short of equipment, including 35 per cent of authorized tanks, 55 per cent of recovery vehicles, 19 per cent of 8-inch howitzers, and 65 per cent of personnel carriers.[8]

Thus both historically and more recently, evidence indicates that the army reserve forces would be unable fully to deploy within the tight schedule demanded by the NATO conventional war and mobilization contingency plans. Furthermore, the increasing likelihood that a Pact attack would be launched after only a brief period of preparation and would be terminated within days or a few weeks raises doubts about the adequacy of U.S. reinforcement plans. If units from the United States are to play a role in any conflict, they probably will have to arrive on the battlefront even sooner than envisioned in Pentagon war plans.

Regardless of whether a conflict were to begin after a shorter or longer warning period than that envisioned in U.S. plans, the army's questionable ability to sustain extended combat operations has many implications. First, the on-site units of the Seventh Army, and other units of the active army that could be quickly flown to Europe, together with the forces of the European NATO allies, may not be strong enough to deter aggression by Soviet and other Pact forces, or to avoid military defeat in the critical early weeks of the war.

Second, a conventional conflict would be much more likely to escalate into a nuclear exchange or be ended through negotiation.

Third, if negotiations were to occur between NATO and Pact leaders, before the outbreak of hostilities, during the initial stages of the conflict, or later, the absence of a strong U.S. war-sustaining capability would greatly reduce NATO's bargaining power.

These conclusions are based, of course, on the assumptions that it would not be in NATO's interest to initiate tactical or general nuclear war or to end a conflict through negotiation, and that it would be in the interest of the Pact to pursue an extended conflict with NATO forces. If NATO leaders are willing to use nuclear weapons, particularly tactical attacks on troops, staging areas, and supply depots, the availability of an extended war capability becomes somewhat of a moot point. Indeed, if the Pact perceives that NATO would rely on nuclear weapons, its forces would be unlikely to initiate any attack, save one for limited objectives which could be achieved quickly before the exhaustion of on-site NATO forces or a decision by NATO to use nuclear weapons.

A sustained war capability would of course be valuable in many situations, particularly if there were a strong commitment on both sides to achieve their goals without a nuclear exchange or negotiated surrender. Other factors may also be influential. For example, as Neville Brown has reminded us, the usefulness of reinforcements is based not only on the time needed to deploy them but also on assumptions about the prospects of strategic warning.[9] And U.S. war plans assume a minimum period of warning before the outbreak of hostilities. If more time were available, various training, equipping, supply, and deployment actions would enhance the value of those active army and reserve units in the United States that are scheduled for late deployment.

Military and civilian officials assume that the U.S. and other NATO countries would have clear indications of probable Soviet or Pact attacks. Indeed, NATO's flexible strategy rests heavily on the assumption that the West would have two kinds of warning. As explained by Harlan Cleveland, "We would have political warning, because a surprise attack not preceded by a build-up of political tensions seems almost inconceivable. We would have strategic warning, because we would see and sense a build-up of Soviet forces."[10]

This view is echoed by Pentagon planners who cite the need for lengthy and visible Pact mobilization and the ability of U.S. intelligence, particularly satellite reconnaissance, to provide adequate advance warning and time for countermobilization activities in the United States and other NATO countries. Many critics, however, doubt whether such actions would be correctly assessed. They point to the Soviet buildup of 1968 which could have been directed at NATO rather than the invasion of Czechoslovakia.[11]

Throughout the 1970's a 23/30 scenario dominated U.S. mobilization planning. In this scenario it is assumed that NATO mobilization lags the Warsaw Pact buildup by about a week, and that war begins about thirty days after the Pact starts to mobilize.[12]

In the latter years of the decade, however, a growing number of analysts argued that the "worst case" threat from the Pact would be the possibility that their forces would attack in two weeks rather than thirty days. Some experts, including the NATO Supreme Commander, have even estimated that Pact forces would launch a surprise attack with less than two weeks' warning.[13]

Thus a variety of positions exists concerning the probable length of warning time. If those who predict a mobilization time shorter than twenty-three days are correct, weaknesses in the army reserve forces and the transportation, equipment, and resupply systems would be compounded, and the ability of the United States to meet its strategic commitments for the defense of Europe would be further diluted. If warning time is greater than twenty-three days, many of the problems inherent in the total force policy would be diminished.

In summary, there can be little doubt that changes in U.S. strategic capabilities as a result of the adoption of the total force policy have resulted in an overall weakening of U.S. defense posture. Whereas stronger on-site forces in Europe and supporting active forces in the United States were available in the years before AVF, the total force decision shifted much of the defense burden to the less ready reserve components. If the United States is to deter aggression to the maximum extent possible, or, in the event of a conflict, sustain operations to a successful conclusion without the use of nuclear weapons, the total force policy will require major improvements—or perhaps abandonment.

The Viability of Maintaining Both a Long-war and a Short-War Capability

The army's inability to sustain combat in Central Europe much beyond the first few weeks is the fundamental change in strategic capabilities which has occurred during the AVF years. But what if reinforcements for the on-site forces were required over an extended period, beyond the initial few weeks when ready divisions of the active army could be quickly flown to Europe? In short, what about the likelihood of a long war, the only conflict scenario in which most units of the reserve forces would play any role?

The army has not publicly stated its planning goals, but indications—such as stockpiling targets for equipment and ammunition—are that army plans are based on preparedness to fight for ninety days or more.[14] Obviously, such planning goals contain a hedge against uncertainty as well as a warning to the Soviets that the United States is serious about defending Central Europe for an extended period.

Despite these planning goals, the emphasis has been on preparations for a shorter war since the mid-1970's. The Nunn Amendment actions, which increased combat strength in Europe at the expense of reductions in support units, and the return to a sixteen-division force structure at the expense of eliminating support elements in the old thirteen-division structure, are two major examples of this change. The conclusion that the army is preparing for a short war at the expense of sustaining capability for a long war also is supported by the army's 1976 publication of a new Operations Manual (FM 100-5) which highlights the changing nature of land warfare, its heightened intensity, deadliness and potentially short duration.

Despite the army's movement toward planning for a shorter war, it is clear that United States strategy in 1978 still assumed a war that could last for several months and a large proportion of the army's resources remained committed to such objectives.[15] And this long-war assumption, which is key to U.S. strategy for the defense of Central Europe, has been maintained regardless of the fact that European NATO forces appear to be oriented toward a much shorter war. While exact figures are classified, various observers have estimated that the European NATO members are not planning for a conventional ground war of much more than thirty days.[16] The commitments of these nations for greater defense expenditures in 1979 and beyond are likely to result in an extension of the thirty-day planning goal, but it is doubtful that the European NATO members will match the U.S. commitment. Indeed, as Richard B. Foster has argued, NATO members in Europe are primarily interested in deterrence. They care little for having to fight a war, long or short.[17] Their concern is to make deterrence as strong as possible, and if it fails, to force the enemy to end the war on terms acceptable to NATO, in the shortest time and with as little damage as possible to Western Europe.

The European NATO forces could not be expected abruptly to withdraw from combat when their equipment and manpower resources were depleted; nevertheless, despite the provision of equipment and ammunition from U.S. sources, their full involvement in an extended NATO defensive effort would by necessity be limited. It therefore seems likely that a conventional conflict extending much beyond the planning and supply limit of the European NATO members would become a struggle primarily between U.S. and Warsaw Pact forces. In this case, the disparity between the NATO and Pact forces would be so great that the conventional phase of the conflict would probably not last very long, a view supported by many observers who believe—regardless of the capabilities of the two forces—that the conflict would be settled either by negotiation within thirty days or would escalate into a nuclear exchange.[18]

Many other experts believe that such a European war would be even shorter. For example, Belgian General R. Close, commander of a NATO tank division, wrote in 1977 that a Pact surprise attack on the central front would find Pact forces at the banks of the Rhine, in control of all of West Germany, within forty-eight hours.[19] Other observers, such as Edward R. Fried, have suggested that Pact forces are designed to achieve victory in thirty and certainly no more than sixty days.[20]

Among all the estimates, official and unofficial, of the probable length of a NATO-Warsaw Pact conventional conflict in Central Europe, only the United States appears to believe in the possibility of a war of longer than sixty days—and makes it the basis for strategic planning. In fact, the weight of evidence supports the likelihood of a shorter war, and raises a fundamental question about maintaining certain support elements of army forces in Europe which might not be needed in a short war, as well as those portions of the army reserve forces structure and the transportation, equipment, and supply resources which would have little impact on the outcome of a conventional conflict of less than sixty days. Of course, such forces could be kept as a hedge against major military crises in other parts of the world.

Taking this approach, however, the United States would miss the potential benefits to be gained from formally adopting a short-war strategy. For in terms of strategic capabilities, a formal short-war strategy would make available added resources to develop and equip a more effective short-war force. Furthermore, it would also avoid the societal disruptions and additional costs that might be caused by the need to forge a national consensus on restoring the army's strategic capabilities to their former levels. On the other hand, there can be no certainty that a conventional conflict in Central Europe would end in less than sixty days, for, as Neville Brown has pointed out, military planning is not a mechanical science which lends itself to exact quantification.[21] Thus if the United States were to endorse a short-war strategy, it might also run the risk of increasing the probability of aggression, though the U.S. nuclear inventory would continue to make such aggression a very remote possibility.

The likelihood of the entire army reserve structure ever being fully involved in a European conflict has always been highly remote. This structure has nevertheless provided insurance against such a possibility, and this insurance would be cancelled if resources were to be shifted to the on-site forces or the early deploying units, or if certain transportation, equipment, and supply capabilities were to be eliminated.

As many now argue that the full reserve structure will never be needed in a conventional conflict, so many men argued before both world wars that modern weapons were so powerful and plentiful that countries could not stand a protracted conflict. There were even those—many eminent men of their time among them—who believed that the dreadful power of modern weapons made war unthinkable. As Oskar Morgenstern has argued, although it is tempting to take this same position now, it could be just as wrong as in previous times.[22] This, then, is the dilemma of supporting reductions in the war-sustaining capabilities of the army reserve in order to justify strengthening the active, national guard, and reserve units which would be moved into combat during the initial weeks of a conflict in Europe.

Conclusion

The anti-militarism which evolved out of the Vietnam War experience, together with a reduction in East-West tensions and severe balance-of-payments problems, were the major reasons for fundamental changes in U.S. military capabilities. Unwilling to continue the draft or to support the force size necessary to involve the nation in major land wars, leaders and followers alike resolved to support a small, NATO-oriented, all-volunteer active force, and to place a much larger portion of the defense burden on the all-volunteer reserve forces. In theory, this total force of the AVF era was to provide a national defense capability equal to that of the pre-Vietnam years. In reality, however, the combination of an active force smaller than expected, loss of key support elements, and quality and manpower problems in the reserve forces prevented the army from reaching this goal, particularly in the areas of reinforcement and war-sustaining capabilities.

For most of almost thirty years of the NATO alliance, the United

States alone among the NATO members had such resources. During this period, though the U.S. capability probably was greater than the U.S.S.R.'s and other Warsaw Pact countries, the U.S. ability to fight a long war was relatively cheap insurance against an error in judgment. By the late 1970's, however, many argued that such insurance was no longer necessary nor affordable. These critics contended that the age of mass armies, supported by industrial bases and large numbers of reserves, had passed and that the United States alone among the NATO and Pact nations had failed to change its strategy by placing increased priority on the combat effectiveness of on-site forces and readily available reinforcements.

Whether a deliberate response to such criticism or an unexpected result of the many changes necessary during the post-Vietnam AVF years, by the end of 1978 the army's reinforcement and war-sustaining capabilities had been severely curtailed. Army actions in 1975–78, as well as those steps scheduled for implementation in later years, will restore the initial combat power of U.S. ground forces in Europe to the pre-Vietnam level. But support units and functions vital to sustaining combat beyond the first thirty days have increasingly been shifted to the less-ready reserves, and reserve units have also been integrated into those active army divisions scheduled for early deployment to Europe. As noted earlier, only two of the ten army divisions in the continental United States do not include reserve combat battalions in their tables of organization. Thus the reliance on reserves for both the initial and the extended reinforcement of the Seventh Army would be very great. And if the army succeeds in pre-positioning additional POMCUS and war reserve stocks in Europe, allowing for faster deployment, the burden on the reserves will be still greater.

Clearly, if the United States is to have a true capability to sustain combat in Europe beyond that which can be supported by on-site forces and some initial airlifted reinforcements, major improvements must be made in the army's war-sustaining capabilities. Such improvements could ultimately cost billions of tax dollars or force a return to some form of conscription, so such steps must not be taken lightly. As Bernard Brodie has concluded, despite the apparent conventional superiority of Pact forces, the United States is committed to using tactical nuclear weapons "if

146 : *The AVF and NATO Defense*

we find ourselves losing without them." This factor, rather than a strong reinforcement and war-sustaining capability, serves as the strongest deterrent to aggression.[23]

Despite such assurances, the relationship between force structures and capabilities and the deterrence of aggression is highly uncertain. Military and civilian leaders repeatedly assess this relationship, but, as Morton H. Halperin has noted, NATO does not know exactly what the Soviet evaluation of forces on the central front is, nor how it would be affected by possible changes in war-sustaining capabilities.[24] Thus the impact on the deterrent value of the armed forces of adopting a short-war strategy cannot be predicted with any certainty. Nevertheless, it seems that, within the limits of public support, it would be prudent for military and civilian leaders to consider what actions might be taken to reconcile the army's capabilities with U.S. strategic commitments. In the following two chapters, which conclude this study, these actions are explored.

Notes

1. The use of reservists by the West German army in the event of mobilization would be similar to current U.S. plans. Some reservists would be used to fill active units, but most would fill cadre or inactive units. In contrast to U.S. policies, however, West German reservists would provide the personnel upon mobilization for some eight hundred replacement battalions which would be organic to brigades, divisions, and corps in the West German army. See Lt. Col. Henry G. Gole, "The Bundeswehr Reserve and Mobilization System," *Military Review*, November 1977, pp. 76–82.

2. It has been argued that President Johnson decided against mobilizing the reserve forces in 1965 (despite a recommendation by his service chiefs that it was the best way quickly to build up the force level in Vietnam) because of political implications and probable adverse reactions. See George H. Gray, "What Are U.S. Reserve Forces Really For?" *Military Review*, June 1975, for a discussion of the Johnson decision. Although the President never fully explained his unwillingness to mobilize the reserve forces, Gray and other writers have submitted a variety of "political" reasons.

3. Herman Boland, "The Reserves," *Studies Prepared for the President's Commission on an All-Volunteer Armed Force* (Washington, D.C., GPO, 1970), pp. IV-2-11, IV-2-12.

4. I. Heymond and E. W. McGregor, *Review and Analysis of Recent Mobilizations and Deployments of U.S. Army Reserve Components* (Washington, D.C., Research Analysis Corporation, 1972), pp. 4–7.

5. *Ibid.*, pp. 55–57.

6. *Military Posture and H.R. 11500: Department of Defense Authorization for Appropriations for Fiscal Year 1977*, Hearings Before the House Committee on Armed Services, February–March 1976, p. 560.

7. The army also uses the Reserve Evaluation System (RES) which assesses readiness based on the unit's performance during annual field training exercises. Although RES results are not correlated with C-ratings, manpower officials believe that they generally parallel but are somewhat lower than the C-ratings received by individual units. According to RES reports for 1976, 25 per cent of reservists were not present for annual training with their units, and only 46 per cent of the crews qualified on their weapons. See General Accounting Office, *Letter Report*, LCD 77–442, 21 December 1977.

8. *Military Posture and H.R. 5068: Department of Defense Authorization for Appropriations for Fiscal Year 1978*, Hearings Before the House Committee on Armed Services, February-March 1977, p. 561.

9. Neville Brown, *Strategic Mobility* (New York, Praeger, 1964), p. 205.

10. Harlan Cleveland, "NATO After the Invasion," *Foreign Affairs*, January 1969, pp. 253–254.

11. While some observers admit that the Soviet buildup in 1968 before the Czech invasion posed a potential "invasion" threat to NATO, others believe that any buildup adequate for an invasion of the West would necessarily be much larger, slower, and difficult to conceal. See, for example, David Calleo, *The Atlantic Fantasy: The U.S., NATO and Europe* (Baltimore, Johns Hopkins Press, 1970). Calleo discounts the possibility of surprise by the Pact in an attack on the Central Front. Conversely, however, Robert Close points out that surprise has almost always succeeded in catching the adversary unprepared. As Close noted: "We need only remember Hitler's offensive against the Soviet Union in June 1941 and the attack on Pearl Harbor." See Robert Close, *The Feasibility of a Surprise Attack Against*

Western Europe, (Rome, NATO Defense College, 1975), p. 77.
12. Speech by Senator Sam Nunn before the New York Militia Association. Reprinted in *Congressional Record*, 13 September 1976, p. S15660.
13. If one accepts the estimate of NATO Supreme Commander General Alexander M. Haig, Jr., of as little as eight days' warning of an attack, the value of U.S.-based reinforcements would be negligible. See "Haig Lifts Estimates of NATO Alert Time," *New York Times*, 15 September 1977, p. A-10.
14. A concern about the need for an even longer "sustaining" capability was expressed by a leading Defense Department official in 1976. Testifying before the Senate Armed Services Committee, the assistant secretary of defense (Manpower and Reserve Affairs) spoke at length about the army's manpower shortfall problems in Europe for the first seven months following a mobilization. See Statement of William K. Brehm Before the Subcommittee on Manpower and Personnel, Senate Committee on Armed Services, 6 February 1976.
15. Despite the steps being taken to improve the initial combat capability of the U.S. Forces in NATO, there has been little overall change in the proportion of the Defense budget allocated to NATO and to the reserve components. And, according to Benjamin F. Schemmer, only 32 per cent of the 1979 Defense budget was devoted to NATO, an increase of some 2 per cent over previous years. As Schemmer also noted, in real terms, overall U.S. defense spending declined about 20 per cent between 1971 and 1977, whereas other NATO members increased theirs by about 13 per cent in the same period. See "Bloody Battle over U.S. Commitment to NATO for 3% Real Budget Increase,"*Armed Forces Journal*, November 1978, p. 9.
16. A special congressional subcommittee determined in 1979 that the European NATO countries lack the capability to fight for thirty days and that plans do not provide for achieving such a capability until 1983. See *Report of the Special Subcommittee on NATO Standardization, Interoperability and Readiness*, p. 2. Also see Sloss, *NATO Reform*, p. 34.
17. Richard B. Foster, et al., *Implications of the Nixon Doctrine for the Defense Planning Process* (Menlo Park, Stanford Research Institute, 1972), p. 51.
18. See, for example, Sir Bernard Burrows and Chistopher Irwin, *The Security of Western Europe* (London, Charles Knight, 1972), pp. 63–64; and Edward L. King, *The Death of an Army: A*

Pre-Mortem (New York, Saturday Review Press, 1972), pp. 140–143.

19. See R. Close, *L'Europe sans Defense? 48 Heures qui Pourraient changer la Face Du Monde* (Paris, Henri Simonet, 1977). Another defender of a Russian "lightning war" conventional attack strategy has been the Mitre Corporation. See W. Gordon Welchman, "An Integrated Approach to the Defense of West Germany," *Journal of the Royal United Services Institute*, March 1975. Also see Hunt, *The Alliance and Europe*, p. 3. Hunt quotes the former Commander in Chief, Allied Forces Central Europe, Graf von Kielmansegg, as saying that Soviet forces, with some luck, could conquer Germany up to the Rhine in three to four days.

20. Edward R. Fried, et al., *Setting National Priorities: The 1974 Budget* (Washington, D.C., Brookings Institution, 1973), pp. 357–358.

21. Brown, *Strategic Mobility*, p. 199.

22. Oskar Morgenstern, *The Question of National Defense* (New York, Random House, 1959), pp. 104–105.

23. Bernard Brodie, "The Development of Nuclear Strategy," *International Security*, Spring 1978, p. 77. Also see Bernard Brodie, *Strategy and National Interests: Reflection for the Future* (New York, National Strategy Information Center, 1971).

24. Morton H. Halperin, *National Security Policy-Making* (Lexington, Mass., D.C. Heath, 1975), p. 162.

Chapter IX

Restoring Strategic Capabilities:
Major Policy Alternatives

The fundamental problem with AVF manpower policies and the army's strategic capabilities is that not enough good men are flowing into the active forces, the selected reserve units, and the individual reserve pools. While this flow will be increased somewhat by various new policy directions and programs, it is not likely to meet necessary levels of quantity and quality required for the "worst case" scenario of a NATO-Warsaw Pact conventional conflict in Central Europe. A return to some form of compulsory service, or another such drastic departure from the AVF policy, could eliminate such problems. This chapter considers the likelihood of such actions.

The Selective Service Alternative

As the 1970's drew to a close, more and more influential lawmakers called for a return to the draft as the means of resolving AVF-related manpower problems. Georgia's Senator Sam Nunn was in the forefront of this group. He was joined by, among others, Senator John C. Stennis, chairman of the Armed Services Committee and one of the defenders of the draft during 1967–71.[1] Even President Jimmy Carter hinted that he would support such a move.[2]

Thus the near universal and sometimes violent opposition to a continuation of the draft which occurred in the fading months of the Vietnam War would appear to have mellowed, at least among a growing minority of national leaders. Strong anti-draft attitudes were nonetheless prevalent in 1978, even though the end of the

Vietnam War and an increasing public awareness of problems within the AVF had softened the depth of opposition. Although two public opinion polls of 1977 and late 1978 indicated that overall opposition to the draft had fallen from 64 to 47 per cent, a closer examination of the data shows that the vast majority of young men surveyed still opposed it.[3] If the draft were reinstituted, many of the deep divisions that beset the country during the Vietnam War would almost certainly re-emerge.

Two other problems would have to be overcome by pro-draft forces. The first concerns the costs to American taxpayers. Whereas the use of Selective Service in the years before 1973 allowed the services to maintain pay rates far below civilian wage scales, the AVF has required that wage rates for new enlistees be substantially raised. Thus, unless wages for conscripts could be reduced, a return to the draft would likely cost the taxpayers more money, due primarily to increased training demands and shorter terms of service of a conscript-volunteer army.[4] Indeed, if inductions under Selective Service were restored, new short-term costs would be avoided only if wage levels were reduced for the conscripts. In the long term, however, most or all of these additional costs could be avoided if conscript wage levels were held constant while inflation took its toll. At the same time, cost-of-living increases could be granted to regulars, and the increasing gap between conscript and regular pay levels would surely have a positive impact on recruiting. During the late 1970's a limited precedent was established as cost-of-living wage increases for military and civil service personnel were limited to percentages somewhat below inflationary gains. In U.S. policies, however, distinctions have never been made between conscript and regular personnel, though precedents abound in other lands.[5] There are also precedents for paying both conscripts and volunteers at low levels; indeed, this option would be the only way in which major cost savings could be realized.[6] Regardless, congressional and service opposition to pay-cutting moves would no doubt crush serious consideration of such economy measures.[7]

The second major problem facing those who would like to restore Selective Service is to overcome the major objection of draft foes during the Vietnam era—that drafting only a small percentage of eligible youth is inequitable. Indeed, even if the strength of the services were raised to the pre-Vietnam level of 2.68 million men and women, yearly draft calls would total only some 300,000 conscripts, with the remainder of the yearly accessions required by the active and reserve forces (approximately 600,000) coming from the ranks of youth desiring to volunteer for military service. Furthermore, if the draft were extended to women, the degree of inequity among non-volunteering youth would become even greater (only about 10 per cent would be inducted). Reinstituting the random selection procedure would ensure impartiality but would not resolve the issue of inequity of service. Thus a return to Selective Service induction policies would require approval of the inequity of drafting only a few of many eligible youths. If the falling level of interest among youth in all things military is any indication, such acceptance would be doubtful.[8]

In sum, the combination of anti-draft feelings and unresolved problems of additional costs and inequity of service make the restoration of Selective Service a highly unlikely event—unless, of course, there are dramatic changes in international tensions or additional problems in the AVF manpower programs.

The Universal Military Training Alternative

Another manpower system which might replace the ailing AVF system is Universal Military Training (UMT). Like other systems of conscription, UMT could guarantee the numbers and quality of personnel required by the armed forces for its strategic capabilities. Yet, as Alan Ned Sabrosky has noted, such "conscripted reserves" would likely produce the worst of both worlds—unenthusiastic and unwilling soldiers free of the leavening influence of regular military service and with few extrinsic incentives to perform well.[9]

Because of its ability to sustain a large though minimally trained force of reserve personnel for major war emergencies, the concept of UMT has appealed to a small but vocal minority of Americans since the closing days of World War II. As early as 1943 a bill for postwar UMT was introduced in Congress, and President Franklin D. Roosevelt, in his first message to the 79th Congress on 6 January 1945, gave his unqualified support to the proposal. Roosevelt died shortly thereafter, but his successor, Harry S. Truman, echoed the plea for the establishment of a

UMT program. The requests of the two Presidents for serious
congressional consideration of UMT promoted a series of extended hearings.[10] While these congressional actions did not result
in authorizing legislation, the door was opened for a continuing
debate on the relative value of a UMT program.

The next major effort to legislate UMT occurred in 1946. Re-
flecting the views of the American Legion and others, the new
Administration proposal called for six months of basic training
followed by one of nine options for completing a twelve-month
period of service. This UMT proposal was supported by the
President's Advisory Commission on Universal Training, commonly called the Compton Commission. The Commission had
heard or consulted with some two hundred individuals represent-
ing all the groups and interests which had taken a public stand
on the subject of UMT. In a lengthy report, the Commission concluded that the sole justification for UMT would be "a demon-
stration that it is needed to insure our safety in a world in which
peace is not yet secure." In recommending approval of UMT, the
Commission urged it as "a matter of urgent military necessity."[11]

Once again, efforts to legislate a UMT program failed. But
momentum was gaining for successful passage of UMT at some
future date. This opportunity came in 1951, when the Truman
Administration proposed that Selective Service legislation be
amended to include a UMT provision. This time, proponents of
UMT were successful as Congress passed the Universal Training
and Service Act (Public Law 51, 82nd Congress). This new law
continued the authority for Selective Service inductions of men
into the active forces but also authorized UMT and created a
National Security Training Commission to explore its implementation. Working quickly, the Commission finished its evaluation
in several months and in its report to Congress enthusiastically
endorsed the concept.[12]

While UMT had been both authorized and judged feasible,
and limited funds earmarked for an experimental program, Congress refused to appropriate the necessary funds for full implementation. Efforts were made in subsequent years to overcome
this funding roadblock, but for all intents and purposes, a full-
scale UMT program died in the early 1950's with this refusal of
Congress to approve necessary funding.

Since then, and until the late 1970's the UMT issue remained dormant, though there were occasional outbursts of support and debate.[13] By 1978, however, because of AVF problems some support had arisen for a reauthorization. Four reasons were most often advanced to justify this move: (1) the guarantee of greater equity in military service among youth; (2) social benefits to individual trainees and to the nation; (3) increases in mobilization capabilities inherent in such a program; and (4) the strengthening of the active forces and the selected reserve because of the better quality and representativeness resulting from UMT-induced enlistments.

"Equity" is the key word in any defense of UMT. Recognizing the lack of equity in Selective Service, it would be necessary to ensure that nearly all youths participated in UMT, with exemptions limited to those clearly unqualified on mental or physical grounds.

The major criticism of UMT is the lack of military necessity for a full-scale program. While critics concede that UMT would resolve most AVF manpower problems and thus assure a near reconciliation of strategic capabilities and strategic commitments, they also point out that UMT would accomplish these tasks at far too high a cost in money and in military service demands.

An examination of the relationship between UMT and the problems of the AVF supports this view. For example, the major thrust of UMT would be to eliminate the IRR shortfall and thus provide the services with a viable mobilization pool. To accomplish this, however, a maximum of some 550,000 trainees would be needed each year. Even allowing for an additional 400,000 youths who each year would volunteer for longer terms of service with the active forces or the selected reserve, and for youths who would be disqualified on mental, physical, or moral grounds, more than two million young men and women still would be eligible each year for UMT but surplus to service needs. These youths would either be trained unnecessarily or be excused by lottery or a system of exemptions, choices which would be either far too costly or politically unacceptable.

Universal National Service Alternative

Yet another manpower system that might be adopted in

lieu of the AVF is a program of Universal National Service (UNS). Like other compulsory alternatives, UNS would guarantee the services their required numbers and quality of personnel.

The UNS program would be the antithesis of the AVF. Under UNS, virtually all youth would be compelled to serve—some in the military, others in the civilian sector. As with all compulsory manpower systems, the government could dictate the quality and quantity of personnel assigned to the armed forces. Thus the mobilization manpower problems of AVF would be resolved, and the nation would be assured of the manpower required to sustain strategic capabilities at a high level regardless of fluctuations in the civilian economy and the attitudes of youth toward military service. Whereas the UMT program would produce a large surplus of minimally trained manpower, the UNS program could limit the numbers assigned to the military forces and keep them on active duty for longer terms.

The degree of compulsion in UNS could vary widely. At one extreme, the compulsion could be limited to a requirement of some undefined service to the nation. At the other extreme, the government could totally manage the assignment of youths to military and civilian programs in accordance with detailed selection and distribution plans.

There could also be wide variations in the periods of required service, ranging from a minimum of four months (the period required for basic military training) up to the two or more years commonly associated with compulsory military service. Civilian service periods could also be weighted in order to prompt greater numbers of volunteers for the military forces.

Supporters of UNS have advanced both philosophical and practical benefits. On the philosophical side, UNS has been seen as a means of creating a new sense of patriotism and individual self-worth. On the practical side, in addition to resolving AVF problems, advocates have claimed that the adoption of UNS would bring an immediate reduction in youth employment (as well as a long-term reduction in adult unemployment).

Another line of argument in favor of UNS emphasizes the benefits to the armed forces. For example, Edward F. Hall has advocated a common initial training program, followed by a choice of military or civilian service, with supply and demand factors balanced through pay adjustments.[14]

Perhaps the greatest problem facing organizers of a UNS program would be to determine how constructively to motivate the large numbers of young men and women who would be involved in civilian service. As about three million young men and women would be available and minimally qualified for civilian service each year, the prospects for finding suitable assignments for all of them would be slight. Even if terms were limited to four months, a million year-round jobs would have to be located. UNS advocates point to the nation's conservation and pollution problems, as well as those of health and education, as main targets of the civilian portion of the UNS program; but there is little detail on the usefulness of generally unskilled eighteen- and nineteen-year-olds in such efforts. A specific inventory of possible endeavors has never been made, nor have any steps been taken to identify new and imaginative ways of challenging youth. And many opponents of UNS believe it is impossible to equate military and civilian service.

UNS also could be expected to cause economic dislocations, as a full-scale program would temporarily remove a large number of employed youth from the workforce. This dislocation also would be felt by colleges and universities.

Involved youths might provide less than full support for the program. One only has to remember anti-draft activities to imagine the possible reaction of young people if they reached a consensus that the UNS program was "a waste of time" or would have an "adverse impact" on their career plans or ambitions. Furthermore, as national defense cannot be used as a justification for a nonmilitary draft, a compulsory program for civilian service could be in violation of the 13th Amendment that forbids "involuntary servitude." Indeed, many scholars have supported the conclusion of Yale Law Professor Charles L. Black who argued that such "large-scale coercion of labor is foreign to our traditions and to our Constitution."[15]

The cornerstone of a successful UNS program would be equity of obligation and service, with exemptions limited to a very few disqualifications on mental, moral, or physical grounds. As this degree of compulsory service would clearly conflict with the values of many Americans, common sense dictates that those who favor it prove their case convincingly. By late 1978, however, very little evidence had been presented to support their position, despite the fact that a reasonably large and consistent number of youths have favored a one-year program of UNS.[16]

Increased AVF Funding Alternative

The abandonment of conscription was made possible largely by the willingness of the American people to pay a higher price for national defense, a price paid not only in terms of reduced strategic capabilities but also in tax dollars. Had Congress been willing to appropriate larger sums for AVF manpower, many of the manpower problems which have afflicted the AVF probably would have been avoided.

As Chapter III noted, the main thrust of the effort to achieve an AVF was based on economics—that salaries could be raised to the levels necessary to attract desired numbers of quality recruits in the volunteer marketplace.[17] In a continuation of this theme, many military and civilian leaders in the late 1970's were calling for still further increases in service salaries and enlistment and retention bonuses. While exact increases could not be predicted with certainty because of the unknowns of the volunteer marketplace, at least several billion dollars in additional manpower funds would be needed each year.[18]

If such additional funds were to be appropriated, no doubt the Pentagon would continue with its traditional approach of using financial incentives to attract and hold quality volunteers for three- or four-year terms of service. A growing number of military scholars, however, have called for a departure from these traditional policies, particularly as they relate to combat arms enlistments. Sociologists Morris Janowitz and Charles Moskos, Jr., have been in the forefront of this group, whose members have been urging the restoration of the "citizen soldier" program, based on the concept of the citizen's obligation for service to the state.

The core of this concept is a broadened base of citizens serving in the armed forces, particularly in combat arms. To achieve this more representative force, Janowitz and Moskos have urged a return to shorter enlistment terms, restriction of more popular technical assignments to those who have served in the combat arms, stabilization of tour lengths and assignments, and linking the military service experience to post-service study and employment. As Janowitz explained to Congress, while funding would be needed for such post-service benefits, many more qualified men and women would likely seek enlistment in the armed forces, thus helping to sustain the AVF and prompting broader participation in the service experience.[19]

Whether for traditional uses or for innovative departures from such policies, the chances of Congress appropriating more tax dollars for AVF manpower are not very good. Competition for funds from non-defense programs is too great, and ceilings on available revenues too strict. Even the honoring of President Carter's pledge to increase defense spending by 3 per cent a year for NATO-related programs will not make much difference, as most of the increased monies will be spent for new weapons or modernization programs.

An examination of trends in AVF expenditures supports this contention. For example, in FY 1964 (the year before the buildup for Vietnam), 8.3 per cent of the GNP went for national defense; by 1978 this level had been cut by more than 30 per cent. Corresponding changes occurred in the federal appropriations. In 1964 almost 42 per cent was allocated to the Department of Defense; by 1978 the proportion had been reduced to less than 25 per cent. Yet within the context of these overall reductions, the manpower portion of the defense budget steadily increased. For example, in 1964 less than 48 per cent of the Department of Defense funds was spent for manpower; by 1978 almost 60 per cent was required. This increased level of spending was necessary despite reductions from 1964 employment levels of more than 700,000 military and civilian personnel.

Increased manpower costs also had an adverse impact on national defense capabilities. For, as the Secretary of Defense explained in 1976, higher AVF manpower costs were causing shifts of some $10 billion each year from research, development, and weapons acquisition programs (about one-quarter of the monies expended each year for such items).[20] As there was no fixed ceiling on such national defense expenditures, the shifting of funds to the manpower account did not necessarily cause a reduction in modernization programs. In reality, the ceiling on total Department of Defense expenditures was determined by many political factors, as well as the state of the economy, expected revenues, and the perceived justification for a stronger or weaker defense in the minds of national leaders. There is a limit, however, on what citizens and businesses are willing to pay in taxes. And in looking to the future, whether additional funds are made available to the services to attract more and better recruits will depend primarily on competition for limited revenues from weapons development and acquisition programs, and from non-defense social, educational, and community development activities.

In terms of such competition, the most vexing problem for the armed forces is the trend toward spending more on nonmilitary training and service schemes aimed at disadvantaged and unemployed youths.[21] These youth have not been prime enlistment candidates; the trend toward spending more federal funds for such programs portends difficulties for AVF manpower funding in future years. As noted earlier, a continuing decline in defense spending occurred during the first five AVF years, while spending for civilian manpower programs increased many times over. Within the context of an overall spending ceiling, the chances of the armed forces obtaining additional manpower funds are thus quite bleak. Indeed, because of the competition, including that from NATO-related weapons development and acquisition programs, the army may have problems in the early 1980's in sustaining its FY 1979 and FY 1980 manpower spending levels. And even if these levels of expenditures are maintained, the gap which began to develop in the late 1970's between service pay and the pay of civilian counterparts (because of the government's failure to keep pace with inflation) would widen, with resulting damage to army recruiting and retention programs.

The Equity Tax Alternative

In the face of increased competition for existing revenues, the armed forces could gain added funds if a new military-service-related tax were imposed. Under such an equity tax concept, men and women who served in the active or reserve forces would be excused from the tax, or even granted tax incentives; those who elected to avoid military service, or were disqualified, would be liable.

The imposition of such a tax scheme could allow the services to obtain additional funds for manpower recruiting and retention programs. Of course, it would not guarantee the elimination of AVF problems. But with a combination of higher service pay and the avoidance of a heavy tax on civilian earnings, volunteers might step forward in required numbers.

Such an equity tax scheme has been working successfully in Switzerland for many decades.[22] A modified form of the Swiss tax system was proposed in 1973 by a governmental commission to the West German legislature, though the German lawmaking body failed to approve it.[23] In the United States, however, the concept has never received serious consideration from civilian or military leaders.[24] While the equity tax would not guarantee a resolution of current and projected manpower problems in the AVF, at least it would bring significant strides in that direction.

Conclusion

The strong opposition to conscription that grew out of the Vietnam War experience—although it has slackened—appears to preclude the restoring of compulsion as a means of resolving AVF manpower problems. While serious weaknesses in strategic capabilities have emerged during the AVF years, many of which could be resolved through a return to the draft, no large body of citizens has been directly threatened by these capability changes; therefore, there has been no widespread concern, nor a groundswell of emotion, for a return to compulsory service, or for the expenditure of large additional sums for AVF manpower programs.

Consequently, and in contrast to events of 1968-71, consideration of AVF policy changes in the early 1980's very likely will be confined to superficial evaluations of the AVF, balanced against similar analyses of alternatives. Barring a military crisis with a sudden demand for greatly increased forces, any fundamental changes in military manpower procurement policies will be the result of a political decision-making process far different from that which occurred when the draft was so abruptly abandoned.

First, priority will be given to those policy options that can "get through the system," and those approved will be characterized by compromise and accommodation among conflicting interests. Second, any changes which finally occur will most likely evolve by a series of small incremental adjustments rather than by a bold, distinctive departure from previous policy (such as occurred in 1971 when the draft was so suddenly abandoned).

Timing also will be a key factor in this process. Each year Congress and the President face a near overwhelming schedule of legislation. There is neither time nor staff resources for a thorough study and investigation of all recommended policy changes. Therefore, only a few key issues are selected, with the rest postponed or given perfunctory attention. And because public interest and political pressures play a large role in selecting those issues for serious consideration, Congress and the President do not always act on those policy problems that are truly of the greatest significance.

Legislation to restore military conscription, or to make major increases in AVF manpower funding levels, will thus be a difficult task, and apathy, inertia, and other priorities will contribute to the problem. The barriers might be overcome, however, by a growing wave of revulsion and strong opposition to existing practices. Such were the events surrounding the decision to abandon the draft. Not only was the decision abrupt, but the preceding discussions by the lawmakers were highlighted by often violent and emotional differences. That experience, however, was unique in American political decision-making, and a similar protest movement against AVF policies is highly unlikely. Most likely, most Americans will agree with Jacques Van Doorn (who relates the end of the draft in the United States to a general decline of all mass armies in Western countries) that the strategic capabilities of the armed forces will be limited to what is possible under AVF policies.[25]

In light of the fact that AVF manpower problems have not reached a crisis stage, it would be unrealistic at this time to expect the Administration or Congress to seriously consider abandoning the AVF, particularly since, as David Segal has observed, the public generally avoids discussion of complex defense issues.[26] Without question, then, the army faces a serious dilemma. On the one hand, AVF recruitment policies have contributed to increasing deficiencies in strategic capabilities. On the other hand, the army has not been able to develop the political support necessary to make major constructive changes.

Time may resolve this dilemma. As noted earlier, there appears to be mounting public support for a stronger military and for a return to the draft. Achievement of these goals, of course, could be hastened by a change in the international situation, particularly as it relates to United States-Russian detente, or by unexpectedly large failures in AVF recruitment programs. In the absence of either, the continuing anti-draft opposition and the memory of almost endless debates in Congress over draft reform and the ending of the draft, make decision-makers wary of a return to conscription. Indeed, while opposition to change has been waning, particularly since the end of the war in Vietnam, most leaders agree with Morris Janowitz that it will prevail at least until the mid-1980's.[27] Despite manpower problems, the AVF policy will be with us, at least for several years.

If this is so, the nation faces a variety of difficult choices. Some of these decisions could result in a stronger AVF, others could compromise the capabilities of the AVF with more demanding requirements. In the following chapter, which concludes this study, these choices are addressed.

Notes

1. In 1976 Stennis advocated a return to the draft "in some few years" so that the armed forces would be assured of enough "talent, dedication, and manpower." See *Washington Post,* 30 December 1976, p. 6. By 1979 his position on the issue had hardened. Declaring that the AVF hasn't worked and that it was weakening the nation's defense, Stennis called for serious exploration of the Selective Service alternative. See *U.S. News and World Report,* 5 March 1979, pp. 55–56.
2. In early 1977 the President stated: "If I consider as President that a restoration of the draft is necessary for the security of the Nation, I will not hesitate one day to recommend it to the Congress." See *Newsweek,* 28 March 1977, p. 20.
3. In the 1977 poll, 82 per cent of men ages eighteen to twenty-four opposed a return to the draft. In the December 1978 poll, 61

per cent of a somewhat broader eighteen to twenty-nine age group opposed it.

4. The Pentagon does not agree with this assessment. In its view, a reutrn to the draft would result in a net savings each year of some $500 million, mostly from reduced recruiting, advertising, and bonus expenditures. The comptroller of the United States, however, believes that the savings would be greater. See *Costs of the All Volunteer Force*, Hearings Before the Subcommittee on Manpower and Personnel, Committee on Armed Services, Senate, 6 February 1978, p. 5.

5. In Germany, volunteers in 1975 were paid at four times the rate of conscripts. During the 1945–70 period of conscription in the United Kingdom, volunteers were paid at a rate approximately 20 per cent higher than national servicemen. In Israel the I.D.F. paid only a subsistence salary to first-termers, and men and women were not allowed to sign up for better paying regular enlistments until they had completed a period of conscript service. See Kenneth J. Coffey with Alan Stovitz, *Manning the U.S. Armed Forces in a Post All-Volunteer Force Era* (Washington, D.C., Selective Service System, 1975), pp. 571–572.

6. Frederick J. Reeg estimated that a yearly cost savings of $6 billion could be realized if the pay of all first-termers were cut to a level where only quarters, food, medical care, and spending money were provided. See Frederick J. Reeg, "The Costs of the All-Volunteer Force and Total Force Mobilization," *Defense Manpower Commission Staff Studies and Supporting Papers*, Vol. III, pp. 8–10.

7. Even in France, where conscripts traditionally have been paid very little, pay was increased ninefold between 1970 and 1976. Michael L. Martin attributes this to the better education and political sophistication of French youth and their ability to make their demands for better treatment felt in the legislature. See Michael L. Martin, "Conscription and the Decline of the Mass Army in France, 1960–1975," *Armed Forces and Society*, May 1977, pp. 373–374.

8. The large proportion of males who expressed opposition to the restoration of conscription in 1977 and 1978 public opinion polls corresponds closely to the proportion of males in three 1975–77 surveys who were not interested in service enlistment opportunities. Indeed, the proportion of males interested in army enlistments fell by almost one-third, from 18.4 per cent in 1975 to 14.5 per cent in 1976 to 12.7 per cent in 1977. See Committee on Armed Services, Senate, *Hearings on the FY 1979 Au-*

thorization for Military Procurement, Research and Development, and Active Duty, Selected Reserve, and Civilian Personnel Strengths, 1978, p. 2722.

9. Alan Ned Sabrosky, *Defense Manpower Policy: A Critical Reappraisal* (Philadelphia, Foreign Policy Research Institute, 1978), p. 53.

10. See U.S. Congress, House of Representatives, Select Committee on Postwar Military Policy, *Universal Military Training* (Washington, D.C., GPO, 1945).

11. Advisory Commission on Universal Training, *A Program for National Security* (Washington, D.C., GPO, 1947), p. 2.

12. See National Security Training Commission, *First Report to the Congress* (Washington, D.C., GPO, 1951). Also see subsequent annual reports.

13. Foremost among the supporters of the UMT concept in the 1960's was former President Dwight D. Eisenhower. Eisenhower defended the UMT proposal on the ground of military preparedness and for reasons of fitness and discipline among American youth. See Dwight D. Eisenhower, "This Country Needs Universal Military Training," *Reader's Digest*, September 1966, pp. 49–55.

14. Edward F. Hall, "The Case for Compulsory National Service," in Donald J. Eberly, ed., *National Service: A Report of a Conference* (New York, Russell Sage Foundation, 1968), pp. 467–483. Another proponent has urged that the service obligation be considered as primarily in the civilian sector, with deferments and exemptions granted for military service. See Harris Wofford, "Toward a Draft Without Guns," *Saturday Review*, 15 October 1966, p. 53. Thirteen years later, in 1979, Wofford was still promoting a UNS program as chairman of the Committee for the Study of National Service. See their report, *Youth and the Needs of the Nation* (Washington, D.C., Potomac Institute, 1979), for a thorough discussion of the UNS issue.

15. Charles L. Black, Jr., "Constitutional Problems in Compulsory National Service," *Yale Law Report*, Summer 1967, p. 21. Grave doubts whether conscription for nonmilitary service is constitutional also have been expressed by the Library of Congress. See Report of the American Law Division, Library of Congress, "Constitutionality of Universal Compulsory Non-Military Service," as printed in the *Congressional Record*, House of Representatives, 1 April 1971, pp. 8996–8997.

16. In Gallup polls of 1972, 1973, and 1977, the proportions of young

people surveyed who favored a one-year UNS program were 58
per cent, 51 per cent, and 50 per cent respectively. See *The
Gallup Poll Index*, Vols. I and II, pp. 21–22, 212, 690.

17. Perhaps the epitome of viewing the AVF in marketplace terms is
to be found in the 1977 Rand study on AVF manpower. Herein,
Cooper advocates a continuation and refinement of service recruitment and retention policies by which military compensation is calibrated to supply and demand conditions in the
civilian economy.

18. Army Chief of Staff General Bernard Rogers proposed in 1977 that
some $800 million dollars be added to the recruiting budget for
the army reserve forces. In Rogers's view, this money was
needed to provide additional enlistment incentives for the
selected reserve units. The proposal did not provide recommendations for resolution of the army's major shortfall
problem in the IRR.

19. U.S. Congress, Senate, Committee on Armed Services, Subcommittee on Manpower and Personnel, Hearing, *The All-Volunteer
Force*, 2 March 1977. Also see Morris Janowitz and Charles
Moskos, Jr., "Five Years of the All-Volunteer Force, 1973–
1978," *Armed Forces and Society*, Winter 1979, pp. 171–218.

20. Secretary of Defense Donald H. Rumsfeld, *Annual Defense
Department Report*, FY 1977 (Washington, D.C., Department
of Defense, 1976, p. 281.

21. The proposal which most closely links civilian programs with the
needs of the armed forces was made in 1977 by William R.
King, who called for mandatory registration, vocational and
medical diagnosis, and counseling. Because of a forced contact
with armed forces recruiters, King submitted that AVF opportunities would be better understood, with a resulting marked
increase in enlistments. See William R. King, *Achieving
America's Goals: National Service or the All-Volunteer Armed
Force?*, Study prepared for the Committee on Armed Services,
U.S. Senate (Washington, D.C., GPO, 1977).

22. Every Swiss citizen of military age who fails to render military service for initial training and follow-up reserve service obligations (which extend to age fifty) is liable for the payment of a
military tax. The tax is based on a fixed amount for each
missed period of service, together with a percentage of earned
income. See H. R. Kurz, *Analysis of the Swiss Military Establishment*, (Zurich, Pro Helvetia Press Service, 1971), p. 4.

23. The Force Structure Commission of the Federal Republic of Germany recommended in 1973 that men conscripted into the

forces be issued tax credit coupons, based on their length of
service, which could be used in later years to reduce their tax
payments. The Commission also recommended that men not
chosen for induction be required to pay an "equalization tax"
as compensation for the burden placed on the conscript who
serves and who is materially impeded in his vocational training
and career. See Force Structure Commission of the Government of the Federal Republic of Germany, *The Force Structure of the Federal Republic of Germany* (Bonn, Federal
Government, 1973), pp. 162–165.

24. A variation of this equity tax concept was proposed to American
military leaders in 1972 by Daniel Newlon, who suggested that
each eighteen-year-old be offered three options: (1) enlistment
in the armed forces, for which he would receive a lifetime tax
reduction; (2) exemption from military duty by payment of a
lifetime tax surcharge; or (3) taking his chances on being
drafted under the Selective Service lottery scheme. See Daniel
H. Newlon, "A Volunteer Draft," *Military Review*, February
1972, pp. 83–89.

25. Van Doorn also believes that the main effect of the adoption of
AVF recruiting policies will be a wider gap between the military and civilian sectors. See Jacques Van Doorn, "The Decline
of the Mass Army in the West," *Armed Forces and Society*,
February 1976, p. 154.

26. David R. Segal, "Civil Military Relations in the Mass Public,"
Armed Forces and Society, Winter 1975, pp. 215–229.

27. Interview with Professor Morris Janowitz, University of Chicago,
Chicago, 2 February 1975.

Chapter X

The AVF and Strategic Capabilities

A new and probably extended era in American military history began with the end of the draft.

For all but one of the previous thirty-two years, the armed forces had been able to rely on the guaranteed and relatively cheap flow of new recruits required to sustain a large mass army. During these years millions of young men were drafted, millions more were motivated to enlist because of draft pressures, and still other millions were channeled into civilian professions and industries vital to a strong national defense through Selective Service deferment and exemption policies. Since the end of the draft, the need for the armed forces to recruit volunteers in the open marketplace has caused fundamental changes in their strength, composition, structure, and strategic capabilities.

The opposition of youth and other citizens to the use of the draft in the Vietnam War gave urgency to a growing unwillingness on the part of many Americans to continue conscription in the post-Vietnam peacetime years. And when Congress and the President finally accepted this mandate, the era of mass armies effectively ended.

Within this context and within the confines of current funding limits, three fundamental questions must be resolved. First, what additional measures can be taken by the armed forces to reduce AVF-related manpower problems? Second, what adjustments can be made in AVF mobilization and deployment policies to provide a more realistic deterrent against a conventional attack on NATO by the Warsaw Pact? And third, what changes should be made in U.S. strategic policies in order to reconcile the capabilities of the AVF with U.S. war-sustaining commitments?

Reductions in AVF-Related Manpower Problems

Several policy changes could be implemented by the army to reduce manpower deficits in the selected reserve and the IRR. These actions also would broaden the representational base of the AVF.

First, physical standards for enlistment could be lowered. There is ample evidence that these standards have been unnecessarily high—a permissible luxury during the draft years but questionable in the limited marketplace of the AVF. The Rand Corporation, for example, found physical standards for enlistment higher than entry standards for the armed forces of other advanced nations as well as for employment in entry-level jobs in the civilian sector.[1] Pointing out that the entry standards also were higher than those for retention in the services or recall in the event of mobilization, the Rand study called for a 40 per cent reduction in the rate of rejection for failure to meet physical standards.

The second management action that could increase the supply of potential recruits for the reserve forces concerns the minimum mental qualifications for entry both into the armed services generally and into specific skill areas. The reserve forces already recruit a large proportion of candidates who rank in the lowest 10 to 30 per cent on the standard intelligence test they administer; yet even more such Mental Group IV candidates could be enlisted. In addition, a great number of other potential recruits do not meet minimum educational and intelligence standards for entry, and consideration could be given to a limited, experimental utilization of individuals from this group.[2] A careful examination of the minimum intelligence standards for assignment to specific occupational areas could provide useful recommendations, for the army may be enlisting over-qualified personnel for some occupations, with a resulting lowering of their effectiveness and an unnecessary restriction of the recruitable pool. In addition, because some candidates refuse enlistment on the ground that they cannot be assigned to desired skill areas, a lowering of minimum entry standards for assignment to various skill or occupational areas would increase the number of enlistments.

As a third possible action, the limited two-year enlistment

program, authorized by the army in late 1978, could be expanded. Whereas enlistments of three years or longer result in smaller training loads and greater efficiency, the longer enlistment term has a direct effect on the size of the IRR. Not only do the men and women who enlist for a longer term have less time remaining for IRR service following their release from active duty, but the longer enlistment term results in fewer new accessions. A return to more two-year enlistments also would broaden the representation of certain groups, for the recruiting gains would be greatest among those sons and daughters of middle-income groups who normally attend post-high school training but could benefit from the savings of a two-year service. Such gains would be particularly evident if the two-year enlistment schemes were tied to post-service educational benefits.

Finally, a much more drastic and perhaps politically unacceptable solution to the shortfall in the individual reserve pools would be to gain approval of a limited draft for the IRR.[3] Such an IRR draft would not only ease the projected IRR shortfall, but might also stimulate more enlistments in the active forces and the selected reserve. The IRR draft scheme also would produce a younger, more viable IRR and would increase the number of trainees being prepared for deployment during the critical initial weeks following a mobilization decision. In addition, the IRR draft would exercise the Selective Service System, getting it ready to function fully, quickly, and efficiently in the event of mobilization.

As noted earlier, the army IRR could be short up to 550,000 personnel by 1980. Under an IRR draft, this manpower could be provided by a variety of training and recall obligation schemes. For example, 550,000 could be trained each year. Following four months of basic and advanced training, participants would be liable for immediate recall, in the event of an emergency, for the following eight-month period. Although the induction each year of these youths would not come close to exhausting the potential pool of inductees (which would total more than three million men and women), the degree of inequity under an IRR draft would be considerably less than under a return to Selective Service inductions for the active forces. Thus the combination of a shorter training period, a limited period of recall obligation, and a greater degree of participation of the nation's youth could make the IRR draft considerably more acceptable to Congress and the public than a return to pre-Vietnam Selective Service policies.

A drawback to the implementation of an IRR draft would be that the army would need authorization for increases in both the numbers of trainees and training staff. Furthermore, an IRR draft scheme would likely prompt a return of much of the bitter polarization over the issue of conscription which beset American society during the Vietnam War years.

In addition to these four approaches to increasing the strength of the selected reserve or the IRR, several internal service policy changes could bring a more effective use of limited AVF manpower resources. In particular, these changes would reduce the army's critical mobilization shortage of trained combat arms replacements.

For example, surpluses within the army IRR pool in noncombat skill areas could be used as combat arms replacements. Indeed, men in all army occupational fields have had at least basic individual training as infantry riflemen; some have had actual combat experience. Such surpluses exist in several occupations that lend themselves to relatively rapid conversions, for example, from military policemen to riflemen, from artillerymen to mortarmen or tank gunners.

In other specialties where conversion is more difficult, a "double change" could be considered—for example, moving someone from administration to military police, thus freeing the latter for combat duty. Physical condition and individual capability would of course have to be considered. But there may be a sufficient number of qualified men in the specialties outside combat arms to help meet the requirements of combat arms mobilization.

A potential also exists for cross-service utilization of reservists, since the navy and the air force do not foresee a great need for fillers but do have IRR pools. In some instances, fairly direct transfers of occupational skills could be made. For example, a former air policeman should be readily adaptable as an army MP; certain supply and engineering jobs are sufficiently similar for cross-branch transfers, as are those of cooks, clerks, medics, drivers, and many others. The other services' individual reservists could seldom directly fill the army's needs in combat arms, but a double switch in common specialties could be accomplished. For example, if the army's pool of truck drivers and clerks were depleted by their transfer to combat duty, drivers and clerks from other services could fill the army's need at least temporarily.

Still another action which could improve the army's mobilization capability concerns the Selective Service System. The ability of the system to provide new trainees immediately following mobilization could be easily restored, either by a return to peacetime registration or by implementation of the proposed EMMPS program allowing for nationally directed emergency induction processing. Additional funds would be required for either alternative, but the sums would be very small in comparison to the gains in war-sustaining capabilities.

Of these two proposals, a return to peacetime registration would provide the army with the highest degree of assurance that the system would be able to deliver inductees on short notice. Under existing statutes, however, the government would have to jail or fine nonregistrants, and this prospect has precluded the Administration from giving serious consideration to restoring peacetime registration though increasing numbers of top Pentagon officials in 1978 and 1979 were calling for such a program. As a compromise, a peacetime program with waivers of prosecution might be initiated. A totally voluntary registration also could be implemented. And in both cases, while the absence of enforcement would allow a small number of resisters to avoid prosecution, the vast majority of youth could be expected to register. Consequently, a registration list to be used for immediate inductions in a military emergency would be maintained.

Implementation of EMMPS also would be a major step toward restoring the induction capability of the system. For if required changes in conscription laws cannot be obtained during peacetime, quick congressional approval at the time of an emergency cannot be guaranteed, and it would be folly to count on an increased flow of conscripts when this hurdle remained.

Adjustments in AVF Mobilization and Deployment Policies

The changes discussed above, together with other improvements initiated by the Department of Defense, could greatly reduce the army's manpower shortfall problems. Still, in the event of full mobilization in response to a probable attack by Warsaw Pact forces in Central Europe, the army probably could not provide the manpower strength called for in the "worst case" contingency. Consequently, before reducing the U.S. commitment or taking some other such drastic action, care should be taken to insure that the army's requirements are valid, both in terms of numbers and time-phasing.

As noted in Chapter V, the army's mobilization plan for the European scenario calls for some 1.725 million pretrained personnel within 120 days of mobilization. As all judgments of shortfalls and corrective actions depend on these figures, we must be sure that all these men and women are needed. In particular, the army's estimate of replacements needed for casualties merits scrutiny. During the manpower-rich draft years, there was little reason for refining the requirements. In fact, as Alan Sobrosky noted, the services tried to hold on to every man and every weapon, without really asking if the number matched the need.[4] Even worse, decision-makers could have been influenced by pressures to justify a large reserve establishment and mobilization role. This is not to say that estimates of manpower requirements are biased, but that such determinations necessarily contain a great number of subjective judgments made by military planners and their leaders. Such judgments, of course, should reflect the lowest level consistent with national security objectives. And in an effort to achieve this goal, the Pentagon in 1977–78 began to examine the validity of the army's requirements. The preliminary results of their study indicate that the army's mobilization requirement may be more than 125,000 higher than necessary. This determination was based on judgments that manpower would not be needed upon mobilization for filling unmanned units (for which there is no equipment), that estimated casualties may be unnecessarily high, and that increases in long-term enlisted schooling programs could be deferred.

During the draft years it made no difference whether requirements for mobilization manpower were precise, because the numbers of surplus reservists and the functioning Selective Service System gave Pentagon leaders the resources easily to adjust the level of the mobilized force. During the AVF years, however, such resources have not been available, and they are not likely to be so in the future. Therefore, if various policy changes still fail to provide the resources required, common sense dictates that a reconciliation take place between the capabilities of the forces and our strategic commitments.[5] A recalculation of requirements could make this possible.

The army's decision that it would need all of the 1.725 million pretrained personnel within 120 days of mobilization also should be subject to careful scrutiny. Newly trained conscripts or volunteers could be available in large number within 150 days of the decision to increase recruit training (even sooner if the decision preceded formal mobilization actions). Furthermore, such a capability could be provided with minimum additional peacetime costs. In addition, even if all the required pretrained individuals are available, there is grave doubt that they could be equipped, trained, transported, and supplied in accordance with the current deployment schedule. Despite these reasons, the army's insistence that its units be filled 100 per cent within 120 days nullifies the question of placing a major mobilization burden on new trainees. Yet this insistence appears to be unrealistic and a legacy from the equipment, supplies, transportation and manpower-rich Vietnam War years. Thus serious consideration should be given to shifting some of the mobilization burden from pretrained individuals to new trainees. This step would require that the induction capability of the Selective Service System be restored to its earlier level and that the training base of the army be improved so that it could quickly train the new personnel.

If a re-evaluation of the army's manpower requirements for the European scenario confirms that a shortfall of pretrained personnel still would exist—a likely conclusion—the Department of Defense could improve the army's capability by "trading off" capabilities in other areas.

First, those army forces reserved for a minor contingency under the 1½ war strategy could be deployed to Europe. The disadvantage of such an action is that the United States would have no remaining military units at home or in non-European overseas bases, and a total absence of capability to respond to a secondary crisis or the expansion of the NATO-Pact conflict.

Second, available manpower in the army reserve forces could be reassigned so that those units with early deploying schedules could be manned at high levels with high quality, well-trained

personnel. Such an action would increase the army's initial reinforcement capability and provide a longer war-sustaining ability
than is currently possible. The expense of this action, however,
would be the removal of any capability for later deployment of
those units whose better personnel were reassigned.

An individual replacement system rather than the planned reserve unit replacement system also could be adopted. As Steven
L. Canby has argued, by eliminating the need for pre-deploy-
ment unit training, such a move would increase the availability
of individual reservists to the maximum extent possible.[6] But such
a policy change also would break up the integrity of army national guard and army reserve units, a move which would eliminate the usefulness of these units in a longer war. Therefore,
whether only certain or all army reserve units were made expendable so that their qualified personnel could be assigned more
quickly as vitally needed reinforcements, the impact would be a
reduction in the nation's long-term war-sustaining capabilities.

Finally, consideration could be given to the abandoment of
those aspects of the total force policy involving the use of fillers
from the individual reserve pools. No doubt the units called up
in the three mobilizations since World War II would have been
able to deploy much more quickly if they had not been required
to absorb and train large numbers of such personnel. If such a
policy were implemented, the trained reservists from later deploying commands could be concentrated after mobilization in
key early-deploying units, or existing units could be restructured
downward so that, for example, presently undermanned, under-
equipped, and undertrained brigades became full-strength battalions. Regardless of which option were chosen, the result would
be the same: the army's initial reinforcement and combat capabilities would be enhanced at the expense of a potential for pro-
longing combat beyond the initial weeks of a conflict.

A strengthening of the army's capability to fight in Europe—at
least during the early weeks of a conflict—also would occur if the
total force policy were redefined so that army reserve forces assumed responsibility for some post-mobilization functions of the
active army. For example, with better planning, more active army
personnel in administrative and support positions could be relieved by reservists so that the readier regulars could be assigned
as fillers for early-deploying units. In addition, if the U.S. de-

cided that the forces reserved for secondary contingencies were not expendable, consideration could be given to replacing them with reserve units. For example, if the army's independent brigades in Alaska and Panama, the vestiges of the 2nd Infantry Division in Korea, and the 25th Infantry Division in Hawaii are reserved for non-European actions, these units could be replaced by reserves. Although such a decision would allow better-trained and equipped active army units to arrive in Europe much faster than their reserve counterparts, the army would be stripped of all available contingency forces for a period of time after their departure and before the arrival of the reserves.

Even these drastic policy changes might not ensure fully manned and trained reinforcements in the early weeks of a conventional conflict in Central Europe. If so, it might be necessary to transfer some of the resources and support now being provided to the army reserve forces to the active army, which could then maintain a larger force-in-being in Europe. This decision would mean abandoning the total force concept and accepting a revised strategy which places much greater emphasis on maintaining a capability to fight a short, intense war after a minimum period of warning and preparation.

Reconciliation of Strategic Capabilities with Commitments

If military and civilian leaders fail to improve the army's mobilization capabilities, the nation will be left with several less than satisfactory choices.

First, it could be agreed that upon mobilization certain units would be manned by less than 100 per cent of their wartime complements, with the reduction directly applied to the requirement for filler personnel. In making this assessment, the services would have to distinguish between units that must be filled quickly to full wartime strength and those that could function at lower levels while awaiting draftees to complete their number. In addition, an assessment could be made of the effectiveness of combat units that function at less than full strength for a while after suffering combat losses and receiving less than one-for-one replacements. The foregoing does not mean that an ideal objective should be any less than 100 per cent, but rather that reassessment would distinguish different degrees of essentiality and provide a better basis for planning. While certain risks would be incurred even by this strategem, distributing manpower shortages among only units better able to sustain them would certainly minimize the effect of the shortfalls.

Second, it could be agreed that the nation will accept the shortages of military manpower. If the need for mobilization does not materialize, or if mobilization occurs early enough before the outbreak of hostilities, the effect of the reserve forces shortfalls would be minimal. If there is little or no warning of war's outbreak, the reserves would in any case have little impact on the critical first weeks of fighting in Europe. Thereafter, however, if combat continued, a serious shortfall would jeopardize the army's capabilities for sustained conventional combat and lower the nuclear threshold accordingly, but U.S. strategic nuclear forces would not be affected.

Third, it could be agreed that a war in Europe would develop only after a period of warning longer than that now anticipated by Pentagon mobilization plans. If this decision were made, it would allow a longer period for reserve retraining, the reconstruction of Selective Service induction machinery, and the training of greater numbers of new conscripts and volunteers.

The judgment on warning time contained in Pentagon contingency plans of 1978 (approximately one month) was at best subjective. Reasonable arguments can be made for either shorter or longer warning periods. Consequently, a re-estimation of the expected warning time may be an acceptable political compromise.

Obviously, however, such a decision would create risks. There would be no guarantee that the nation's leaders could determine a war probability in advance, or that they would be able or willing to act on the basis of such a warning.

A policy based on an extended period of warning also could open the door for still further reductions in mobilization capabilities and a resulting greater reliance on nuclear weapons. This is because many in Congress believe that the conventional warfare balance has shifted in favor of Warsaw Pact forces, and that the only realistic option open to NATO is the quick use of nuclear weapons.

Finally, and most sensibly, the nation could agree that U.S. strategic policy for the defense of Western Europe must be reconciled with the changed capabilities of the AVF. For within the context of a continuing commitment to a long war-sustaining capability, it is an unfortunate paradox that the AVF has fostered both the total force policy and the progressively worsening ability of the army to meet the obligations of that policy.

Perhaps, then, the total force policy and the commitment to maintain a long war-sustaining capability are anachronisms of a past era when a large mass army was the order of the day. In any case, in an era of volunteerism, the willingness of the American people to support the armed forces and to participate therein should determine the level of strategic commitments.

At least for the forseeable future, the nation's commitments should be reduced in order to reflect the level of capabilities possible under the AVF system and steady-state funding levels. In particular, the commitment to maintain a long war-sustaining capability should be replaced by a more realistic short-war policy allowing the concentration of available resources in on-site combat power and readily available fully manned, trained, and equipped reinforcements.

In more specific terms, the personnel, equipment and funds of the army total force should be redistributed with the following goals in mind: (1) a larger and better equipped active army, whose sixteen divisions would be fully manned with full complements of first-line equipment; (2) a larger and more self-sufficient combat force in Europe, with less dependence on transported reinforcements, equipment, and supplies; (3) improved strategic mobility forces and larger war reserve stocks; and (4) a much smaller but far better manned, trained, and equipped reserve, whose "ready" units would be able to deploy in support of the active army on short notice.

Such compromising actions should not be taken lightly. Certain risks would accrue. Yet in an era when there are inadequate personnel and funding resources to support both a short-war and long-war capability, the continuation of such efforts will only perpetuate the inability of the army to perform its assigned missions.

Unless and until the nation is willing to provide the resources to restore an effective war-sustaining capability, the army must concentrate on providing the forces necessary to respond fully to the initial demands of a sudden intense attack by Warsaw Pact forces in Central Europe. To do less within the realistic confines of the resources available would be to continue a deception dangerous to our allies, to the provision of an adequate deterrent in Central Europe, and to the maintenance of world peace.

Notes

1. See David S. C. Chu, et al., "Physical Standards in the All-Volunteer Force," Report No. R-1347, April 1974, p. 49. A report prepared in 1973 for the Senate Armed Services Committee also recommended a lowering of physical standards. See Martin Binkin and John D. Johnston, *All-Volunteer Armed Forces: Progress, Problems and Prospects* (Washington, D.C., GPO, 1973, p. 53).
2. The Department of Defense in the late 1960's conducted such an experimental program. Called "Operation 100,000," the program allowed the enlistment of up to 100,000 sub-standard recruits. Provided with special training programs, the recruits were assigned to regular service positions. This program was stopped after the election of Richard Nixon and the departure of Defense Secretary Robert S. McNamara. The views of knowledgeable Defense officials on the relative success of this program are mixed. Some point to increased expense and higher attrition rates of the participants as a mark of failure; others point to individuals who successfully completed their enlistment terms as a mark of success.
3. The Army Chief of Staff in March 1979 publicly called for the adoption of an IRR draft in which the active duty portion would be limited to initial skill training. General Bernard Rogers's endorsement of the IRR draft scheme was quickly repudiated by the Secretary of the Army, Clifford Alexander. See *Washington Post*, 15 March 1979, p. 1.
4. Sabrosky, *Defense Manpower Policy*, p. 65.
5. Pointing out that many of the units of the army reserve forces (particularly the army reserve) evolved out of World War II experience and would not be needed in a modern-day conflict, critics such as Martin Binkin have called for reductions in the force structure of up to 150,000 billets. Receiving strong criti-

cism from Binkin were units that would play no role in a short-
term conventional conflict, such as those training for civil
affairs, public information, and various other support functions.
See Martin Binkin, *U.S. Reserve Forces: The Problem of the
Weekend Warrior* (Washington, D.C., Brookings Institution,
1974).
6. See Steven L. Canby, "European Mobilization: U.S. and NATO
Reserves," *Armed Forces and Society*, February 1978, pp.
227–244.

Bibliography

Part I: The Draft Era

BOOKS AND MONOGRAPHS

Boulding, Kenneth, et al., *The Draft?* (New York, Hill and Wang, 1968).

Chapman, Bruce K., *The Wrong Man in Uniform: Our Unfair and Obsolete Draft and How We Can Replace It* (New York, Trident Press, 1967).

Cohen, Carl, *Civil Disobedience, Conscience, Tactics and the Law* (New York, Columbia University Press, 1971).

Davis, James W., and Kenneth M. Dolbeare, *Little Groups of Neighbors: The Selective Service System* (Chicago, Markham, 1968).

Falk, Stanley, L., *Defense Military Manpower* (Washington, D.C., Industrial College of the Armed Forces, 1969).

Ferber, Michael, and Staughton Lynd, *The Resistance* (Boston, Beacon Press, 1971).

Foot, M. R. D., *Men in Uniform* (New York, Praeger, 1961).

Garrett, Banning, and Katherine Barkley, eds., *Two, Three . . . Many Vietnams: A Radical Reader on the Wars in Southeast Asia and the Conflicts at Home* (San Francisco, Canfield Press, 1971).

Gaylin, William, *In the Service of Their Country: War Resisters in Prison* (New York, Viking Press, 1970).

Gerhardt, James M., *The Draft and Public Policy: Issues in Military Manpower Procurement 1945–1970* (Columbus, Ohio State University Press, 1971).

Ginzberg, Eli, with James K. Anderson and John L. German, *The Optimistic Tradition and American Youth* (New York, Columbia University Press, 1962).

Gray, Francine du Plessix, *Divine Disobedience: Profiles in Catholic Radicalism* (New York, Knopf, 1970).

Greig, Ian, *Today's Revolutionaries: A Study of Some Prominent Modern Revolutionary Movements and Methods of Sedition in Europe and the United States* (London, Foreign Affairs Publishing Co., 1970).

Haskins, Jim, *The War and the Protest: Vietnam* (Garden City, Doubleday, 1971).

Hendel, Samuel, ed., *The Politics of Confrontation* (New York, Meredith, 1971).

Hoffman, Paul, *Moratorium: An American Protest* (New York, Tower, 1970).

Horowitz, Irving L., *The Struggle is the Message: The Organization and Ideology of the Anti-War Movement* (Berkeley, Glendessary Press, 1970).

Jacobs, Clyde E., and John F. Gallagher, *The Selective Service Act: A Case Study of the Governmental Process* (New York, Dodd, Mead, 1967).

Killmer, Richard L., Robert S. Lecky, and Debrah S. Wiley, *They Can't Go Home Again* (Philadelphia, Pilgrim Press, 1971).

Kim, Kwan Ho, Susan Farrell, and Ewan Clague, *The All-Volunteer Army: An Analysis of Demand and Supply*, Praeger Special Studies in U.S. Economic and Social Development (New York, Praeger, 1971).

Leinwand, Gerald, *The Draft* (New York, Washington Square Press, 1970).

Liddell Hart, B. H., *Defence of the West* (London, Cassell, 1950).

Liston, Robert A., *Dissent in America* (New York, McGraw-Hill, 1971).

Liston, Robert A., *Greeting: The Draft in America* (New York, McGraw-Hill, 1970).

Little, Roger W., ed., *Selective Service and American Society* (New York, Russell Sage Foundation, 1969).

Lynd, Alice, ed., *We Won't Go* (Boston, Beacon Press, 1968).

Marmion, Harry A., *Selective Service: Conflict and Compromise* (New York, Wiley, 1968).

Miller, James C. III, ed., *Why the Draft? The Case for a Volunteer Army* (Baltimore, Penguin, 1968).

O'Sullivan, John, and Alan M. Meckler, eds., *The Draft and Its Enemies: A Documentary History* (Chicago, University of Illinois Press, 1974).

Prasad, Devin, and Tony Smythe, *Conscription: A World Survey* (London, War Resisters' International, 1968).

Reedy, George E., *Who Will Do Our Fighting for Us?* (New York, World, 1969).

Reeves, Thomas, and Karl Hess, *The End of the Draft* (New York, Random House, 1970).

Rothenberg, Leslie S., *The Draft and You* (Garden City, Doubleday, 1968).

Saunders, Jacquin, *The Draft and the Vietnam War* (New York, Walker, 1966).

Shapiro, Andrew O., and John M. Striker, *Mastering the Draft* (New York, Avon, 1971).

Stafford, Robert T., et al., *How to End the Draft: The Case for an All-Volunteer Army* (Washington, D.C., National Press, 1967).

Suttler, David, IV-F, *A Guide to Draft Exemption* (New York, Grove Press, 1970).

Tax, Sol, ed., *The Draft: A Handbook of Facts and Alternatives* (Chicago, University of Chicago Press, 1967).

GOVERNMENT PUBLICATIONS

Civilian Advisory Panel on Military Manpower Procurement, *Report to the Committee on Armed Services, House of Representatives* (90th Congress, 1st Session) (Washington, D.C., GPO, 1967).

Coffey, Kenneth J., with Alan Stovitz, *Manning the U.S. Armed Forces in a Post All-Volunteer Era* (Washington, D.C., Selective Service System, 1975).

Comptroller General of the United States, *Report to the Congress: Problems in Meeting Military Manpower Needs in the All-Volunteer Force* (Washington, D.C., GPO, 1973).

Congressional Record, various dates.

Department of Defense, Directorate for Information Operations, *Selected Manpower Statistics,* updated and issued yearly by Office of Assistant Secretary of Defense (Comptroller).

Laird, Melvin R., Secretary of Defense, *Progress in Ending the Draft and Achieving the All-Volunteer Force* (Washington, D.C., Department of Defense, August 1972).

Morris, Thomas D., Assistant Secretary of Defense (Manpower), Statement before the House Committee on Armed Services, *Report on Department of Defense Study of the Draft,* 30 June 1966.

National Advisory Commission on Selective Service, *Report* (Washington, D.C., GPO, 1967).

President's Commission on an All-Volunteer Armed Force, *Report* (Washington, D.C., GPO, 1970).

President's Commission on an All-Volunteer Armed Force, *Studies Prepared for the President's Commission on an All-Volunteer Armed Force,* Vols. I and II (Washington, D.C., GPO, 1970).

Secretary of Defense, *Manpower Requirements Report,* published annually (Washington, D.C., Department of Defense).

184 : *Bibliography*

Selective Service System, *Annual Report of the Director of Selective Service*, published annually, 1963–1968.

Selective Service System, "Attacks on Selective Service Facilities," special survey of National Headquarters, March 1971.

Selective Service System, "Channeling," information brochure issued by the National Headquarters, March 1971.

Selective Service System, *Conscientious Objection,* Monograph No. 11 (Washington, D.C., GPO, 1950).

Selective Service System, "Disposition of Defendants Charged with Violation of Selective Service Acts Showing Type of Sentence for Fiscal Years 1945 through 1971" (corrected to include 1972), issued by National Headquarters, October 1972.

Selective Service System, "Disruption of Selective Service Local Board Operations," 7 September 1970.

Selective Service System, *Fourth Report of the Director of Selective Service: 1944–1945* (Washington, D.C., GPO, 1945).

Selective Service System, *Outline of Historical Background of Selective Service* (Washington, D.C., GPO, 1965).

Selective Service System, "The Purposes of Selective Service," information brochure issued by the National Headquarters, 1 July 1965.

Selective Service System, *Selective Service*, published monthly by the National Headquarters, January 1941 through October 1969.

Selective Service System, *Selective Service News,* published monthly by the National Headquarters, November 1969 through 1976 (replaced *Selective Service*).

Selective Service System, *Selective Service Under the 1948 Act,* Report of the Director of Selective Service (Washington, D.C., GPO, 1951).

Selective Service System, *Semi-Annual Report of the Director of Selective Service,* published semi-annually since 1969.

Task Force on the Structure of the Selective Service System, *Report* (Washington, D.C., GPO, 1967).

Supreme Court of the United States, *Breen* v. *Local Board No. 16,* 396 U.S. 295 (1970); and *Gutknecht* v. *U.S.,* 396 U.S. 295 (1970).

Supreme Court of the United States, *United States* v. *O'Brien,* 391 U.S. 367 (1968).

Supreme Court of the United States, *United States* v. *Seeger,* 380 U.S. 163 (1965); and *Welsh* v. *United States,* 398 U.S. 333 (1970).

U.S. Congress, *The Selective Training and Service Act of 1940* (Public Law 783, 76th Congress).

U.S. Congress, *The Selective Service Act of 1948* (Public Law 759, 80th Congress).

U.S. Congress, *The Selective Service Extension Act of 1950* (Public Law 599, 81st Congress).

U.S. Congress, *The Universal Military Training and Service Act of 1951* (Public Law 51, 82nd Congress).

U.S. Congress, *The 1955 Amendments to the Universal Military Training and Service Act* (Public Law 118, 84th Congress).

U.S. Congress, *The 1957 Amendments to the Universal Military Training and Service Act* (Public Law 62, 85th Congress).

U.S. Congress, *An Act to Extend the Induction Provisions of the Universal Military Training and Service Act* (Public Law 4, 86th Congress).

U.S. Congress, *An Act to Extend the Induction Provisions of the Universal Military Training and Service Act* (Public Law 2, 88th Congress).

U.S. Congress, *The Military Selective Service Act of 1967* (Public Law 40, 90th Congress).

U.S. Congress, *The Selective Service Amendment Act of 1969* (Public Law 124, 91st Congress).

U.S. Congress, *The 1971 Amendments to the Military Selective Service Act* (Public Law 129, 92nd Congress).

U.S. Congress, House of Representatives, Committee on Armed Services, Hearings, *Extend Draft Provisions Through July 1, 1967, Including Those Applying to Physicians and Dentists,* 1 March 1963.

U.S. Congress, House of Representatives, Committee on Armed Services, *Analysis and Explanation of Universal Military Training and Service Act,* Document #2236, 1 March 1966.

U.S. Congress, House of Representatives, Committee on Armed Services, Hearings, *Extend Draft Provisions Through July 1, 1971, Including Those Applying to Physicians and Dentists,* 2–11 May 1967.

U.S. Congress, House of Representatives, Committee on Armed Services, Hearings, *Modify System of Selection to Random Selection,* 16 October 1969.

U.S. Congress, House of Representatives, Committee on Armed Services, Hearings, *Review of the Administration and Operation of the Selective Service System,* 22 June–30 August 1966.

U.S. Congress, House of Representatives, Committee on Armed Services, Subcommittee on the Draft, Hearings, *Review of the Administration and Operation of the Draft Law,* 23 July–18 November 1970.

U.S. Congress, House of Representatives, Committee on Armed Services, Hearings, *Extension of the Draft and Bills Relating to the*

Voluntary Force Concept and Authorization of Strength Levels, 23 February–9 March 1971.

U.S. Congress, House of Representatives, Committee on Armed Services, Subcommittee on Investigations, *Hearings on the Selective Service System,* 21–26 January 1976.

U.S. Congress, Senate, Committee on Armed Services, Hearings, *Extend Draft Provisions Through July 1, 1967, Including Those Applying to Physicians and Dentists,* 12 March 1963.

U.S. Congress, Senate, Labor and Public Welfare Committee, Hearings, *Investigation of Existing Draft System as It Affects Manpower and Poverty with View to Possible Needed Revision,* 20 March–6 April 1967.

U.S. Congress, Senate, Committee on Armed Services, Hearings, *Extend Draft Provisions Through July 1, 1971, Including Those Applying to Physicians and Dentists,* 12–19 April 1967.

U.S. Congress, Senate, Committee on Armed Services, Hearings, *Modify System of Selection to Random Selection,* 30 September–16 October 1969.

U.S. Congress, Senate, Committee on Armed Services, Subcommittee on Volunteer Armed Force and Selective Service, Hearings, *Volunteer Armed Force and Selective Service,* 10–13 March 1972.

ARTICLES

Altman, Stuart, and Alan Fletcher, "Military Manpower Procurement: The Supply of Military Manpower in Absence of a Draft," *American Economic Review,* May 1967.

"Amnesty for War Exiles," *Time,* 17 January 1972.

Baldwin, Hanson W., "New Attitude on Peacetime Draft," *New York Times,* 8 March 1963.

Barnes, Peter, "All Volunteer Army?" *New Republic,* May 1970.

"A Call to Resist Illegitimate Authority," *New York Review of Books,* 12 October 1967.

"C.O. Court Ruling: Added Work for Local Boards," *Selective Service News,* June–July 1970.

Davis, James W., Jr., and Kenneth M. Dolbeare, "Selective Service: Present Impact and Future Prospects," *Wisconsin Law Review,* Fall 1967.

Duscha, Julius, "Should There Be Amnesty for the War Resisters?" *New York Times Magazine,* 24 December 1972.

Editorial Research Reports, "Resistance to Military Service," *Congressional Quarterly*, 20 March 1968.

Evans, Robert, Jr., "The Military Draft as a Slave System: An Economic View," *Social Science Quarterly*, December 1969.

Fisher, Anthony C., "The Cost of the Draft and the Cost of Ending the Draft," *American Economic Review*, June 1969. Klotz, Benamin P., "The Cost of Ending the Draft: Comment," *American Economic Review*, December 1970. Fisher, Anthony C., "The Cost of Ending the Draft: Reply," *American Economic Review*, December 1970.

Friedman, Milton, "The Case for Abolishing the Draft and Substituting for It an All-Volunteer Army," *New York Times Magazine*, 14 May 1967.

Friedman, Milton, "Milton Friedman on the Volunteer Army," collection of articles by Milton Friedman reprinted at the request of Hon. Mark O. Hatfield, *Congressional Record*, 18 August 1970, pp. S-13613–S-13616.

Friedman, Milton, "Why Not a Volunteer Army?" in Sol Tax, ed., *The Draft: A Handbook of Facts and Alternatives* (Chicago, University of Chicago Press, 1967).

Gillam, Richard, "The Peacetime Draft," *Yale Review*, Summer 1968.

Glass, Andrew J., "Defene Report: Draftees Shoulder Burden of Fighting and Dying in Vietnam," *National Journal*, 15 August 1970.

Goodman, Walter, "They March to Different Drummers," *New York Times Magazine*, 27 June 1966.

Hatfield, Mark O. "The Draft Should be Abolished," *Saturday Evening Post*, 1 July 1967.

Hershey, Lewis B., "Enforcement of the Law," *Selective Service*, December 1967.

Hershey, Lewis B., "Responsible Reporting," *Selective Service*, September 1968.

Hershey, Lewis B., "United We Stand . . ." *Selective Service*, March 1968.

Huston, James A., "Selective Service as a Political Issue," *Current History*, October 1968.

Jackson, Donald, "Evading the Draft: Who, How and Why," *Life*, 9 December 1966.

Janowitz, Morris, "The Decline of the Mass Army," *Military Review*, February 1972.

Johnson, Haynes, "Peace Fires Amnesty Issue," *Washington Post*, 4 February 1973.

Kennedy, Edward M., "Random Selection: An Alternative to Selective

Service," *Current History*, August 1968.

Large, Arlen J., "When the U.S. Gives Up Conscription," *Wall Street Journal*, 1 October 1971.

"Law Violators Plagued Nation in Past Wars," *Selective Service*, May 1968.

Lubell, Samuel, "Draft Sired Youth Revolt," *Washington Post*, 21 June 1970.

McFadden, Robert D., "C.O.'s Find a Rise in Acceptance," *New York Times*, 23 April 1971.

Mitrisin, John, "The Pros and Cons of a Voluntary Army," *Current History*, August 1968.

Moore, John L., "Defense Report: Draft, Volunteer Army Proposals Head for Showdown in Congress," *National Journal*, 6 March 1971.

Moore, John L., "Defense Report: Pentagon Turns to Ad Campaign, Minimizes 'Mickey Mouse' in Zero Draft Program," *National Journal*, 13 March 1971.

Oi, Walter Y., "The Economic Cost of the Draft," *American Economic Review*, May 1967.

Oi, Walter Y., and Brian E. Forst, "Manpower and Budgetary Implications of Ending Conscription," in *Studies Prepared for the President's Commission on an All-Volunteer Armed Force* (Washington, D.C., GPO, 1970).

Pemberton, John De J., Jr., "The War Protester," *Current History*, July 1968.

Poppy, John, "The Draft: Hazardous to Your Health?," *Look*, 12 August 1969.

Schaffer, Patricia, and David Weissbrodt, "Conscientious Objection to Military Service as a Human Right," *The Review of the International Commission of Jurists*, December 1972.

Scott, Richard, "Draft Dodging in U.S. Now Socially Acceptable," *Guardian*, 12 April 1966.

Sherk, J. Harold, "The Position of the Conscientious Objector," *Current History*, June 1968.

"Survey Shows CO's Talented," *Selective Service News*, January 1973.

Swomley, John M., Jr., "Why the Draft Should Go," *The Nation*, 11 August 1969.

Tarr, Curtis W., "End of Channeling Marks Change of Times," *Selective Service News*, June-July 1970.

Tyler, Gus, "Dangers of a Professional Army," *The New Leader*, 24 April 1967.

"U.S. Draft Policy and Its Impact," *Congressional Quarterly Service*, July 1968.

"Volunteer Army Gains Support But Passage is Doubtful," *Congressional Quarterly*, 3 April 1970.

Wilson, Richard, "Problems of Ending the Draft and Waging War," *Washington Evening Star*, 3 February 1969.

Ziegler, Mel, "Selective Service Meets Massive Resistance," *New York Magazine*, 29 June 1970.

NEWSPAPER CITATIONS

Army Information Digest, November 1946, August 1947.

Chicago Tribune, 30 December 1969.

Christian Science Monitor, 22 May 1967, 3 October 1969, 29 January 1970, 30 August 1972.

Cleveland Plain Dealer, 30 August 1972.

Denver Post, 27 March 1967.

Guardian, 12 April 1966, 18 October 1967, 19 October 1967.

Harvard Crimson, 15 January 1968.

International Herald Tribune, 8 March 1968, 26 February 1971, 19 December 1972, 15 August 1973.

Keesing's Contemporary Archives, 14–21 December 1968, 27 December 1969–3 January 1970; 25 March–1 April 1972, 5–12 August 1972.

Knickerbocker News, 1 September 1972.

London Times, 17 October 1967, 19 October 1967.

Los Angeles Times, 9 January 1967.

Miami Herald, 18 April 1971.

Part II: The AVF Era

BOOKS AND MONOGRAPHS

Baldwin, Hanson W., *Strategy for Tomorrow* (New York, Harper and Row, 1970).

Binkin, Martin, *U.S. Reserve Forces: The Problem of the Weekend Warrior* (Washington, D.C., Brookings Institution, 1974).

Binkin, Martin, and Shirley J. Bach, *Women and the Military* (Washington, D.C., Brookings Institution, 1977).

Binkin, Martin, and John D. Johnston, *All Volunteer Armed Force: Progress, Problems, and Prospects*, Report Prepared for the Committee on Armed Services, U.S. Senate (Washington D.C., GPO, 1973).

Blechman, Barry, and Robert Berman, et al., *The Soviet Military Buildup and U.S. Defense Spending* (Washington, D.C., Brookings Institution, 1977).

Bliven, Bruce, Jr. *Vounteers, One and All* (New York, Reader's Digest Press, 1976).

Bonestell, Charles H., *The Army's Contribution to National Security Policy-Making and Force Posture Analysis* (Menlo Park, Stanford Research Institute, 1971).

Bradford, Zeb B., Jr., and Frederic J. Brown, *The United States Army in Transition* (Beverly Hills, Sage, 1973).

Brodie, Bernard, *Strategy and National Interests: Reflections for the Future* (New York, National Strategy Information Center, 1971).

Brown, Neville, *Strategic Mobility* (New York, Praeger, 1964).

Brown, Neville, *Strategy and the Atlantic Alliance: A Critique of United States Doctrine* (Princeton, Princeton University Press, 1964).

Burrows, Sir Bernard, and Chrisopher Irwin, *The Security of Western Europe* (London, Charles Knight, 1972).

Burt, Richard, *New Weapons Technologies: Debate and Directions,* Adelphi Papers No. 126 (London, International Institute for Strategic Studies, 1976).

Calleo, David, *The Atlantic Fantasy: The U.S., NATO and Europe* (Baltimore, Johns Hopkins Press, 1970).

Canby, Steven L., *Military Manpower Procurement: A Policy Analysis* (Lexington, Mass., D.C. Heath, 1972).

Canby, Steven L., *NATO Military Policy: The Constraints Imposed by an Inappropriate Military Structure* (Santa Monica, Rand, 1972).

Canby, Steven L., *NATO Military Policy: Obtaining Conventional Comparability with the Warsaw Pact* (Santa Monica, Rand, 1973).

Canby, Steven L., and R. B. Rainey, *Rand Working Note WN-7078/1, ISA,* unpublished manuscript (Santa Monica, Rand, 1972).

Carpenter, William M., and S. P. Gilbert, *Integrated Global Force Postures: An Overview* (Menlo Park, Stanford Research Institute, 1973).

Cater, Douglass, *Power in Washington: A Critical Look at Today's Struggle to Govern in the Nation's Capital* (New York, Random House, 1964).

Chu, David S. C., et al., *Physical Standards in the All-Volunteer Force,* Rand Report No. R-1347, April 1974.

Cliffe, Trevor, *Military Technology and the European Balance,* Adelphi

Papers No. 89 (London, International Institute for Strategic Studies, 1972).

Close, R., *L'Europe sans Defense?: 48 Heures Qui Pourraient Changer la Face du Monde* (Paris, Henri Simonet, 1977).

Close, Robert, *The Feasibility of a Surprise Attack Against Western Europe* (Rome, NATO Defense College, 1975).

Collins, John M., *Imbalance of Power* (San Rafael, Presidio Press, 1978).

Committee for the Study of National Service, *Youth and the Needs of the Nation* (Washington, D.C., Potomac Institute, 1979).

Cooper, Richard V. L., *Military Manpower and the All-Volunteer Force* (Santa Monica, Rand, 1977).

Deitchman, Seymour J., *Limited War and American Defense Policy: Building and Using Military Power in a World at War*, 2nd ed. (Boston, MIT Press, 1969).

Eberly, Donald J., ed., *A Profile of National Service* (Washington, D.C., National Service Secretariat, 1966).

Enthoven, Alain C., and K. Wayne Smith, *How Much is Enough?: Shaping the Defense Program 1961–1969* (New York, Harper and Row, 1971).

Fischer, Robert Lucas, *Defending the Central Front: The Balance of Forces*, Adelphi Papers No. 127 (London, International Institute for Strategic Studies, 1976).

Fligstein, Neil D., "Who Served in the Military, 1940–1973?," unpublished monograph, July 1976.

Force Structure Commission of the Government of the Federal Republic of Germany, *The Force Structure in the Federal Republic of Germany* (Bonn, Federal Government, 1973).

Foster, Richard B., *Implications of the Nixon Doctrine for the Defense Planning Process* (Arlington, Va., Stanford Research Institute, 1972).

Ginzberg, Eli, James K. Anderson, Sol. W. Ginzburg, and John L. Herma, *The Lost Division* (New York, Columbia University Press, 1959).

Graham, Daniel O., *A New Strategy for the West: NATO After Detente* (Washington, D.C., Heritage Foundation, 1977).

Hackel, Erwin, *Military Manpower and Political Purpose*, Adelphi Papers No. 72 (London, International Institute for Strategic Studies, 1970).

Halperin, Morton H., *National Security Policy-Making* (Lexington, Mass., D. C. Heath, 1975).

Hauser, William, *America's Army in Crisis: A Study in Civil-Military Relations* (Baltimore, John Hopkins Press, 1973).

Heymont, I., and E. W. McGregor, *Review and Analysis of Recent Mobilizations and Deployments of U.S. Army Reserve Components* (Washington, D.C., Research Analysis Corporation, 1972).

Hoag, Malcolm W., *Rationalizing NATO Strategy* (Santa Monica, Rand, 1964).

Hunt, Kenneth, *The Alliance and Europe: Part II: Defense with Fewer Men*, Adelphi Papers, No. 98 (London, International Institute for Strategic Studies, 1973).

Janowitz, Morris, *U.S. Forces and the Zero Draft*, Adelphi Papers No. 94 (London, International Institute for Strategic Studies, 1973).

Johnson, David T., and Barry R. Schneider, *Current Issues in U.S. Defense Policy*, Center for Defense Information (New York, Praeger, 1976).

Keeley, John, ed., *The Military in American Society* (Charlottesville, University of Virginia Press, 1978).

King, Edward L., *The Death of an Army: A Pre-Mortem* (New York Saturday Review Press, 1972).

Kurz, H. R., *Analysis of the Swiss Military Establishment* (Zurich, Pro Helvetia Press Service, 1971).

Lampson, Edward T., *The United States and NATO: Commitments, Problems and Prospects* (Washington, D.C., Congressional Reference Service, 1972).

Lawrence, Richard D. and Jeffrey Record, *U.S. Force Structure in NATO* (Washington, D.C., Brookings Institution, 1974).

Levantrosser, W. F., *Congress and the Citizen Soldier: Legislative Policy-Making for the Federal Armed Forces Reserve* (Columbus, Ohio State University Press, 1967).

Liddell Hart, B. H., *Deterrent or Defence: A Fresh Look at the West's Military Position* (London, Stevens and Sons, 1960).

Luttwak, Edward, *Strategic Power: Military Capabilities and Political Utility* (Beverly Hills, Sage, 1976).

Maiziere, Ulrich de, *Armed Forces in the NATO Alliance* (Washington, D.C., Center for Strategic and International Studies, 1976).

Marton, Laurence W., *Arms and Strategy: The World Power Struggle Today* (New York, McKay, 1973).

Martin, Michael L., *The Changing French Military: A Sociological Study of Men and Organization* (Chapel Hill, N.C., University of North Carolina Press, 1980).

McDonough, James R., ed., *Senior Conference on National Compulsory Service* (West Point, United States Military Academy, 1977).

Newhouse, John, with Melvin Croan, Edward R. Fried, and Timothy W. Stanley, *U.S. Troops in Europe: Issues, Costs, and Choices*

(Washington, D.C., Brookings Institution, 1971).

Osgood, Robert E., *NATO: The Entangling Alliance* (Chicago, University of Chicago Press, 1962).

Ramati, Sgan Aluf Shanl, *Israel Today: The Israel Defense Forces* (Jerusalem, Israel Digest, 1966).

Russett, Bruce M., *What Price Vigilance? The Burdens of National Defense* (New Haven, Yale University Press, 1970).

Sabrosky, Alan Ned, *Defense Manpower Policy: A Critical Reappraisal* (Philadelphia, Foreign Policy Research Institute, 1978).

Schiller, Warner R., William T. R. Fox, Catherine M. Kelleher, and Donald J. Puchala, *American Arms and a Changing Europe: Dilemmas of Deterrence and Disarmament* (New York, Columbia University Press, 1973).

Sloss, Leon, *NATO Reform: Prospects and Priorities*, Washington Papers, Vol. III, Center for Strategic and International Studies (Beverly Hills, Sage, 1975).

Stanley, Timothy W., *NATO in Transition: The Future of the Atlantic Alliance* (New York, Praeger, 1965).

Stanley, Timothy W., and Darnell M. Whitt, *Detente Diplomacy: United States and European Security in the 1970's* (New York, Dunellen, 1970).

Stillman, Edward, et al., *Alternatives for European Defense in the Next Decade* (Harmon-Hudson, N.Y., Hudson Institute, 1964).

Sukovic, Olga, et al., *Force Reductions in Europe*, A SIPRI Monograph (Stockholm, Almqvist and Wiksell, 1974).

Tarr, David W., *American Strategy in the Nuclear Age* (New York, Macmillan, 1966).

U.S. Army War College, Faculty, *War Dynamics in National Strategy* (New York, Thomas Y. Crowell, 1975).

Williams, G. L., and A. L. Williams, *Crisis in European Defense: The Next Ten Years* (London, Charles Knight, 1974).

GOVERNMENT PUBLICATIONS

Abellera, James W., and Mimi Y. Dunham, "Prospects for Sustaining the Peacetime All-Volunteer Force, 1976–1985," *Defense Manpower Commission Staff Studies and Supporting Papers*, Vol. III (Washington, D.C., GPO, 1976).

Abellera, James W., with Mimi Y. Dunham, and Richard K. Kuzmack, "Job Selection Standards in the Armed Forces," *Defense Manpower Commission Staff Studies and Supporting Papers*, Vol. III (Washington, D.C., GPO, 1976).

Advisory Commission on Universal Training, *A Program for National*

Security (Washington, D.C., GPO, 1947).

Assistant Secretary of Defense (Manpower and Reserve Affairs), *Volunteer Force Status* (Washington, D.C., Department of Defense, 1974).

Battle, Delores, "Women in the Defense Establishment," *Defense Manpower Commission Staff Studies and Supporting Papers,* Vol. II (Washington, D.C., GPO, 1976).

Boland, Herman, "The Reserves," *Studies Prepared for the President's Commission on an All-Volunteer Armed Force* (Washington, D.C., GPO, 1970).

Brehm, William K., Assistant Secretary of Defense (Manpower and Reserve Affairs), Statement Before the Subcommittee on Manpower and Personnel, Senate Armed Services Committee, 6 February 1976.

Central All-Volunteer Task Force, Office of the Assistant Secretary of Defense (Manpower and Reserve Affairs), *Utilization of Military Women* (Washington, D.C., Department of Defense, 1972).

Coffey, Kenneth J., "Standby Draft Capabilities," *Defense Manpower Commission Staff Studies and Supporting Papers,* Vol. III (Washington, D.C., GPO, 1976).

Coffey, Kenneth J., and James W. Abellera, "The Availability of Individual Ready Reserves (IRR) upon Mobilization," *Defense Manpower Commission Staff Studies and Supporting Papers,* Vol. III (Washington, D.C., GPO, 1976).

Coffey, Kenneth J., and Frederick J. Reeg, "Representational Policy," *Defense Manpower Commission Staff Studies and Supporting Papers,* Vol. III (Washington, D.C., GPO, 1976).

Coffey, Kenneth J., Edward Scarborough, Frederick J. Reeg, Audrey J. Page, and James W. Abellera, "The Impact of Socio-Economic Composition in the All-Volunteer Force," *Defense Manpower Commission Staff Studies and Supporting Papers,* Vol. III (Washington, D.C., GPO, 1976).

Collins, John M., *Defense Trends in the United States, 1952–1973* (Washington, D.C., Congressional Reference Service, 1974).

Congressional Budget Office, *Assessing the NATO/Warsaw Pact Military Balance* (Washington, D.C., U.S. Congress, 1977).

Congressional Budget Office, *Improving the Readiness of the Army Reserve and National Guard: A Framework for Debate* Washington, D.C., U.S. Congress, 1978).

Congressional Budget Office, *Planning U.S. General Purpose Forces: Army Procurement Issues* (Washington, D.C., U.S. Congress, 1976).

Congressional Budget Office, *Planning U.S. General Purpose Forces:*

Overview (Washington, D.C., U.S. Congress, 1977).

Congressional Budget Office, *Planning U.S. General Purpose Forces: The Tactical Air Forces* (Washington, D.C., U.S. Congress, 1977).

Congressional Budget Office, *The Selective Service System: Mobilization Capabilities and Options for Improvement* (Washington, D.C., U.S. Congress, 1978).

Congressional Budget Office, *U.S. Army Force Design: Alternatives for Fiscal Years 1977–1981*, staff working paper (Washington, D.C., U.S. Congress, 1976).

Congressional Budget Office, *U.S. Air and Ground Conventional Forces for NATO: Mobility and Logistics Issues* (Washington, D.C., U.S. Congress, 1978).

Congressional Research Service, Library of Congress, *United States/ Soviet Military Balance: A Frame of Reference for Congress* (Washington, D.C., GPO, 1976).

Defense Manpower Commission, *Defense Manpower: The Keystone of National Security* (Washington, D.C., GPO, 1976).

Department of the Army, National Guard Bureau, *After Action Report: Mobilization of Reserve Forces 1968* (Washington, D.C., Department of Defense, 1969).

Department of Defense, *Defense Manpower Quality Requirements*, Report to the Senate Armed Services Committee, as required by Report No. 93-385, January 1974.

Department of Defense, *Department of Defense Manpower, FY 64– FY 77: The Components of Change* (Washington, D.C., Department of Defense, 1975).

Department of Defense, *Navy Accelerated Sealift Study: Project Sea Express* (Washington, D.C., Department of Defense, 1974).

Department of Defense, Office of Deputy Assistant Secretary of Defense (Reserve Affairs), "Reserve Forces Manpower Charts," 30 September 1978 (published quarterly).

Department of Defense, Secretary of Defense, *Report to the Congress on the FY 1977 Budget and Its Implications for the FY 1978 Authorization Request and the FY 1977–1981 Defense Programs* (Washington, D.C., Department of Defense, 1976).

Department of Defense, *Reserve Forces Manpower Requirements Report, FY 1976* (Washington, D.C., Department of Defense, 1975).

Enthoven, Alain, Assistant Secretary of Defense (Systems Analysis), *Evaluation of NATO* (Washington, D.C., Department of Defense, 1968).

General Accounting Office, *Airlift Operations of the Military Airlift Command During the 1973 Middle East War*, 16 April 1975.

Goldrich, Robert L., "Military Manpower Policy and the All-Volunteer Force," Issue Brief No. IB77032, Library of Congress, Congressional Research Service, 28 June 1977.

Israel, Ministry of Defense, *Chen* (Tel Aviv, I.D.F. Spokesman, 1969).

McNamara, Robert S., Secretary of Defense, *The Fiscal Years 1969–1973 Defense Program and the 1969 Defense Budget* (Washington, D.C., Department of Defense, 1968).

National Security Training Commission, *First Report to the Congress* (Washington, D.C., GPO, 1951).

Nunn, Sam, "Gearing Up to Deter Combat in Europe," *Congressional Record,* 13 September 1976.

Nunn, Sam, and Dewey F. Bartlett, *NATO and the New Soviet Strength,* Report to the Senate Committee on Armed Services, 24 January 1977.

Office of the Assistant Secretary of Defense (Equal Opportunity), *The Negro in the Armed Forces: A Statistical Factbook* (Washington, D.C., Department of Defense, 1971), supplemented by *Blacks in the Armed Forces,* unpublished 1973, 1974, and 1978 updates.

Office of the Assistant Secretary of Defense (Manpower, Reserve Affairs and Logistics), *America's Volunteers: A Report on the All-Volunteer Armed Forces* (Washington, D.C., Department of Defense, 1978).

Office of the Assistant Secretary of Defense (Manpower and Reserve Affairs), *The All-Volunteer Force: Current Status and Prospects* (Washington, D.C., Department of Defense, 1976).

Office of Management and Budget, *Report of Informal Study Group, Budget Concept for Selective Service System, FY 76,* 19 September, 1974.

Office of the Secretary of Defense, *A Report to Congress on U.S. Conventional Reinforcements for NATO* (Washington, D.C., Department of Defense, 1976).

President's Reorganization Project of the Office of Management and Budget, "Selective Service Reorganization Study, Final Report," August 1978.

Richardson, Elliot L., secretary of defense, *The All-Volunteer Force and the End of the Draft* (Washington, D.C., Department of Defense, 1973).

Scarborough, Edward, "Minority Participation in the Department of Defense," *Defense Manpower Commission Staff Studies and Supporting Papers,* Vol. IV (Washington, D.C., GPO, 1976).

Secretary of Defense, *Annual Report of the Secretary of Defense on*

Reserve Forces, Fiscal Year 1972 (Washington, D.C., Department of Defense, 1973). These reports are published yearly in January for the preceding year.

Secretary of Defense, *FY 1977 Defense Report* (Washington, D.C., GPO, 1976).

Secretary of Defense, *The Guard and Reserve in the Total Force,* unclassified portions of secret document (Washington, D.C., Department of Defense, 1975).

Sitterson, John D., Jr., and William A. Lindsay, "Individual Reserves," *Defense Manpower Commission Staff Studies and Supporting Papers,* Vol. II (Washington, D.C., GPO, 1976).

U.S. Congress, House of Representatives, Appropriations Committee, *Department of Defense Appropriations for 1976* (Washington, D.C., GPO, 1975).

U.S. Congress, House of Representatives, Committee on Armed Services, Hearings, *Extension of the Draft and Bills Relating to the Voluntary Force Concept and Authorization of Strength Levels,* 23 February–9 March 1971.

U.S. Congress, House of Representatives, Committee on Armed Services, *Hearings Before and Special Reports Made by Committee on Armed Services on Subjects Affecting the Naval and Military Establishments, 1971* (Washington, D.C., GPO, 1972).

U.S. Congress, House of Representatives, Committee on Armed Services, *Hearings on the Selective Service System,* 27–29–2–23 February 1976.

U.S. Congress, House of Representatives, Committee on Armed Services, *Hearings of Special Committee on North Atlantic Treaty Organization Commitments,* 14 October 1971–24 March 1972.

U.S. Congress, House of Representatives, Committee on Armed Services, Hearings, *Military Posture and H.R. 11500: Department of Defense Authorization for Appropriations for Fiscal Year 1977* (Washington, D.C., GPO, 1976).

U.S. Congress, House of Representatives, Committee on Armed Services, Subcommittee on Investigations, *Hearings on the Selective Service System,* 21–26 January 1976.

U.S. Congress, House of Representatives, Committee on Armed Services, Special Subcommittee on NATO Standardization, Interoperability and Readiness, *NATO Standardization, Interoperability and Readiness* (Washington, D.C., GPO, 1979).

U.S. Congress, House of Representatives, Committee on Armed Services, Special Subcommittee on Recruiting and Retention of Military Personnel, Hearings, *Recruiting and Retention of*

Military Personnel, 29 July 1971–6 March 1972.

U.S. Congress, House of Representatives, Committee on Merchant Marines and Fisheries, Hearings, *National Defense and Economic Benefits of the U.S. Flag Merchant Marine* (Washington, D.C., GPO, 1975).

U.S. Congress, House of Representatives, Select Committee on Postwar Military Policy, *Universal Military Training* (Washington, D.C., GPO, 1945).

U.S. Congress, Senate, Committee on Armed Services, Hearings, *Fiscal Year 1978 Authorization for Military Procurement, Research and Development, and Active Duty, Selected Reserve and Civilian Personnel Strengths,* 25 January–24 February 1977.

U.S. Congress, Senate, Committee on Armed Services, *Hearings on the FY 76 Defense Budget* (Washington, D.C., GPO, 1975).

U.S. Congress, Senate, Committee on Armed Services, Hearings, *Military Manpower Training Report for Fiscal Year 1977, DOD Authorization,* 4 February–19 March 1976.

U.S. Congress, Senate, Committee on Armed Services, *Hearings on Department of Defense Authorization for Appropriations for Fiscal Year 1979* (Washington, D.C., GPO, 1978).

U.S. Congress, Senate, Committee on Armed Services, Subcommittee on Manpower and Personnel, Hearings, *Costs of the All-Volunteer Force* (Washington, D.C., GPO, 1978).

U.S. Congress, Senate, Committee on Armed Services, Subcommittee on Manpower and Personnel, Hearings, *The All-Volunteer Force,* 2 March 1977.

U.S. Congress, Senate, Committee on Armed Services, Subcommittee on Manpower and Personnel, Hearings, *Military Manpower Issues of the Past and Future,* 13–14 August 1974.

U.S. Congress, Senate, Committee on Armed Services, Subcommittee on Volunteer Armed Force and Selective Service, Hearings, *Volunteer Armed Force and Selective Service,* 10–13 March 1972.

Walton, Hugh M., Ray A. Dunn, Jr., and John D. Sitterson, Jr., "Selected Reserve Issues," *Defense Manpower Commission Staff Studies and Supporting Papers,* Vol. II (Washington, D.C., GPO, 1976).

Walton, Hugh M., "Overview of the Reserve Components," *Defense Manpower Commission Staff Studies and Supporting Papers,* Vol. II (Washington, D.C., GPO, 1976).

West Germany, Minister of Defense, *Security and Defence: The Policy of the Federal Republic of Germany* (Bonn, Ministry of Defence, 1977).

White, John P., Statement of the Assistant Secretary of Defense (Manpower, Reserve Affairs, and Logistics), *Hearings Before the Task Force on National Security,* House Budget Committee, 13 July 1977.

White House, National Security Council, *National Security Decision Memo 208,* 16 March 1973.

ARTICLES

Allen, Robert S., and John A. Goldsmith, "Would All-Volunteer Army Be Mostly Black?" *New York Daily News,* 5 March 1969.

Bingham, Jonathan B., "Replacing the Draft," *New Republic,* 16 January 1971.

Bird, Robert, "The Case for Voluntary Service," in Donald J. Eberly, ed., *National Service: The Report of a Conference* (New York, Russell Sage Foundation, 1968).

Black, Charles L., Jr., "Constitutional Problems in Compulsory National Service," *Yale Law Report,* Summer 1967.

Blanchard, George S., "CENTAG/USAREUR Interoperability—A Total Program: From the Bottom Up," *Strategic Review,* Winter 1977.

Borden, Donald F., "Inflexibility in NATO's Flexible Response," *Military Review,* January 1976.

Bradley, K., "NATO Strategy and the Security of Western Europe," *Journal of the Royal United Services Institute,* December 1974.

Brayton, Abbott A., "The Transformation of U.S. Mobilization Policies: Implications for NATO," *Journal of the Royal United Services Institute,* March 1975.

Brodie, Bernard, "The Development of Nuclear Strategy," *International Security,* Spring 1978.

Burt, Richard, "U.S. Analysis Doubts There Can Be Victor in Major Atomic War," *New York Times,* 6 January 1978.

Canby, Steven L., "European Mobilization: U.S. and NATO Reserves," *Armed Forces and Society,* February 1978.

Canby, Steven L., "NATO Muscle: More Shadow Than Substance," *Foreign Policy,* Fall 1972.

Canby, Steven L., "Regaining a Conventional Military Balance in Europe," *Military Review,* June 1975.

Carver, Sir Michael, Remarks/lecture/interview at the London School of Economics, 28 January 1977.

Chapman, William, "White Males and Reverse Discrimination," *Washington Post,* 20 March 1977.

Cleveland, Harlan, "NATO After the Invasion," *Foreign Affairs,* January 1969.

"A Conventional Strategy for the Central Front in NATO," A Report of a Seminar Held at the Royal United Services Institute on 23 October 1974 and 26 May 1975 (London, Royal United Services Institute, 1975).

Cooper, Richard V. L., "Defense Manpower Issues," Rand Paper #P-5364 (Santa Monica, Rand, 1975), as presented to the Defense Manpower Commission 28 January 1975.

Corcoran, Edward A., "Military Support for NATO Political Strategy," *Military Review,* August 1976.

Cortright, David, "Economic Conscription," *Society,* May/June 1976.

Davison, Michael S., "The Role and Capability of United States Ground Forces in Europe," report of a lecture given at the Royal United Services Institute on 17 January 1973, *Journal of the Royal United Services Institute,* December 1973.

Dellums, Ronald, "Don't Slam the Door," *Focus,* June 1975.

Department of Defense, "Deploying U.S. Forces to NATO," *Commanders Digest,* 20 January 1977.

Eberly, Donald J., "National Needs and National Service," *Current History,* August 1968.

Eisenhower, Dwight D., "This Country Needs Universal Military Training," *Reader's Digest,* September 1966.

Enthoven, Alain C., "U.S. Forces in Europe: How Many? Doing What?" *Foreign Affairs,* April 1975.

Etzold, Thomas H., "Short-War Theorem: Cliche or Strategy?" *Army,* September 1977.

Fishel, John T., "Effective Use of the Reserve Components," *Military Review,* May 1977.

Foster, Charles R., "American Elite and Mass Attitudes Toward Europe," *NATO Review,* June 1975.

Fowler, Delbert M., "How Many Divisions," *Military Review,* November 1972.

Fritchey, Clayton, "Serving One's Country," *Washington Post,* 19 March 1975.

Fritchey, Clayton, "Volunteer Army: The New Deserters," *Washington Post,* 25 December 1976.

Galen, Justin, "Restoring the NATO-Warsaw Pact Balance: The Art of the Impossible," *Armed Forces Journal,* September 1978.

Gans, Daniel, "The Israeli Way and U.S. Reserve, Guard Readiness," *Army,* February 1977.

Getler, Michael, "Study Insists NATO Can Defend Itself," *Washington Post,* 7 June 1973.

Gole, Henry G., "The Bundeswehr Reserve and Mobilization System," *Military Review*, November 1977.

Gray, George H., "What Are U.S. Reserve Forces Really For?," *Military Review*, June 1975.

Hall, Edward F., "National Service and the American Tradition," *Current History*, August 1968.

Harrison, Stanley L., "Congress and President: NATO Troop Resolution Conflict," *Military Review*, September 1971.

Janowitz, Morris, "Focus on Blacks in Military," *Focus*, June 1975.

Janowitz, Morris, "The Decline of the Mass Army," *Military Review*, February 1972.

Janowitz, Morris, and Charles Moskos, Jr., "Racial Composition of the All-Volunteer Force," *Armed Forces and Society*, Fall 1974.

Jordan, Vernon E., Jr., "Black Volunteer Army?," *Atlanta Constitution*, 14 August 1974.

Landrum, Cecile, "Policy Dimensions of an Integrated Force," *Armed Forces and Society*, August 1978.

Ludvigsen, Eric C., "Huskier NATO Heads '79 Defense Priorities," *Army*, March 1978.

Marmion, Harry A., "Selective Service: Are There Any Alternatives?," *Educational Record*, Spring 1967.

Martin, Michael L., "Conscription and the Decline of the Mass Army in France, 1960–1974," *Armed Forces and Society*, May 1977.

Mead, Margaret, "The Case for Compulsory National Service," *Current History*, August 1968.

Moskos, Charles C., Jr., "The Enlisted Ranks in the All-Volunteer Army," in John Keeley, ed., *The Military in American Society* (Charlottesville, University of Virginia Press, 1978).

Moskos, Charles C., Jr., and Charles W. Brown, "Race Attitudes and Military Commitment in the All-Volunteer Army," paper presented at the Biennial Conference of the Inter-University Seminar on Armed Forces and Society, Chicago, 16–18 October 1975.

Moulton, Harland B., "The McNamara General War Strategy," *Orbis*, Summer 1964.

Ognibene, Peter J., "Must We Revive the Draft?," *Parade*, 12 June 1977.

Osgood, Robert E., "The Reappraisal of Limited War," in Eugene J. Rosi, ed., *American Defense and Detente: Readings in National Security Policy* (New York, Dodd, Mead, 1973).

Paone, Rocco M., "The Last Volunteer Army, 1946–1948," *Military Review*, December 1969.

Plattner, Andy, "All Volunteer Force May Be in Trouble," *Army*

Times, 14 March 1977.

Polk, James H., "The New Short War Strategy," *Strategic Review,* Summer 1975.

Reid, Sydney A., "Race and the Military: The Problem of Black Representation," paper prepared for presentation to the Defense Manpower Commission, 6 February 1976.

Santilli, Joseph F., Jr., "NATO Strategy Updated: A First Use Policy," *Military Review,* March 1974.

Schemmer, Benjamin F., "Bloody Battle over U.S. Commitment to NATO for 3% Real Budget Increase," *Armed Forces Journal,* November 1978.

Schexnider, Alvin J., "Expectations from the Ranks: Representativeness and Value Systems," paper presented at the 1975 Biennial Conference of the Inter-University Seminar on Armed Forces and Society, Chicago, 16–18 October 1975.

Schexnider, Alvin J., "Race, Quality, and Quantity in the All-Volunteer Force," statement prepared for presentation to the Defense Manpower Commission, 6 February 1976.

Schexnider, Alvin J., and John Sibley Butler, "Race and the All-Volunteer System," *Armed Forces and Society,* Spring 1976.

Schlesinger, James R., "A Testing Time for America," *Fortune,* February 1976.

Seamans, Robert C., Jr., "Planning the Total Force Concepts for the 1970's," *Air Force Magazine,* November 1970.

Segal, David R., "Civil-Military Relations in the Mass Public, *Armed Forces and Society,* Winter 1975.

Stevens, Phil, "A Four-Sided Argument Over Ye Old Draft," *Federal Times,* 16 February 1976.

Stevens, Phil, "Must Armed Forces Reflect U.S. Society?" *Air Force Times,* 24 September 1975.

Tarr, Curtis W., "The Obligation to Serve," *Air University Review,* July/August 1972.

"U.S. Ground Forces: Inappropriate Objectives, Unacceptable Risks," *Defense Monitor,* November 1978.

Van Doorn, Jacques, "The Decline of the Mass Army in the West," *Armed Forces and Society,* February 1975.

Von Kielmansegg, J. A. Graf, "A German View of Western Defense," *Journal of the Royal United Services Institute,* March 1974.

Welchman, W. Gordon, "An Integrated Approach to the Defense of West Germany," *Journal of the Royal United Services Institute,* March 1975.

Werner, Roy A., "The Other Military: Are U.S. Reserve Forces Viable?," *Military Review,* April 1977.

Westcott, Diane N., "The Nation's Youth: An Employment Perspective," *Worklife*, Department of Labor, June 1977.
Westerman, T. G., and Wayne C. Knudsen, "Bold Thinking Is Needed to Revitalize the Ready-Reserve," *Army*, May 1976.
Wilson, George C., "Reactivated Draft Seen as Way to Fill Reserves," *Washington Post*, 9 February 1977.
Wofford, Harris, "Toward a Draft Without Guns," *Saturday Review*, 15 October 1966.
Yochelson, John, "The American Military Presence in Europe: Current Debate in the United States," *Orbis*, Fall 1971.

NEWSPAPER AND MAGAZINE CITATIONS

Chicago Defender, 8 May 1975.
Congressional Digest, May 1971.
International Herald-Tribune, 15 August 1973, 4 December 1974.
London Financial Times, 30 December 1975.
London Times, 26 February 1952, 22 May 1971.
Newsweek, 31 January 1977, 28 March 1977.
New York Times, 30 November 1954, 26 February 1970, 23 November 1974, 5 February 1975, 30 May 1975, 5 June 1976, 28 January 1977.
U.S. News and World Report, 5 March 1979.
Washington Post, 19 December 1966, 1 July 1973, 14 August 1973, 9 June 1976, 30 December 1976, 15 March 1979.
Washington Star, 13 July 1975.

Index